CFA® Basics

PRE-LEVEL 1

THE SCHWESER STUDY GUIDE TO GETTING STARTED

By Dr. Bruce Kuhlman
Associate Professor of Finance
University of Toledo

Edited by

Dr. Greg Filbeck, CFA
Senior Vice President
Schweser Study Program

and

Dr. Andrew Temte, CFA
President and Chief Executive Officer
Schweser Study Program

Simon & Schuster

NEW YORK · LONDON · SINGAPORE · SYDNEY · TORONTO

Kaplan Publishing
Published by Simon & Schuster
1230 Avenue of the Americas
New York, New York 10020

For bulk sales to schools, colleges, and universities, please contact:
Order Department, Simon & Schuster, 100 Front Street, Riverside, NJ 08075.
Phone: (800) 223-2336. Fax: (800) 943-9831.

Contributing Editor: Jeff Manzi, Ph.D.
Project Editor: Eileen Mager
Cover Design: Cheung Tai
Interior Page Layout: Laurel Douglas
Production Editor: Maude Spekes
Production Manager: Michael Shevlin
Editorial Coordinator: Dea Alessandro
Executive Editor: Del Franz

Special thanks to Karen Quackenbush

Manufactured in the United States of America
Published simultaneously in Canada

September 2001
10 9 8 7 6 5 4 3 2

ISBN 0-7432-2472-8

Contents

CFA® Basics

Appendixes

Foreword

CFA®. Each year, students and investment professionals from around the world invest considerable time and energy in their quest to include those three letters behind their names. Those who are able to achieve this goal show that they have acquired a well-rounded understanding of the tools of investment finance and have made a pledge to the investing public to uphold the highest ethical conduct. If you are reading this book, chances are that you, too, are considering joining the thousands of students and professionals who are currently working toward their Charter.

Who Should Use this Book?

This book is for those who are interested in becoming a Chartered Financial Analyst™ but who might not be prepared to enter the CFA Program™ right away. One of the requirements for entry into the CFA Program™ is a bachelor's degree from a four-year college or university (graduating seniors may also enter the program, but their graduation date must be no later than the summer term following their first crack at the CFA® Level 1 examination). But what if you received your degree in chemistry or political science? Or what if you have been out of school for 10 years and cannot recall much from your undergraduate days? The purpose of this text is to help you gain (or regain) the basic accounting, economic, and financial background that is necessary to *begin* your studies in the CFA Program™.

What Is the Structure of the CFA Program™?

The CFA Program™ is a series of three examinations that are given once per year on the first Saturday after Memorial Day (typically the first Saturday in June) by the Association for Investment Management and Research® (AIMR®). Each exam is a *six-hour experience* (three hours in the morning and three hours in the afternoon). In your first year of the program, you prepare for the CFA® Level 1 examination. If you pass the Level 1 exam, you are allowed to take the Level 2 exam the following year. Pass the Level 2 exam, and you can take the Level 3 exam. However, if you *fail* an examination along the way, you must wait until the next year to retake it. It takes a minimum of three years and a maximum of seven years to pass all three levels (although the seven-year deadline may be extended by re-registering for the program).

- *Level 1–Investment Tools* (100 percent multiple-choice): The Level 1 curriculum focuses on the tools of investment finance. The five main topic areas that are covered are: ethical and professional standards; quantitative methods; economics; financial accounting/corporate finance; asset valuation (includes equity, debt, derivatives, and alternative investments); and portfolio management. The Level 1 exam is all about breadth, not depth. As a result, each question is relatively short and focuses on a particular concept—almost to the point of seeming like the exam is an exercise in minutiae. There are 240 multiple-choice questions on the Level 1 exam.

- *Level 2–Analysis and Valuation* (combination essay and multiple-choice): The purpose of the Level 2 exam is to apply and expand upon the tools that were introduced at Level 1. For example, at Level 1, you learn about the basics of derivative securities in the asset valuation section. The Level 2 derivatives curriculum is much more in depth, introducing additional tools and instruments and applying those tools to investment analysis. The primary areas of coverage are: ethics; quantitative methods; economics; financial accounting; asset valuation; and portfolio management. Also, the questions focus on a deeper treatment of the material and are much more difficult in comparison to the Level 1 exam.

- *Level 3–Synthesis and Portfolio Management* (combination essay and multiple-choice): The main focus of the Level 3 exam is portfolio management. Here, you will use the tools and analysis from the previous two levels to develop investment policies and appropriate portfolios for both individual and institutional investors (pension funds, endowments, and life insurance companies). Also, you will learn to protect existing investment positions from the effects of market volatility through the use of debt and derivative instruments (hedging).

Since the structure of the exam is subject to change on an annual basis, we urge you to visit www.aimr.org to download informational pamphlets and learn more about the specifics of the CFA Program™.

In addition to passing the three exams, you must also have accrued three years of relevant work experience prior to the award of your Charter (though you do not have to have any relevant work experience while you are taking the CFA® exams).

How Do I Register for the CFA Program™?

Registration for the CFA Program™ involves completing an application form, which can be obtained from AIMR®. After registering, you will have three years in which to take the Level 1 exam. The easiest way to contact AIMR® is by visiting their Website at www.aimr.org. AIMR® has offices in Charlottesville, Virginia, and Hong Kong, SAR.

What Can the CFA® Designation Do for Me?

If you are serious about a career as an investment analyst, portfolio manager, high-net worth money manager, credit analyst, or any of several other careers that deal primarily with the "investment decision-making process," the CFA® designation is for you. There are many firms that *require* their employees to attain the designation. Just look in the *Wall Street Journal* at the job listings that are posted. Most of the positions that you will see will ask for or require that the applicant hold the Charter. In addition, AIMR® periodically publishes a survey of its members regarding their income. The global median income (you'll learn more about the median in the Quantitative Methods chapter of this book) of an AIMR® member with more than 10 years of experience is well over $200,000. The bottom line is that your investment in the CFA Program™ will pay off in the long run.

How Can Schweser Study Program™ Help Me Achieve my Goals?

Schweser is the premier provider of study tools for the CFA® examination. Our core product is our Study Notes, but we also provide live seminars around the world, produce instructional videos, audiotapes, and flashcards, and host a world-class online educational program. No matter what your preferred learning method, Schweser can help you pass the CFA® exams. Please visit our Website at www.schweser.com for more information.

How Should I Use this Book?

This study guide will help you understand the basics of the critical content areas that are covered in the CFA Program™. The chapters are broken down by topic: economics; financial statement analysis; quantitative methods; corporate finance; capital markets; security valuation; and portfolio theory. Depending on your educational background and work experience, you can start to build an understanding of the fundamentals by working through the book chapter by chapter, or you can target your particular areas of weakness by going straight to the relevant chapters or sections. You can further target your studying by using the glossary in the back of the book to learn or review important concepts. The learning objectives outlined in each chapter and the practice questions and answers at the end of every chapter will help to reinforce the concepts you are studying.

Make no mistake, the road to success in the CFA Program™ is not easy. Each exam is like running a marathon: training and pace are critical. Dedication and hard work are the hallmarks of CFA® exam preparation. From the breakdown given above, you can see that the CFA Program™ is a *growth* process. We are confident that when you are finished with all three exams, you will not only breathe a well-deserved sigh of relief, but you will also have grown significantly–both professionally and academically.

Best regards,

Dr. Carl Schweser, CFA
Chairman
Schweser Study Program

Dr. Andrew Temte, CFA
President and Chief Executive Officer
Schweser Study Program

CFA® Basics:
Content Review

Economics

Merriam Webster's Collegiate Dictionary defines **economics** as "the social science concerned chiefly with the description and analysis of production, distribution, and consumption of goods and services." **Economical**, on the other hand, is defined as "operating with little waste or at a savings; a thrifty use of material resources." [1]

In *Economics: Private and Public Choice*, Gwartney, Stroup, and Sobel contend that "economics is about how people choose."[2] From the most important to the most mundane, any decision is economic in nature. Every choice is made in terms of the decision maker's **utility**, which can be thought of as satisfaction. In every choice we make, we try to find that combination of cost and benefit, which maximizes our utility (satisfaction).

> Every choice is made to maximize **utility**, which is satisfaction derived from the choice.

The economic implications of business decisions are usually fairly obvious. Their results often include increased revenues or reduced costs. But what about the small, seemingly insignificant decisions we make every day? Consider the simple choice of crossing the street in the middle of the block or walking to the corner to use the crosswalk. How did we make the decision? It probably had to do with the reason we

> "Economics is about how people choose."

[1] *Merriam Webster's Collegiate Dictionary, 10E,* 1998.

[2] Gwartney, Stroup, and Sobel, *Economics: Private and Public Choice, 9E* (The Dryden Press, 2000).

wanted to cross the street, the distance to the nearest crosswalk, how quickly we needed to get to the other side, and the amount of traffic.

Is this decision economic in nature? Did we try to maximize our utility? Most certainly! If we cross in the middle of the block, we might save valuable time (a benefit) and get to our goal (making it to the other side) more quickly. That's very satisfying! On the other hand, if traffic is heavy, we might have to wait a long time to cross, we might get stuck in the middle of the street, or we might even be hit by a car and never make it to the other side. That's not very satisfying! Is the potential cost of crossing in the middle of the block worth the potential benefit? There is much less risk if we take the time to walk to the corner, wait for the signal, and use the crosswalk, but it takes longer to get to the other side.

> Every time we make a choice, we balance the potential **costs** with potential **benefits**.

In fact, any decision we make can be summed up in very much the same terms. The decision maker weighs the potential gains (benefits) against the potential losses (costs) and makes the decision that maximizes utility. Once you have accepted the fact that each decision you make is economic in nature, it is a fairly simple step to make the jump to understanding the importance of economics in business decision-making. Referring to Webster's definition of economics, we see the clear orientation to the business world. All production, delivery, and consumption decisions are based upon a perceived benefit. However, costs must always be considered.

Section 1 of this chapter discusses the evolution of economic thought from the era of Sir Francis Bacon to John Maynard Keynes, one of the most widely studied and respected economists of modern times. Section 2 provides examples and discusses some of the most widely used economics terms.

In this chapter, your learning objectives are the following:

1. To understand the origin and development of economics as a discipline.
2. To understand the three most important forms of government: capitalism, socialism, and communism.
3. To master an essential economics vocabulary.

Schweser
Study Program™

SECTION 1: A HISTORICAL OVERVIEW OF ECONOMICS

Although he most certainly did not think of it in those terms, earliest man made economic decisions; the cost of a decision made little difference when the benefit was eating, or even survival. To walk many miles to gather food versus taking it from some great beast was not really a decision. If food was not otherwise readily available, he was willing to walk whatever distance necessary. Risking his life to try to take food from a lion or other man-eating beast would have been insane if an alternative had been available. Thus, his decision was easy. The pervasiveness of economics in our lives from the very earliest period cannot be debated.

To truly understand any subject, you must first study its origins. The exact time when scholars started to take notice of the economic nature of decision making (and started to call it economics, for that matter) is anybody's guess, but many early philosopher/economists wrote on the nature of business and the lengths to which man will go to achieve wealth. Let's investigate the writings of four well-known economists who have made significant contributions to the development of economics.

Sir Francis Bacon

Sir Francis Bacon (1561–1626) was an English politician, barrister, scientist, and philosopher. The writings of early philosophers were typically based in religious doctrine, and Bacon was no exception. In 1597, Bacon wrote *The Essays*. In this collection of his opinions, which is laced throughout with his religious and philosophical beliefs, Bacon seems to have a fairly good grasp of the mind of modern man and the concept of economics. For instance, in the essay titled "Of Truth," Bacon states, " to think what should be in it, that men should love lies; whether neither they make for pleasure, as with poets, nor for advantage, as with the merchant; but for the lie's sake." Of course, Bacon is addressing the overall concept of truth versus lies, and questions why man would "embrace" lies. He seems to believe the reason business people lie is to gain an advantage. (Surely not a unique opinion!)

The Bible passage, "What is a man profited, if he shall gain the whole world, and lose his own soul?" (Matthew 16:26) speaks about the fashion in which wealth is accumulated. Although not always on religious

Most early economists were in fact philosophers.

Sir Francis Bacon was an early philosopher/ economist. His writings were based in religious doctrine. He spoke against waste and greed (wealth for wealth's sake).

grounds, most philosophers embrace honesty and integrity, and these ideals flow through their writings. In "Of Riches," Bacon writes, "For as the baggage is to an army, so is riches to virtue. It cannot be spared nor left behind, but it hindereth the march; yea and the care of it sometimes loseth or disturbeth the victory." Is he implying that virtue hinders or even stops the "march" toward wealth? Or is he implying that, although virtue makes the march longer and harder, it should accompany the march? His opinion of the accumulation and use of wealth is quite clear. "Seek not proud riches, but such as thou mayest get justly, use soberly, distribute cheerfully, and leave contentedly." He continues: "Therefore measure not thine advancements by quantity . . . and defer not charities till death . . . ."

In "Of Expense," Bacon writes, "Riches are for spending, and spending for honor and good actions . . . . A man had need, if he be plentiful in some kind of expense, to be as saving again in some other." In this passage, Bacon recognizes the concept of a limit to spending, or a budget, as we would call it today. This belief was most certainly embraced by our next philosopher/economist.

Adam Smith

Adam Smith was a **classical economist**. They believe in strict **laissez-faire**; government should not interfere with the natural working of the economy.

Adam Smith (1723–1790), a Scottish economist and philosopher, is regarded as the founder of economics as a separate discipline and is probably the most famous of all early economists. He was Professor of Moral Philosophy at Edinburgh from 1748 to 1751 and published his *Theory of Moral Sentiments* in 1759. In *Theory*, Smith, as most philosophers before and after him, dealt with the role of standards of ethical conduct as the glue that holds society together. In 1776, he published what would be his greatest work and one of the most influential works of all time, *An Inquiry into the Nature and Causes of the Wealth of Nations*. *Wealth of Nations* introduces us to the "invisible hand" and the idea of a "free enterprise" system. In a free enterprise system, private business is free to operate without governmental interference (beyond regulation necessary to protect the public interest).

Smith puts into words what many others of the time suspected but were unable to articulate. Smith contends that in a free market, participants' actions are controlled by competition. Competition is widely understood and accepted today, but it was quite an enlightening concept at that time. Smith makes the point that participants in the market make selfish decisions as if an "invisible hand" were guiding them. This invisible hand, or **market pressure**, will ultimately direct the self-seeking activities of the individual to the betterment of society as a whole. The end result is that only those goods and services that society needs are provided.

With the common goal of maximizing personal wealth, market participants (sellers and buyers) will strive to buy or sell at the best possible price. As long as there is no price collusion, each seller will try to attract new customers by offering a lower price than other sellers' prices (**collusion**, which is illegal, occurs when competitors secretly agree to maintain high prices or agree not to compete on price, so as to keep prices high). Since manufacturers want to pay the lowest possible price, they will naturally buy from the supplier offering the best prices. When the high-priced suppliers realize that they are losing business, they will lower their prices in order to remain competitive.

However, there is a minimum price at which a supplier is willing to sell. This price depends upon the price that the supplier, as a customer, must pay for the product. His suppliers are in the same competitive struggle with rival suppliers. The process continues in this way until prices reach a minimum, or **equilibrium** level. When they can no longer compete using price, suppliers begin competing on the basis of service and product quality. The process continues in both directions, backward up the chain of suppliers, and forward through the chain of customers. Theoretically, consumers are guaranteed the highest possible quality product at the best possible price.

The same argument can be applied to ensure society produces only those products it needs and wants. Products that are in high demand get the most attention from manufacturers, and the supply of these products will increase. Products with relatively low demand receive less attention, and their supply is reduced. In this way, the supply of all products will reach an equilibrium level with their respective demands.

To illustrate this concept, assume your company manufactures equal quantities of two products, forks and spoons. Now assume soup suddenly becomes very popular, and your customers rush to buy more spoons. Although your customers still occasionally eat with forks, they

Adam Smith's **invisible hand** is **market pressure**, the unseen force that affects individuals' choices.

Equilibrium: opposing forces are perfectly balanced.

When consumer tastes change, the demand for new products increases. Producers and suppliers will shift resources to supply those products.

don't have to buy new forks. Since your customers are buying only spoons, and your production mix of spoons and forks has not changed, your inventory (supply) of forks increases. Thus, you reduce fork production and shift much of your fork-making resources into producing spoons. You now produce more spoons, which are in higher demand, and fewer forks, which are in lower demand. Society is happy, due to the ready supply of reasonably priced spoons, and you spend less of your scarce resources (labor, raw materials, and cash) on a product that no one wants to buy. Of course, your competitors will shift production to spoons, and all suppliers will compete on price, quality, and service. This ensures consumers the best quality spoons at the best possible price. If and when the demand for forks increases, you and your competitors will once again realign your production resources.

Capitalism is synonymous with free enterprise.

Smith's "invisible hand" (market pressure) makes sense to us today, as it probably did to readers in his day. As a result of the widespread respect and acceptance for his contribution to economic thought, Smith is considered the "father" of the free enterprise system, what we call **capitalism** today. There are, however, economists with other ideas of the ideal system. Our next economist is well known, not only for his considerable intellect and understanding of capitalism, but also for his willingness to display both.

Karl Marx

Karl Marx believed in a natural social decay to communism. Capitalism leads to class struggle, which leads to revolution and socialism. Unequal distribution within socialism leads to revolution and communism.

Karl Marx (1818–1883) was born in Trier, Germany. Marx spent much of his time analyzing capitalism, and is widely known as the chief antagonist of the capitalist economic system. His devotion to **dialectic materialism**[3] led him to study the workings of the capitalistic economic system as it relates to the working man (the **proletariat**). In the spring of 1847, Marx and his closest friend, Frederick Engels, joined a society called the Communist League. It was at the request of the League's Second Congress (London, November, 1847) that they drew up *The Communist Manifesto*,[4] which appeared in February 1848. The *Manifesto* outlines a new world order based upon materialism.

[3] **Dialectics** is the method of reasoning, which tries to understand things by form and substance, rather than appearance. **Materialism** is the philosophy that asserts that the material world is the foundation of thought. In this context, materialism does not mean what it means today.

[4] Although *The Communist Manifesto* is probably the best-known work of Karl Marx, *Das Capital*, 1867, his study and analysis of capitalism, is his most influential work.

Marx was chiefly concerned with what he saw as the glaring flaw in capitalism: the conflict inherent to a system that encourages social classes. Rather than the elite being more important and controlling society, Marx believed the working people themselves should hold this position. He saw ownership and control of industry by individuals as causing an irreversible class struggle, which ultimately leads to revolution. His thoughts are best summarized in his own words:

> And now as to myself, no credit is due to me for discovering the existence of classes in modern society or the struggle between them. Long before me bourgeois[5] historians had described the historical development of this class struggle and bourgeois economists, the economic anatomy of classes. What I did that was new was to prove:
>
> (1) that the existence of classes is only bound up with the particular, historical phases in the development of production,
>
> (2) that the class struggle necessarily leads to the dictatorship of the proletariat, and
>
> (3) that this dictatorship itself only constitutes the transition[6] to the abolition of all classes and to a classless society.[7]

As you can imagine, Marx was not typically welcomed with open arms wherever he went. In fact, he spent a lot of time in exile from one country or another, where leaders felt his ideas were dangerous. It was with both spoken and written words that Marx drew the attention—and ire—of governments:

> From the moment all members of society, or at least the vast majority, have learned to administer the state themselves, have taken this work into their own hands, have organized control over the insignificant capitalist minority, over the gentry who wish to preserve their capitalist habits and over the workers who have been thoroughly corrupted by capitalism—from this moment the need for government of any kind begins to disappear altogether. The more complete the democracy, the nearer the moment when it becomes unnecessary. The more

Under **communism**, there is no formal government.

---

[5] **Bourgeois** refers to business owners, capitalists. Collectively, they are called the **bourgeoisie**.

[6] **Transition** is Marx's mild word for change, not necessarily peacefully.

[7] Letter to Weydemeyer, March 5, 1852.

democratic the 'state' which consists of the armed workers, and which is 'no longer a state in the proper sense of the word,' the more rapidly every form of state begins to wither away.[8]

John Maynard Keynes

In *The General Theory of Employment, Interest, and Money*, **John Maynard Keynes** changed the way we look at macro-economics.

Completely opposed to Marxist thought, John Maynard Keynes (pronounced "canes") (1883–1946) was devoted to capitalism. Philosopher, economist, and mathematician, Keynes was born in Cambridgeshire, England. It is interesting to note that while Keynes remains one of the most influential modern economists, his formal education was in mathematics and statistics. In fact, his fellowship dissertation at King's College was in probability theory. In the field of economics, Keynes was largely self-educated.

Keynes taught economics at Cambridge during World War I, and in 1915 went to work in the Treasury. Never a dedicated politician, Keynes was always quick and blunt with his comments and criticism. At one point he called the comments of Lloyd George, then Chancellor of the Exchequer,[9] "rubbish." In 1919 he even attacked the leading political figures of the Versailles Peace Conference in *The Economic Consequences of the Peace*, in which he strongly criticizes the peace terms that punished the defeated Germany. He would probably respond to the later rise of Adolph Hitler with an admonishing, "I told you so!"

Unlike **classical economists**, Keynes believed the government needs to intervene during a recession by increasing its expenditures.

Keynes recognized the importance of government intervention during the Great Depression of the 1930s. In 1936, he published *The General Theory of Employment, Interest, and Money* in which he revolutionized the way economists think about macroeconomics.[10] He clearly laid out how and why recessions happen and what must be done to recover from them. His very controversial strategy for recovery from a recession was for government to run deficits in order to stimulate demand and employment. In this, he varies widely from classical economists, such as Adam Smith, who advocate a strict "hands off" approach to government.

---

[8] Karl Marx, *The State and Revolution*, September 1917.

[9] The Exchequer is the department of state in Great Britain charged with the receipt and care of the national revenue.

[10] **Microeconomics** focuses on the effects of human behavior on households or individual firms, while **macroeconomics** focuses on how human behavior affects entire, aggregate markets. Both are discussed in Section Two.

Classical economists argue that market wages and prices will decline quickly enough during a recession to bring about economic recovery.

Classical economists favor a school of thought referred to as **supply-side economics**. Supply-side economics holds that supply creates demand by providing jobs and wages. The prices of goods for which there is excess supply will fall, and the prices of goods in demand will rise. Deficient demand can never be a problem, because the production of goods will always generate (through employment) sufficient demand to purchase the goods produced. The markets will always adjust quickly to direct the economy to full employment. It is argued that if unemployment is temporarily high, wages will fall, which will reduce costs and prices. Reduced prices will increase product demand, which will increase the demand for labor until the excess supply of labor is eliminated. Keynes, however, believed that wages and prices are "sticky," meaning they will resist downward adjustment. It is only through the help of the national government's spending that demand is stimulated and employment increased.

Keynes's views can be summarized with the following quote: "Businesses will produce only the quantity of goods and services they believe consumers, investors, governments, and foreigners will buy . . . . When aggregate expenditures are deficient, there are no automatic forces capable of assuring full employment. Prolonged unemployment will persist."[11] Keynes argues that the aggregate expenditures of these four sectors (consumers, investors, governments, and foreigners) determine the extent of employment, and that the government must step up expenditures during a recession to make up for deficiencies in the other three sectors. This concept, whether universally accepted or not, should be recognized as at least partially responsible for recovery from the Great Depression of the 1930s.

We've looked at four of the most respected and widely read philosopher/economists in history. Whether they are completely right, partly right, or completely wrong, they remain very influential in economics today. The writings of these four individuals, among many others, led people to think, discuss, and debate economics as a true and separate discipline.

Keynes: The level of employment in society is determined by the aggregate spending of consumers, investors, government, and foreigners.

[11] Gwartney, Stroup, and Sobel, *Economics*, 272.

SECTION 2: IMPORTANT CONCEPTS AND TERMS IN ECONOMICS

In this section we will explore some of the more commonly used economics terms, without employing graphs and charts. A basic understanding of these terms will not only aid in your preparation for the CFA® exam, but will also prove invaluable for arguments with co-workers and relatives!

The easiest way to impress your associates is to share your knowledge of the three most important economic systems: capitalism, socialism, and communism.

Capitalism

Capitalism is based upon free enterprise.

The writings of Sir Francis Bacon, Adam Smith, and John Maynard Keynes focused on the concept of capitalism. A capitalistic society (economy) is characterized by free enterprise: private ownership of productive resources with prices determined by market forces (supply and demand). Government has the limited role of developing and enforcing a structure of laws. The laws define and enforce contracts, protect private ownership rights, and protect individuals from fraud, misrepresentation, and violence.

Capitalism is the economic system that the United States defends and promotes. The individual's opportunities for success within a capitalist system are limited only by his or her imagination and determination.

Socialism

With **socialism**, the government owns all income-producing assets, and allocation of wages and goods is done according to effort.

What we now know as Russia and the former communist-bloc nations were once collectively known as the Union of Soviet Socialist Republics. In a socialist nation, the government owns all income-producing assets and determines which products will be produced and in what quantities. Unlike capitalism, which calls for no or very limited intervention by government, allocation of resources is done through a centralized planning committee or agency rather than by market forces.

In the writings of Karl Marx, socialism is the intermediate step between capitalism and communism. It is characterized by the distri-

bution of goods and pay according to the amount of work done. Marx says this leads to unequal distribution and the continued evolution toward a communist system.

Communism

The communist doctrine mandates, "From each according to his abilities, to each according to his needs." Communism is the final stage of society in Marx's decline of capitalism. It is characterized by having no formal government. As with socialism, a single authoritarian party controls all state-owned means of production, though the inequities of allocation are removed. There is no private ownership of property, as all property is communally owned and available to each, according to need.

Communism has no formal government. Allocation is "from each according to his abilities, to each according to his needs."

Supply

Supply and **demand** are probably two of the most commonly used words in our economics vocabulary, so a discussion of each is quite appropriate. Although the textbook definition for supply might include such terms as *aggregate production*, *marginal cost*, or *marginal revenue*[12], let's think of supply as the amount of an item available for purchase. The amount of an item available for purchase is based upon factors such as the number of producers, the profit from producing the item, the number of customers, the selling price, and the costs for shipping the item around the country or globe. For the typical consumer, these factors don't really mean much. What is important is whether the item we want is available when and where we want it and at the price we want to pay. Many variables must be considered here, so let's take a look at an example.

Supply is the amount of a good or service available for purchase.

Assume that you are a wholesaler and your company supplies two products: gerbil bedding and gold necklaces. You purchase gold chain directly from the manufacturer in 1,000-inch rolls at $2.00 per inch. It costs you another $25.00 per necklace to cut the chain to length, add clasps, and prepare it for shipping. The bedding material is actually

---

[12] In economics, a good synonym for the word *marginal* is *last*. Marginal cost is the total cost to produce the last item produced. Marginal revenue is the revenue received from selling the last item. Since production costs may increase or decrease with the amount produced, the marginal cost may be higher or lower than that for the second to the last item. A similar argument would apply to marginal revenue.

wood chips and mulch left over from a lumberyard. It costs you $0.10 per pound and comes by truckload. (A pound of the bedding material is about two cubic feet, enough for the typical gerbil cage.) It costs you another $0.15 to put one pound in a labeled plastic bag and prepare it for shipping.

Shipping presents an interesting problem for these vastly different products. Since shipping costs are based upon weight and size (volume), a small, heavy item costs no more than a large (bulky), light item. This makes gold necklaces very value-intensive products, meaning they are valuable, light, and small. The bedding, on the other hand, is very cost intensive. It is very light and inexpensive, but must be shipped in much larger containers. The result is that 100 necklaces can be shipped for about the same cost as 20 bags of bedding. (Let's assume the shipping cost for each is $10.00.) So where is this discussion going? Let's take a look at the total cost to prepare and ship one necklace versus one bag of bedding.

The gold for a 20-inch necklace costs $40.00, and the clasps and packaging cost another $25.00, resulting in a total of $65.00 to assemble and prepare one necklace for shipping. Since jewelers place orders for 100 necklaces at a time, and 100 necklaces can be shipped for $10.00, shipping adds only an additional $0.10 to the cost of each necklace, bringing the total costs to assemble and ship one necklace to $65.10. In turn, we assume that we can sell the necklace to a jeweler for $100.00.

Next, let's look at the bedding. The costs for the material and packaging for one bag of bedding is $0.25. Since it costs $10.00 to ship 20 bags, the cost to ship one bag is $0.50. This brings the total to $0.75 per bag. Let's assume that you can sell them to pet stores for $0.65. The result? It is very cost effective for you to ship gold necklaces just about anywhere. The bedding, on the other hand, can only be sold locally, since to package, prepare it for shipping, and ship it costs more than the price you can sell it for.

What is the point of all this? Of course, you will not ship your gerbil bedding any distance. In fact, unless you can distribute the bedding locally at a total cost that is lower than your selling price, you won't supply gerbil bedding. And, as long as costs are about the same for all suppliers of gerbil bedding, all suppliers are faced with the same situation.

> When a finished product is **cost intensive**, handling, packaging, and shipping cost more than the product itself.

> When a finished product is **value intensive**, handling, packaging, and shipping are a small portion of its final value.

Now, let's assume it costs about $0.10 per bag to distribute bedding locally, as opposed to $0.50 to ship it longer distances. That means it costs a total of $0.35 per bag ($0.25 material and packaging plus $0.10 transportation) to supply bedding locally. If you can sell it for $0.65, a gross profit of $0.30 per bag will be realized. As long as you don't try to charge local retailers more than $1.00 or so, out-of-town suppliers won't be enticed to compete with you. (Remember, out-of-town suppliers can ship it in to your local market at a total cost of $0.75 per bag. As long as the local selling price doesn't make it profitable for outside suppliers to sell in your market, they won't.)

Local suppliers want to maximize profits, so they want to sell at the highest price possible, without reaching the estimated $1.00 that would attract nonlocal competition. Note that price is the only thing that matters when gerbil-bedding suppliers compete among themselves in the local market. Gerbil bedding is gerbil bedding; customers don't care about the label on it or who provides it, so suppliers can't compete on quality or service.

The bottom line is that the supply of bedding is constrained by the amount the local suppliers can provide. Gold chains, on the other hand, are a totally different product. Since it is profitable to ship them anywhere, the gold chains consumers see in stores can be from anywhere in the world. This makes the supply of gold chains limited only by the worldwide supply of gold.

The above arguments are completely dependent upon the price suppliers receive. If the total cost to make and ship an item is sufficiently below the selling price, that item will be supplied. When the selling price does not provide revenues sufficient to cover all costs and provide a profit, the item is not supplied. Therefore, the selling price is crucial, and it was simply assumed in the arguments.

> The amount of a good or service supplied will depend upon the price received compared to the total costs to supply it. The higher the price received by suppliers, the greater the supply.

Demand

Demand is how much society wants of a good or service. Let's assume you have a bicycle you want to sell, and there is only one person interested in buying it.

Demand is the total amount of a good or service society wants. The higher the price, the lower the demand.

That person comes to you in response to your advertisement in the newspaper. He asks how much you want for it. When you respond with $100, he backs away a little and says, "I'm thinking about replacing the bicycle I have, but I'm not interested in paying more than $50." You consider the offer for a moment and counter with, "I'll sell it to you for $75." Eventually, the two of you settle on $60. Why did you lower your price so much?

The answer is quite straightforward. Since you have had only one person show interest in the bike, you fear he is the only person in the market for a bicycle. You probably believe that if you let this buyer "get away," you might as well put the bike in your attic or give it away.

Equilibrium is reached when supply equals demand.

Now let's assume that several interested parties arrive simultaneously to consider the purchase of the bicycle you're selling at your garage sale. One of these individuals offers you $50.00. Since there are several people standing around to hear the offer and see your disappointment, someone else steps up and says, "I'll give you $60.00 for it! That's a great bike! And it's in great shape!" Now you have two buyers interested in your bicycle, and the bidding begins. Bidder Number One ($50 bid) goes to $65, and Bidder Number Two goes to $70. Bidder Number One now offers $75, and Bidder Number Two walks away saying, "Nice bike, but I won't pay $80 for it."

If demand is greater than supply (excess demand), prices rise.

With two interested buyers, your selling price has gone to $75, due to the additional buyer. Buyer Number One knows there is another bidder and decides he doesn't want to lose the opportunity to get this nice bicycle at a good price. Had there been three or more interested buyers, the price might have reached your asking price of $100, or higher! Why the drastic change over the case with only one customer? Since there are several interested buyers but only one bicycle, there is "excess demand." There is more demand for the product than there is supply. Your neighbor, who watched the whole thing and saw what great success you had, decides to sell her bicycle at her garage sale the next weekend. She enjoys very nearly the same experience, so all your other neighbors join the selling frenzy, and they all plan garage sales for the following weekend.

If supply is greater than demand, (excess supply), prices fall.

The weekend arrives and all the garage sales open at once. Unfortunately for the neighborhood sellers, there are only a few buyers interested in bicycles. Your neighbors do not have multiple buyers simultaneously bidding on their bicycles. In fact, they actually have to compete for the few interested buyers by lowering their prices. Since there are many more bicycles available than buyers to buy them, we now have "excess supply": There is more supply of the product than there is demand. Our conclusion? If demand is greater than supply, prices increase. If supply is greater than demand, prices decrease.

Hopefully, you related the garage sale discussion to our previous examples of gold chains and gerbil bedding. In the gold chain and bedding discussions, we took the selling price as a given. Whether gerbil bedding was shipped or not depended upon the total cost to package and ship the bags compared to the given selling price. We assumed a sufficiently low price such that it was not feasible to ship the bags of gerbil bedding cross-country. On the other hand, the gold necklaces sold at a high enough price that you could ship them anywhere and still make a profit. Just what determined the selling prices for those items?

Gold, as you probably are aware, is considered a precious metal. There is a limited (actually, carefully controlled) supply of gold on the world market at any time. Since gold is highly sought after worldwide, there is a more or less constant demand. As long as the supply of gold does not run ahead of demand, its price will remain relatively high.[13]

Gerbil bedding, on the other hand, is not a precious commodity. Although gerbil owners might consider commercial bedding superior, they will substitute newspaper if the commercial product gets too expensive. **Substitutes** are products that provide about the same use for the consumer. If one of the products goes up in price, consumers will purchase (substitute) the other. **Complements**, on the other hand, are products usually purchased together, like peanut butter and jelly. Reduction in the demand for one will usually cause reduced demand for the other. Having the option of substituting newspaper for gerbil bedding means there is a maximum retail price that consumers are willing to pay, so the costs to package and ship gerbil bedding become extremely important. Even though gerbil bedding is a very inexpensive product to produce, package, and ship, its limited demand constrains possible sales opportunities and profits.

> The demand for some products is far more sensitive to price changes than the demand for some other products.

---

[13] The prices for gold and other precious metals are determined not solely by the supply of and demand for jewelry. They are sometimes considered a hedge against inflation, which reduces the buying power of currencies and currency-denominated investments.

From our discussions of supply and demand, you have probably come to the conclusion that it is the interaction of these two economic conditions that sets prices. Neither supply nor demand alone is sufficient. We see that regardless of whether a product is expensive or cheap to produce, if no market exists (no demand for the product), it won't sell at any price. If a strong market exists for the product, it will sell, regardless of the cost to produce it. However, profits depend upon the price received. That price, in turn, depends upon the number of buyers relative to the number of sellers (i.e., the demand relative to the supply).

We have discussed supply and demand and have seen how it is the interaction of the two that sets market prices. There are other forces at work, however, and one of the most infamous is **inflation**.

Inflation

Inflation is a very commonly used word, but does everyone who uses it really know what it means? "Inflation is the continuing rise in the general level of prices of goods and services. The purchasing power of the monetary unit, such as the (American) dollar, declines when inflation is present."[14] It is easier to think of inflation as the artificial increase in prices due to excess demand, usually caused when there is too much money present in the economy.

Inflation: Too many dollars chasing too few goods.

Let's think about that for a moment. If you received a totally unexpected large sum of money, an inheritance or lottery prize, for example, wouldn't you spend at least some of it? Now, are you contributing anything of value to the economy that warrants your receipt of this extra money? Is your increase in spending due to an increase in your productivity or an increase in your work output? If not, you could say the spending creates demand (Keynes's expenditures) that is not related to need, but to excess spending ability.

This excess spending usually increases demand for luxury goods such as cars, electronic equipment, and housing. The increased demand for those items increases their prices. Meanwhile, the rest of us are sitting around wondering why in the world prices are going up! There hasn't

---

[14] Gwartney, Stroup, and Sobel, *Economics*, 272.

been an increase in the overall output of the economy. No more goods and services are being supplied that can absorb the excess spending. The result is an increased demand for a relatively constant supply.

Of course, you can argue that the inheritances of one or even several individuals shouldn't be sufficient to cause such dire results, and you are probably correct. The point is that whenever we see more money in the system than the system justifies on the basis of its productive output, the result is inflation (i.e., a general rise in the level of prices in the economy, caused by excess demand for goods and services). Whenever the level of spending in the economy is not due to economic reasons such as increased productivity (increased output from increased effort), the result is "artificial" demand. In other words, if wage increases are not due to economic reasons (e.g., increased efficiency, better or more work), the money added to the system causes "unearned" increased demand. Let's look at a very simple example.

Bob is a carpenter who works rather slowly and is not all that dependable, but when the rest of the carpenters on the job get a raise, Bob also gets one. Is Bob getting a raise because he deserves it? Has his work improved? Does he do more in a given day that would justify the increase in his wages? Whether or not Bob deserves the raise, his spending will increase, causing increased demand. This is the "artificial" demand referred to above. Whether real or artificial, increased demand causes prices to rise.

> An increase in **real income** means the percentage increase in income is greater than the rate of inflation. Buying power has increased.

There is a seemingly logical argument in support of Bob receiving a raise along with his productive and dependable coworkers. If Bob doesn't get a raise, his "real" income declines. Due to the inflation already in the economy, the dollars Bob earns are worth slightly less each week. After a while, without a raise, this constant erosion of his buying power will reduce Bob's ability to make ends meet.

Does this mean that inflation causes inflation? No. When raises are only sufficient to cover inflation, there is no new demand. Bob is able to buy only the amount of goods and services he could before the raise. Only if Bob's raise exceeds the current rate of inflation (the current rise in prices) does it cause increased demand.

Now, even if it is more than the current rate of inflation, Bob's raise doesn't necessarily have to cause inflation. If Bob has become more productive or if he does more or better work in a given day, his raise is due to increased productivity. He has increased his input to the system, thus justifying the extra money. He has not only increased his demand, he has also added more value (goods and/or services) to the economy. His work is "worth" more. We don't see more money "chasing" the same amount of goods and services. We see more money "chasing" more goods and services. The result? Stable prices—no inflation.

Unemployment

To be classified as **unemployed**, an individual must be actively seeking employment or waiting to return to work after being laid off.

The U.S. civilian work force is the total number of people over 16 years of age who are either employed or unemployed. Notice the distinction between the total population over 16 and those who are either employed or unemployed. To be considered unemployed, an individual must be actively seeking employment or waiting to go back to work after a layoff. Missing from unemployment data are those classified as **discouraged workers**. An individual is classified as discouraged if he or she is unemployed but has given up trying to find work. Although they may be at least 16 years of age, individuals who have never been employed or have no intention of seeking employment are not considered among the country's work force. These individuals would include children living at home, students, and retirees.

The U.S. Bureau of Labor Statistics maintains many different types of employment data. To measure and present the number of unemployed during a given month, the Bureau first estimates the total civilian work force. Then the number of unemployed is estimated and stated as a percentage of the total. The table below, which shows the monthly unemployment rate from January 1991, can be found online at *http://stats.bls.gov/cpshome.htm.*

Year	Jan	Feb	Mar	Apr	May	Jun	Jul	Aug	Sep	Oct	Nov	Dec
1991	6.4	6.6	6.8	6.7	6.9	6.9	6.8	6.9	6.9	7.0	7.0	7.3
1992	7.3	7.4	7.4	7.4	7.6	7.8	7.7	7.6	7.6	7.3	7.4	7.4
1993	7.3	7.1	7.0	7.1	7.1	7.0	6.9	6.8	6.7	6.8	6.6	6.5
1994	6.6	6.6	6.5	6.4	6.1	6.1	6.1	6.0	5.9	5.8	5.6	5.5
1995	5.6	5.4	5.4	5.8	5.6	5.6	5.7	5.7	5.6	5.5	5.6	5.6
1996	5.6	5.5	5.5	5.6	5.6	5.3	5.5	5.1	5.2	5.2	5.4	5.4
1997	5.3	5.3	5.2	5.1	4.9	5.0	4.9	4.8	4.9	4.7	4.6	4.7
1998	4.7	4.6	4.7	4.4	4.4	4.5	4.5	4.5	4.5	4.5	4.4	4.4
1999	4.3	4.4	4.2	4.4	4.2	4.3	4.3	4.2	4.2	4.1	4.1	4.1
2000	4.0	4.1	4.0	4.0	4.1	4.0	4.0	4.1	3.9	3.9	4.0	4.0
2001	4.2	4.2	4.3									

There are actually three types of unemployment. **Frictional unemployment** is the result of employers' not being aware of qualified workers and workers' not being aware of available jobs. In other words, frictional unemployment exists because the location of the jobs and the workers has not been conveyed to interested parties, so they don't connect. The implication is that with proper information and willingness to relocate, this form of unemployment is avoidable.

Frictional unemployment is caused by the inability to connect the workers to the available jobs. It is due to the lack of information.

When the structural characteristics of the economy change, the result is **structural unemployment**. It becomes difficult for those seeking employment to find jobs, because they are not qualified. The economy has changed structurally, so that new qualifications are required for jobs. Under these circumstances, employers also find it difficult to find qualified workers, because they need people with different skills.

Structural unemployment is due to changes in the structure of the economy. Workers are not qualified for the available jobs.

The third type of unemployment is **cyclical unemployment**, which is due to decreases in the aggregate demand for goods and services. During such periods, firms produce less output and need fewer employees. Employees are typically laid off and return to their positions when the economy improves.

Cyclical unemployment is due to lack of aggregate demand. It usually involves layoffs.

Full employment is the natural level of employment resulting from the efficient utilization of the work force.

Full employment is the rate of employment resulting from the efficient utilization of the total labor force. This takes into consideration such factors as the levels of frictional and structural unemployment, which are to be expected in an expanding and evolving economy. In the United States, full employment is thought to be around 95 percent. This means that at full employment, approximately 5 percent of the U.S. labor force will be unemployed. Related to full employment is the concept of a **natural rate of unemployment**. It is the long-run, average unemployment rate caused by structural and frictional factors. In the U.S. the natural rate of unemployment is approximately 5 percent (i.e., 100 percent minus the full employment rate).

Macroeconomics

An official definition for macroeconomics is "the branch of economics that focuses on how human behavior affects outcomes in highly aggregated markets, such as the markets for labor or consumer products."[15] That's really a complicated way of saying macroeconomics refers to large, or economy-wide forces. A **macroeconomic variable** (e.g., inflation, unemployment, or government policies) is a factor that affects the entire economy or a major portion of it (a variable is something, such as inflation, that can have different values. For instance, inflation might be 2% one year, 4% the next, 7% the next, 3% the next, and so on).

Macroeconomics deals with economy-wide factors, such as inflation.

Macroeconomic variables are beyond the control of individuals or individual companies. For instance, no matter how much money you save or spend, you will have no affect on the rate of inflation in your country. However, the aggregate[16] spending or saving habits of the entire population of a country greatly affect that country's inflation or even overall economic growth.

For the individual company, macroeconomic variables are simply something with which to contend. For example, an increase in inflation increases input costs, which increases the total cost to manufacture goods. Whether the company can raise the selling price to absorb the increased cost is not certain since that will depend upon con-

---

[15] Gwartney, Stroup, and Sobel, *Economics*, 272.

[16] Aggregate is an economics term for "all together."

Schweser Study Program

sumers' willingness to pay a higher price. Whether caused by inflation or not, consumers tend not to blindly accept price increases.

We now return to our discussion of gerbil bedding and gold chains. Remember, gerbil bedding is very inexpensive to manufacture, but it is relatively costly to ship, and it has a readily available substitute (i.e., newspaper). If the retail price of gerbil bedding gets too high, even when the increase is due to the effect of inflation on manufacturing costs, consumers will simply not buy it.

Gold, however, is a different product. Recall our discussion of the supply and demand for gold as a precious metal used in jewelry. There seems to be a substantial profit built into selling gold necklaces, but even gold has its limits. As inflation increases the costs of mining, milling, and processing gold into chains, the wholesale[17] cost of gold chain will obviously increase. This means the gold chain distributor must now sell the chains to jewelry stores at higher prices. In turn, the jewelry store must charge consumers more. As this process continues, it will reach a point where consumer demand is reduced and sales of gold chains decreases.

As a gold chain wholesaler, you had nothing to do with the increase in inflation, nor can you do anything about it. You must simply live with it, even though you're not too happy with what it does to your costs and sales! There are also other economic variables that affect the entire economy, or at least very large sectors within it, and each of these variables has an economic impact similar to that of inflation. Also, like inflation, these variables are beyond the control of individuals or individual companies, though there may be very large companies within an economy that may be in a position to control prices and, hence, at least indirectly affect inflation.

Microeconomics

Microeconomics is "the branch of economics which focuses on how human behavior affects the conduct of affairs within narrowly defined units, such as individual households or business firms."[18] In other

Microeconomics deals with factors within a single firm or household, such as wages.

---

[17] Think of wholesale as the cost retailers, such as department stores, jewelry stores, and others pay for goods. They then sell the product to the final consumer at retail.

[18] Gwartney, Stroup, and Sobel, *Economics*, 272.

words, microeconomic variables are such things as wages at your company, the number of people you employ, your rent, your manager's salary, or any other item (variable) that pertains to your firm and no other. Notice that you ultimately have control over all of these variables because you own the company![19]

For example, as a supplier of gerbil bedding and gold necklaces, you employ twenty people to process the products and prepare them for shipping or delivery. Ten of these people work on bedding and ten on necklaces. In times of very high inflation, increases in your wholesale costs cause you to increase your price to retailers, which causes demand for your products to decline.

The bedding is far more sensitive to inflationary pressures, and the demand for it will almost disappear if its price rises. The result is that ten people who used to work processing the bedding for delivery are now idle. As owner/manager of the firm, you don't like to see people unemployed, but you must think of your family and other obligations. You hold on as long as you can, but ultimately you must lay off most of the bedding workers. You reassign the most senior bedding processors to the gold necklace line for as long as possible. Finally, as the effects of inflation begin to show on the demand for gold necklaces, you must lay off the reassigned bedding processors as well as some of the gold processors.

Assume the gerbil bedding is processed in a separate building. You can close down that building to avoid paying for heating and cooling and some maintenance. This reduces much of your utility expenses and allows you to reduce your maintenance costs too. Hopefully, increased inflation and unexpected cost increases are temporary, and you can bring back the people you laid off and reopen your gerbil bedding building and production line.

Generally, individuals or single firms have at least some control over micro-economic factors.

We could continue with this example, but the point should be clear: Macroeconomic factors (variables), such as inflation, are out of your control. With adverse changes, you simply try to maintain operations, absorbing profit reductions and increasing prices as much as you can.

---

[19] Of course, there are contractual considerations. For example, you might sign a contract for a period of time, during which you can't change your rent. Also, you may be subject to union contracts, which limit changes in wages and the number of people employed.

Schweser
Study Program

Microeconomic factors, such as the number of employees and certain overhead costs, are within your control to some degree. In hard times you may have some room to navigate; you can reduce some costs, and temporarily eliminate others.

Classical Economics

Economists from Adam Smith to those preceding John Maynard Keynes are considered to be **classical economists**. The most distinguishing characteristic of classical economists is their staunch belief in **laissez-faire**. This doctrine holds that government should not interfere in economic affairs beyond providing protection for its cities and maintaining property rights.

Classical economists contend that the economy needs no governmental interference during recessions. They believe that demand is fueled by supply, and that during a recession, prices and wages will fall quickly enough to stimulate the economy and bring it back to full employment. John Maynard Keynes is not considered a classical economist, since his model of the economy is based upon expenditures (demand), not supply. He argues that prices and wages are "downward sticky." This means that during a recession, there is no force that pushes prices and wages down, so the government must stimulate the economy through additional expenditures.

Equilibrium

We've discussed supply, demand, and inflation and the relationships among them. Another term you will often hear is **equilibrium**, which can be thought of as two equal and opposing forces. As an example, consider a tug-of-war contest between two five-person teams with exactly the same "pull" strength. Once the contest starts, with each five-person team pulling on opposite ends of the rope, the rope will not move in either direction. It is in equilibrium because the opposing forces are equal. If one team member loses footing and can no longer contribute to the team's pulling force, the system will no longer be in equilibrium. The rope will move in the direction of the greater force—toward the team with five contributing members.

What in the world is this all about? Well, supply and demand must be in equilibrium for prices to be stable (for simplicity, we'll ignore inflation

Classical economists feel the government should not interfere with the economy.

Supply and demand
must be in **equilibrium**
for prices to be stable.

for a moment). For example, if everyone in the world suddenly wanted a gold necklace, the demand would far outstrip the supply of necklaces, and the price of gold bullion, the raw material for gold necklaces, would increase dramatically. In a similar fashion, if the huge increases in gold bullion prices caused an abnormally large number of gold suppliers to increase their supply, the price would stabilize, or maybe even drop. As long as demand and supply are equal, the price for gold will remain about the same (though inflation may still cause the price of gold to increase steadily).

Without resorting to too much economic jargon to explain equilibrium, let's just leave it as meaning equal forces or pressures. In our example, the demand and supply for gold are equal. This means that the upward pressure on price caused by demand (buying) and the downward pressure on price caused by supply (selling) are perfectly balanced. And in this equilibrium state, prices are stable, since there is no pressure to push them higher or lower.

Costs (Factors) of Production

Fixed costs, such as rent,
are costs that are
incurred regardless of
your level of output.

Let's categorize manufacturing costs (factors) as either fixed or variable. **Fixed costs** are independent of production output. They occur each period regardless of whether your firm is actually producing anything. Rent is a good example of a fixed cost. Assume you are leasing (renting) your building and equipment. It doesn't matter if you ever turn the equipment on to produce your product, you must still pay the rent. When you begin production, the amount of rent you pay does not increase or decrease, so it is independent of production.

In the short run, **fixed
costs** cannot be
changed.

Alternatively, **variable costs** are associated with production, not the passage of time. Variable costs include the direct labor and material costs incurred in assembling the final product. Consider the production line you use to assemble gold necklaces and prepare them for shipping. There is a station where the chain is measured and cut. The 20-inch pieces then go to another station, where clasps are attached. At the last station, the necklaces are packaged for shipping, and then moved to the shipping area.

Variable costs, such as
wages and raw materials
move up and down as
production rises and
falls.

Now, consider the individual costs that are incurred in assembling one necklace: the cost of the material (gold chain), the cost of the clasps, the wages paid to the individuals at each station, the packaging material, and the shipping costs. All of these costs are related directly to the production of the gold necklaces, not the passage of time. They clearly are variable, not fixed, costs of production, since, if you produce no gold necklaces, none of these costs are incurred.

A concept, which may not be immediately obvious, is that classifying costs as fixed depends upon the time frame. In the **short run**, there is nothing that can be done to alter the classification of fixed costs. Fixed costs, such as rent and mortgage payments, cannot be changed in the short run. Given a long enough time period, however, fixed costs can change. For instance, we can pay off or refinance our mortgage, or we can negotiate a different rent. Thus, we refer to the period of time necessary for us to change our fixed costs as the **long run**. In the long run, all costs are variable.

> In the **long run**, all costs are variable.

Economies of Scale

The ability to produce more efficiently (cheaply), based upon size is known as **economies of scale**. For instance, let's assume your gerbil bedding and gold necklace company is doing so well that your regular purchases of gold chain and bedding have gotten very large. Since you are purchasing in larger quantities, the gold chain that used to cost you $2.00 per inch now costs you $1.80, a ten percent reduction. Similarly, bedding used to cost you $0.10 per pound, but, due to your increased purchases, your supplier now charges you only $0.08 per pound.

> **Economies of scale:** The ability to produce more efficiently (cheaply) as the size of the company increases.

In many cases, larger firms can purchase supplies and raw materials at relatively lower prices because of the willingness of their suppliers to sell to them at "quantity" discounts. This is an economy of scale, since the reduced price is attributable to the size of the purchases that are necessary to support the production of the larger firm.

Capital

Any resource that has value because it assists in the production or supply of goods and services is considered capital. From this definition, you can see there are many different things that may be classified as capital.

> **Capital** is considered to be any resource that has value because it helps in the production or supply of goods and services.

Human capital refers to the characteristics of people (e.g., physical strength, intelligence, education, manual dexterity, honesty, and

Human capital refers to the people employed in the supply of goods or services.

reliability) that make them valuable to a company. Obviously, at your gerbil bedding and gold necklace company, you value reliability and honesty above strength. Shipping companies tend to place value on strength for most of their employees in addition to reliability and honesty. Engineering firms value intelligence and education, as do universities.

Physical capital refers to the equipment, buildings and other physical items used in the supply of goods and services.

Physical capital refers to the non-human resources employed by the company (e.g., equipment, buildings, tools, and raw materials). Obviously, the amount of physical capital employed by a firm depends upon the industry. For instance, steel producers and auto manufacturers employ great amounts of physical capital. On the other hand, real estate development firms or brokers have little need for equipment, buildings, and tools.

The **value** of a firm depends upon its ability to fill a need in society, to provide a necessary function or product. In turn, that ability is dependent upon how well the firm uses its capital, people, equipment, and other resources. When you value a firm, whether currently operating or not, you value it as if it is performing at its full potential. That is, you value it as though it is using all of its employed capital in the most efficient and productive manner. To illustrate this concept of value, consider the following situation.

You are at the beach one day, and you notice that a local sandwich and ice cream shop has gone out of business. You say to yourself, "How in the world could that place go out of business? That place has so much potential!" However, your estimate of the value of the sandwich and ice cream shop is dependent upon the collective potential value of all the capital it employed (the location, the building, the equipment, the people, the supplies, and the money). If the shop went out of business, it is a good indication that it was not using its capital in the most efficient and productive manner. In other words, it was not using its capital to its full potential.

Monopolies and Oligopolies

When a single supplier controls the entire supply of a product, that supplier is said to enjoy a **monopoly**. Typically, there are very high barriers to entry in markets that create monopolies. For instance, assume you have control over land that holds a vast supply of gold. Next, assume that searching for gold in other parts of the world is extremely expensive, because the world's supply of gold is nearly depleted. In a situation such as this, the possibility of new suppliers exploring for gold and being able to compete with you is very low. You effectively control the world's supply of gold.

Now, let's make the simplifying assumption that your costs to supply gold are more or less stable, so that your profit equals total revenues less some constant cost, where total revenue equals the amount of gold you sell multiplied by its selling price. Your goal is to find the combination of price and quantity supplied that maximizes total revenue. The optimal price-quantity combination is at the point where the price increase resulting from a reduction in the amount of gold that your company supplies will not offset the accompanying reduction in demand. Similarly, the price decrease associated with an increased supply will not be offset by the increased demand at the lower price. You have maximized your profit, and it has nothing to do with competition.

An **oligopoly** is comprised of a small number of suppliers who totally control the supply of a good or service. As with a monopoly, an oligopoly seeks that combination of supply and price that maximizes profits. Unlike a monopoly, however, the success of the oligopoly is dependent upon its members' ability to reach and maintain supply agreements. Although not technically an oligopoly, OPEC[20] is an appropriate and very familiar example of the concept of oligopoly. OPEC faces an interesting problem, since they do not control the entire supply of crude oil. Member countries control only a very large portion of it, which they maintain carefully to manipulate prices. However, if they limit supplies too much, prices will rise to the point where potential competitors (drillers in Texas, the Gulf of Mexico, the North Sea, etc.) will be enticed to reopen their drilling and exploration sites (In most other areas of the world, exploration and extraction are far more expensive than they are in the OPEC nations. These other sites will only supply oil if the selling price is sufficient to cover costs and provide a profit). Even though OPEC does not have total control over the supply of crude oil, their hold is very strong.

In a **monopoly,** one supplier controls the entire supply of a good or service.

An **oligopoly** is a small group of suppliers who collectively enjoy a monopoly.

---

[20] Since they do not totally control the world's supply of crude oil, OPEC, The Organization of Petroleum Exporting Countries, is actually a cartel. Member countries include Algeria, Indonesia, Iran, Iraq, Kuwait, Libya, Nigeria, Qatar, Saudi Arabia, United Arab Emirates, and Venezuela.

Cartels, such as OPEC, are groups who conspire to control the price of a good or service.

Another interesting aspect of oligopolies is that each member is better off by secretly increasing its supply (cheating!). For instance, if OPEC agrees on a certain supply from each country, all member countries are bound by that agreement. Once the agreement has been reached, the price of crude oil reacts based on the expected supply. Since each member's best interests are served by maximizing revenues, each member will want to do so. The way a member nation maximizes revenues is by increasing supply above that specified in the agreement. In other words, what is best for the group is not necessarily best for the individual member, and vice versa.

The increased supply from one member that violates the agreement is probably not enough to affect world prices, as long as it is not publicly announced. If that member can be quiet and not boast too loudly, other members will not be aware of the transgression and will be no worse off. Of course, this is exactly why cartels and oligopolies must police themselves.

Fiscal and Monetary Policy

Fiscal policy refers to the government's use of spending and taxation to attain macro-economic goals.

The government may try to stimulate or dampen the economy in order to achieve certain macroeconomic goals. There are two primary methods that can be used to stimulate the economy: fiscal policy and monetary policy.

Fiscal policy refers to the government's use of taxation and spending policies to achieve various macroeconomic goals. Taxation affects disposable income. To stimulate the economy, the government can reduce taxes, which increases disposable income, thus increasing expenditures (demand) in the private sector (you and me). Alternatively, increasing taxes reduces disposable income and private sector spending.

Monetary policy refers to the government's use of changes in the money supply to attain macro-economic goals.

Government spending was used extensively during the Great Depression to stimulate the economy of the United States, due in no small measure to the work of John Maynard Keynes. During the Depression, the government started public works projects, such as the Hoover Dam in Nevada, a series of drainage canals running through St. Louis, Missouri, and hundreds of other major projects throughout the country. This fiscal policy had the effect of putting people to work. It increased overall expenditures in the economy, which eventually brought the economy back toward full employment.

The government also uses **monetary policy** to help achieve macroeconomic goals by changing the amount of money in circulation. Like any other product, the higher the demand for money relative to supply, the higher its cost. The cost of money is the rate of interest. The Federal Reserve (Fed) can actually change the supply of money in the U.S. economy by buying and selling U.S. Treasury securities in **open market operations**. For example, to slow the economy in times of rising inflation due to excess (unbalanced) demand, the Fed can reduce the supply of money in circulation by selling Treasury securities from its inventory. The amount of money corporations and other institutional investors,[21] foreign countries,[22] and individuals use to purchase these securities will no longer be in circulation. The resulting reduction in the money supply causes interest rates to rise. Consequently, companies and individuals who need to borrow money may have to postpone expansion plans or large purchases until interest rates decline.

If the economy is weak and unemployment is high, the Fed can buy Treasury securities, effectively increasing the money supply. This will cause interest rates to fall, and, hopefully, the companies that put expansion plans on hold and the individuals who decided to delay their large purchases can go ahead with their plans. This increases expenditures in the private sector and helps the economy move back to full employment.

Another way the Fed can control (adjust) the money supply is by changing the discount rate. When banks face short-term cash shortages, they borrow from the Fed. By increasing the discount rate, the Fed effectively makes money more expensive. The increase in the discount rate ultimately affects all other interest rates, so we see an economy-wide increase in rates. Since money is now more expensive, we again have a situation where some borrowers may have to postpone their plans. There is less money in the economy, money is now more expensive, and the economy slows. To stimulate the economy, the Fed can lower the discount rate, causing the general level of interest rates to decline.

The **discount rate** is the rate the Fed charges member banks for short-term loans.

[21] Institutional investors include pension funds, mutual funds, insurance companies and other large businesses, which are capable of making very large trades.

[22] All U.S. Treasury securities are denominated in U.S. dollars, so even foreign investors must use U.S. currency to purchase them.

CHAPTER SUMMARY

Learning Objective 1: *To understand the origin and development of economics as a discipline.*

A. All choices are economic in nature.
   1. Decision makers weigh the costs against the benefits of the choice.
   2. Decision makers try to find the combination of cost and benefit that maximizes their personal utility (the satisfaction they derive from the choice).
B. **Sir Francis Bacon** (1551–1626) was an early philosopher/economist whose writings were firmly based in religious doctrine.
   1. Most economists of his era were actually philosophers.
   2. They studied the way men and women made decisions in the context of religious doctrine.
C. **Adam Smith** (1723–1790) is considered the father of the **free enterprise system**. He brought economics out of the realm of the church and showed it to be a discipline separate from philosophy. He published *The Wealth of Nations* in 1776 and is considered to be the first "true" classical economist.
   1. **Classical economists** believe in **laissez-faire**.
      a. Government should only provide and protect peace and property rights.
      b. Government should not interfere in the economy.
   2. During a recession, classical economists advocate that prices and wages will drop quickly enough to bring the economy back to full employment.
   3. According to classical economics, individuals' actions in a free market are controlled by competition.
      a. Individuals making selfish decisions will lead ultimately to the betterment of society.
      b. Only those products and services actually needed by society will be provided.
D. **Karl Marx** (1818–1883) was a staunch opponent of the capitalist system, referring to capitalists as the **bourgeoisie** and the working masses as the **proletariat**. Marx believed that the proletariat should control all means of production. Marxists advocate the following:
   1. Capitalism is doomed to evolve into socialism then into communism.

2. There should be no private property.
   a. Private property is the source of economic classes.
   b. Private property leads to greed and avarice.
   c. Private property ultimately leads to revolution.
3. Revolution leads to socialism.
   a. The government owns all income producing assets.
   b. Private property has been abolished.
   c. Goods and pay are allocated according to effort, not need.
   d. This leads to unequal distribution.
4. Further revolution leads to a classless society (communism).
   a. There is no formal government.
   b. A central party controls the distribution of goods and pay.
   c. All property is owned collectively and is available to each according to need.

E. **John Maynard Keynes** (1883–1946) was a devoted capitalist whose views differed greatly from the classical economists. He believed that during a recession, wages and prices will not automatically go lower, and that the only way to recover from a recession is to increase expenditures.
1. When total expenditures from the public and private sectors are deficient, government spending should increase.
2. During a recession, government needs to run a deficit to stimulate demand and bring the economy back to full employment.

Learning Objective 2: *To understand the three most important forms of government: capitalism, socialism, and communism.*

A. **Capitalism** is characterized as **free enterprise**, which is characterized by the following:
1. Private ownership of productive resources.
2. Prices determined by market forces.
3. Limited interference by government, which provides and protects peace and private property, and develops and enforces a system of laws.
B. **Socialism** follows the revolution against capitalism (according to Marx).
1. Socialism is usually characterized as a dictatorship.
2. The government owns all income producing assets (no private property).

  3. Allocation is based upon effort, which leads to unequal distribution. This leads to another revolution (according to Marx).
D. **Communism** follows the revolution against socialism (according to Marx).
  1. Communism is characterized by no formal government.
  2. The proletariat has seized and collectively controls all property.
  3. No economic classes exist as the bourgeoisie has been eliminated.
  4. Distribution is done by a central committee. ("From each according to his abilities, to each according to his needs.")

Learning Objective 3: *To master an essential economics vocabulary.*

A. **Supply**
  1. Supply is defined as the amount of an item available for purchase.
  2. An item is supplied only if the price received from selling it is sufficiently greater than the total cost to provide it. Total cost to supply an item includes the costs of raw materials, labor, overhead, and shipping.
  3. An increase (decrease) in supply usually decreases (increases) price.
  4. The combination of supply and demand sets market prices.
B. **Demand**
  1. Demand is defined as the total amount of an item society wants to purchase, which depends upon several factors (the number of potential consumers, price, the availability of substitutes, whether a necessity or a luxury, and the amount of money in the economy).
  2. An increase (decrease) in demand usually increases (decreases) price.
  3. The combination of supply and demand sets prices.
C. **Inflation**
  1. Inflation is an artificial increase in prices due to excess demand.
  2. Inflation is usually caused by too much money in the economy. The increase in spending is not offset by an increase in the amount of goods and services supplied.

D. **Unemployment**
1. The civilian work force is defined as those above the age of 16 who are employed or unemployed. Those under 16 and those over 16 who are not trying to work are not considered to be a part of the civilian work force.
2. To be classified as unemployed, an individual must be actively seeking employment or waiting to return after a layoff.
3. **Frictional unemployment** is due to the inability to convey information that qualified workers for particular jobs are available.
4. **Structural unemployment** is due to changes in the structure of the economy (i.e., newly created jobs requiring different qualifications).
5. **Cyclical unemployment** is caused by a decrease in aggregate demand for goods and services. The usual result is temporary layoffs.

E. **Macroeconomics**
1. Macroeconomics focuses on large, economy-wide forces. Forces that affect most or all companies and individuals include inflation, unemployment, and government policies.
2. Companies can only adjust output and/or their workforce in response to macroeconomic factors.

F. **Microeconomics**
1. Microeconomics focuses on forces within a single firm or household.
2. There are some ways that companies may be able to control microeconomic forces.
   a. Payroll—reduce/increase number of employees.
   b. Costs of production—reduce/increase purchases of raw materials or shut down individual production lines.
   c. Overhead—reduce utilities, reduce/increase management, or change terms of equipment leases or building rent.
3. The following factors may not be controllable in the short run: labor contracts, long-term lease or rent agreements, or management contracts.

G. **Classical economics**
1. Economists before John Maynard Keynes (1883–1946) believed in a **laissez-faire** approach.
   a. Government should only provide and protect peace and property rights.
   b. Government should not interfere in the economy.

2. During a recession, prices and wages will drop quickly enough to bring the economy back to full employment.

H. **Equilibrium**

1. Equilibrium occurs when equal opposing forces act against one another in such a way that neither gives ground to the other.
2. Relationships between supply and demand affect prices.
   a. If supply of goods matches demand for goods, the result is stable prices.
   b. If supply of goods is greater than demand for goods, the result is a drop in prices.
   c. If supply of goods is less than demand for goods, the result is increasing prices.

I. **Costs (factors) of production**

1. Costs of all resources that go into producing the final product include raw materials, labor, management, equipment and buildings, and intellectual property.
2. **Fixed costs** (e.g., rent, management salaries, and depreciation) are related to passage of time, not production. These costs cannot be changed in the short run. They can be changed if given sufficient time (long run).
3. **Variable costs** (e.g., raw goods and wages) are related to production, not passage of time.

J. **Economies of scale**

1. The ability to produce more efficiently (cheaply) due to size.
2. Large firms can buy in quantity because of volume discounts.
3. Overhead costs can be spread over greater output because of equipment costs (e.g., depreciation, maintenance) and management salaries/bonuses.

K. **Capital**

1. Physical capital includes equipment, buildings, raw materials, location, and money.
2. Nonphysical capital includes human capital (e.g., education, strength, reliability, honesty) and intellectual property (e.g., patents).

L. **Monopoly**

1. Monopolies are characterized by one supplier with no competitors and high barriers to market entry. Companies try to set supply to maximize profit.
   a. More supply reduces profits—increased demand not sufficient to offset reduced price.

      b. Less supply reduces profits—increased price not sufficient to offset reduced demand.

   2. Natural monopolies include public utilities. Natural monopolies reduce total costs to society but must be regulated.

M. **Oligopoly**

   1. Oligopolies occur in markets characterized by a small number of suppliers that enjoy monopoly control. This situation can result in **collusion** (price setting).

   2. A **cartel** is a group that controls most of the supply and the price.

N. **Fiscal policy**

   1. Governments use taxation and spending to achieve macroeconomic goals by either slowing or stimulating an economy.

   2. Tax policies change disposable income.

      a. Increasing taxes reduces disposable income, slows the economy, and reduces expenditures.

      b. Decreasing taxes increases disposable income, stimulates the economy, and increases expenditures.

   3. Spending policies affect work force.

      a. Increased government spending stimulates the economy by increasing employment, which leads to increased private expenditures.

      b. Decreased government spending slows the economy by decreasing employment and decreasing private expenditures.

O. **Monetary policy**

   1. Government controls the money supply.

      a. Increased money supply reduces interest rates, which:
- stimulates borrowing.
- stimulates the economy.
- increases expenditures.

      b. Decreased money supply increases interest rates, which:
- reduces borrowing.
- slows the economy.
- decreases expenditures.

   2. Open market operations occur when the Federal Reserve buys or sells U.S. Treasury securities.

      a. Buying securities increases money supply.

      b. Selling securities reduces money supply.

3. The discount rate can be altered to affect interest rates.
   a. Increasing the discount rate increases all interest rates, which:
      - reduces borrowing.
      - slows the economy.
      - decreases expenditures.
   b. Decreasing the discount rate reduces all interest rates, which:
      - increases borrowing.
      - stimulates the economy.
      - increases expenditures.

PRACTICE QUESTIONS

1. Which of the following people is known as father of the free enterprise system?

   A. Sir Francis Bacon.
   B. Adam Smith.
   C. Karl Marx.
   D. John Maynard Keynes.

2. Which of the following would be considered a violation of laissez-faire?

   A. Government should only provide and protect peace and property rights.
   B. Government should employ a "hands-off" approach to the economy.
   C. Government should only provide fiscal and monetary policy adjustments in times of high unemployment.
   D. All the above would be considered part of the laissez-faire doctrine.

3. Which of the following is **not** in accordance with Marxist theory?

   A. There should be no social class.
   B. Revolution leads to socialism.
   C. The proletariat should control the means of production.
   D. During a recession, prices and wages will drop quickly enough to bring the economy back to full employment.

4. What type of economic system exists in the United States?

   A. Capitalism.
   B. Socialism.
   C. Communism.
   D. Laissez-faire.

5. Under which economic system does the government own all income producing assets and determine which products will be produced and in what quantities?

   A. Capitalism.
   B. Socialism.
   C. Communism.
   D. Industrialism.

6. Which economic system has no formal structure?

    A. Capitalism.
    B. Socialism.
    C. Communism.
    D. Laissez-faire.

7. Inflation could best be defined as an:

    A. artificial decrease in prices due to excess demand.
    B. artificial decrease in prices due to excess supply.
    C. artificial increase in prices due to excess demand.
    D. increase in prices.

8. Which of the following statements is correct?

    Statement M: Macroeconomics focuses on large, economy-wide forces.

    Statement N: Microeconomics focuses on forces within a single firm or household.

    A. M.
    B. N.
    C. Both M and N.
    D. Neither M nor N.

9. We refer to the period of time necessary to change fixed costs as the:

    A. short run.
    B. home run.
    C. long run.
    D. fiscal year.

10. Which term best describes the relationship outlined below?

    One pencil costs $1.00.

    One hundred pencils cost $90.00.

    A. Economies of scope.
    B. Economies of scale.
    C. Diseconomies of scope.
    D. Synergistic economic scaling.

11. Which of the following is a form of human capital?

    A. Experience.
    B. Intelligence.
    C. Education.
    D. All of the above are considered human capital.

12. Which of the following is **not** an example of physical capital?

    A. Equipment.
    B. Physical strength.
    C. Tools.
    D. Raw materials.

13. Which of the following terms describes a situation in which one supplier controls the entire supply of a good or service?

    A. Monopoly.
    B. Oligopoly.
    C. Cartel.
    D. Collusion.

14. Under which type of policy does the government use taxation and spending policies to achieve macroeconomic goals?

    A. Monetary policy.
    B. Fiscal policy.
    C. Laissez-faire.
    D. Open market transactions.

15. Changing the amount of money in circulation is example of what type of government policy?

    A. Monetary.
    B. Fiscal.
    C. Laissez-faire.
    D. Public.

16. Which of the following is **not** an example of a fixed cost?

    A. Rent.
    B. Management salaries.
    C. Depreciation.
    D. Wages.

17. Which of the following is typically classified as a variable cost?

    A. Depreciation.
    B. Management salary.
    C. Wages.
    D. Building expense.

18. When supply is greater than demand, prices:

    A. rise.
    B. fall.
    C. stabilize.
    D. revert.

19. Under which situation would prices rise?

    A. Supply = demand.
    B. Supply > demand.
    C. Supply < demand.
    D. Laissez-faire.

20. Which of the following represents a way in which the federal government can stimulate the economy?

    A. Lower the discount rate.
    B. Increase the interest rate.
    C. Increase the discount rate.
    D. Increase taxes.

ANSWERS AND SOLUTIONS

1. B. Adam Smith is considered the father of the free enterprise system, in which private business is free to operate without government interference (beyond regulation necessary to protect the public interest) and prices are determined by market forces.

2. C. Laissez-faire is strict "hands-off" by the federal government, except for providing and protecting peace and private property.

3. D. This idea is part of classical economics.

4. A. The United States embraces the system of capitalism. Laissez-faire is an approach used within the system of capitalism.

5. B. The correct answer is socialism. Capitalism allows private ownership and under communism, all means of production are owned by the masses.

6. C. Communism has no formal structure. Capitalistic and socialist societies both have formal governments, although those governments serve very different functions.

7. C. We say artificial because the price increases are due to excess money in the system, which is not offset by increased productivity.

8. C. Macroeconomics focuses on large, economy-wide forces. Microeconomics focuses on forces within a single firm or household.

9. C. The definition of "long run" is the time period necessary to adjust fixed costs. Fixed costs cannot be changed in the short run.

10. B. Scale refers to "size." Being able to save money by purchasing single items in larger quantities is a characteristic of firm size. Scope, although also due to size, refers to breadth of coverage (e.g., supplying many different products).

11. D. Human capital refers to the characteristics of people that make them valuable to a process.

12. B. Physical capital refers to non-human resources employed (e.g., equipment, buildings, tools, raw materials).

13. A. In a monopoly, one supplier controls the entire supply of a good or service.

14. B. Fiscal policy refers to the government's use of taxation and spending policies to achieve macroeconomic goals.

15. A. The government uses monetary policy to achieve macroeconomic goals by changing the amount of money in circulation.

16. D. A fixed cost is a function of the passage of time. Even without production, fixed costs must be met.

17. C. Wages are mostly a function of production. If the plant stands idle (no production), wages may be reduced, if not eliminated.

18. B. When supply is greater than demand, suppliers must reduce prices to sell their products.

19. C. If demand is greater than supply, buyers will compete by offering (i.e., be willing to pay) higher prices.

20. A. The discount rate is the rate the Federal Reserve charges member banks for short-term loans. By lowering this rate, the Fed actually makes money cheaper, which stimulates production.

Financial Statement Analysis

Financial statements are useful in helping investors and creditors evaluate firms. They give a snapshot of the firm's assets, liabilities, and equity at a point in time (the **balance sheet**) as well as a summary of the firm's operating performance over a specified period of time (the **income statement**). They show the firm's operating, investing, and financing cash flows over a specified period (the **statement of cash flows**) and the amounts of and changes in ownership (the **statement of owners' equity**).

The Financial Accounting Standard Board (FASB) establishes the form and content of financial statements. The intent is to generate standardized, comprehensible information "for those with a reasonable understanding of business and economic activities [who] are willing to study the information with reasonable diligence."[1]

Before evaluating financial statements, you need a reasonable understanding of the major accounts contained in the statements and the accounting methods used to generate them. Section 1 gives you an overview of the four principal financial statements. Section 2 follows with a discussion of accounting methods and procedures.

> The **four principal financial statements** are the balance sheet, income statement, statement of cash flows, and statement of owners' equity.

SECTION 1: FINANCIAL STATEMENTS

In this section, your learning objectives are:

1. To understand the form and substance of the four principal financial statements.

> The **income statement**, sometimes called the statement of earnings, shows the firm's operating results for a period of time.

[1] Financial Accounting Standards Board, *Statement of Financial Concepts 1, Objectives of Financial Reporting by Business Enterprise,* paragraph 34.

2. To understand the relationships between the four financial statements.
3. To understand the difference between cash and non-cash expenses.
4. To understand the rationale for capitalizing and depreciating the costs of large assets instead of expensing them.
5. To understand the procedure for classifying cash inflows and cash outflows.

Income Statement

From an accounting standpoint, the focus in evaluating a company's performance is usually on "the bottom line," or **net income**. Net income is the difference between **revenues** and **expenses** after the payment of taxes. **Revenues** represent cash or credit inflows from sales of products or services. Simply put, revenues are *inflows*. Any cost associated with running a business is usually considered an expense. Expenses are *outflows*. **Net income** is what is left after deducting all expenses paid (including relevant taxes) from all revenues received.

For example, let's take a look at a young child named Lucy, who sells lemonade in front of her house. The only expense for this business enterprise is the price of the lemonade mix. (Her mother doesn't charge her for the use of measuring spoons, bowls, or pitchers, and her father makes a concession stand for her out of an old box and extra lumber.) Revenue is the money received from selling glasses of lemonade, and net income is what is left in her change box after paying for the lemonade mix. **Exhibit 1** represents Lucy's income statement. It shows the revenues from selling lemonade, the costs associated with selling the lemonade, and net income (i.e., the "bottom line").

Revenues are the cash inflows generated by operations; the sale of goods or services.

Exhibit 1: Lemonade Stand

Lucy's Income Statement
Weekend Ending July 9, 200X

Revenue	$2.00
Less:	
Cost of Goods Sold:	
Mix	$0.50
Net Income	$1.50

Schweser
Study Program™

Of course, reality is far more complex. By expanding upon this simple example, we will show how complicated business record-keeping can get.

Assume Lucy, now age 13, has enlisted several of her friends to help prepare and sell lemonade. With her friends, she is capable of producing and selling a much greater quantity of lemonade at stands throughout her neighborhood. Her income statement is now slightly different, as shown in **Exhibit 2**. Revenues are again the inflows from selling lemonade, but now her costs have been expanded to include the costs of lemonade mix, pitchers, cups, signs, coolers to transport and store the lemonade, and the wages she must pay her helpers.

You may be asking yourself about the leftover cups, pitchers, and coolers. What about the stands and the signs? As you will see later, these items are not used up in mixing and selling the lemonade. The initial costs associated with these items are not considered costs of sales or operating expenses. They are considered company assets and will be recorded in the balance sheet and expensed a little bit in each of the next few years through a process called **depreciation**.

Exhibit 2: Multiple Lemonade Stands

Lucy's Income Statement
Weekend Ending July 9, 200X

Revenue	$15.00
Less:	
Cost of Goods Sold:	
Mix	3.00
Cups	1.00
Operating Expenses:	
Wages	8.00
Net Income	$ 3.00

As Lucy's business gets larger, the challenges get larger, and the accounting gets more complicated. Now a sophomore in college, Lucy sees great opportunities in the lemonade business and strives to expand her business by opening a location inside the local shopping mall.

The mall store presents a new set of challenges for Lucy, who estimates she will need $10,000 to open her business. She will use $5,000 of her own money (equity) and $5,000 which she can borrow from her parents at 8.00 percent (debt). She will make interest-only payments at the end of each month.

Lucy will need to purchase equipment and pay rent in the amount of $12.00 per square foot of space per year. Since she will need 1,000 square feet, her rental cost will be $12,000 per year. Payments of $1,000 are due at the beginning of each month. (For simplicity, we will assume the site already has a counter with stools and storage space for inventory, i.e., no additional improvements are needed.)

Lucy invests $1,500 in machinery but soon realizes that her customers would like pretzels to go with their lemonade. To sell pretzels, Lucy needs to purchase an oven ($1,350) and a heated display case ($250). (We assume that the purchase of the oven and heated display case occur the *day after* Lucy opens for business. As a result, these purchases *do not* affect Lucy's opening balance sheet.)

Her $10,000 will cover the first two months' rent, her beginning inventory of mix, paper cups, straws, napkins, etc., and the cost of an ice-making machine. In addition, she needs to purchase insurance, which costs $7,200 per year, payable every six months. She will sell her lemonade at $1.00 per cup and pay her employees minimum wage. Her business opened July 1, and the income statement after the first month is shown in **Exhibit 3**.

Cost of goods sold includes the costs of all "raw" inputs, which are combined into the final product.

Revenue for the month is the total of all cash inflows from sales. **Cost of goods sold (COGS)** includes the "raw" inputs, which are combined into the final product sold to the customer. Lucy's typical customer buys one pretzel and a cup of lemonade. In this case, the final product includes one pretzel, eight ounces of lemonade, the cup to hold the lemonade, a straw, and the napkins the customer picks up on the way out.

Costs associated with keeping the business open and putting together and selling the final product are considered **operating expenses**.

Costs associated with keeping the business open and putting together and selling the final product are included under **operating expenses**. Lucy's operating expenses include:

- Wages of $2,500 that she pays three part-time employees (for simplicity, we are ignoring payroll taxes)
- Power and light costs of $800
- One month's rent and insurance

Exhibit 3: Lemonade Business in the Shopping Mall

Lucy's Lemonade
Income Statement
Month Ending July 31, 200X

Revenue	$8,500
Less:	
Cost of Goods Sold:	
Mix: Lemonade	975
Mix: Pretzel	350
Paper Goods	625
Operating Expenses:	
Wages	2,500
Utilities	800
Rent	1,000
Insurance	600
Depreciation*	36
Income From Operations	1,614
Less:	
Interest Expense**	33
Net Income**	$1,581

* Depreciation = (Cost of Equipment) $\times$ (depreciation %)(1/12)
= $(1,500 + 1,350 + 250) \times (14\%)(1/12) = \$434(1/12) = \$36.16$
(One month's depreciation is calculated only for a more accurate picture of operations for the first month. For simplicity, we ignore the half-year convention. See MACRS Table 2.)

** Interest Expense = (Amount Borrowed) $\times$ (Monthly Interest Rate)
= $(\$5,000) \times (.08)/12 = \$33.33$

*** Lucy's Lemonade, structured as a sole proprietorship, does not incur an income tax liability. Net income is fully taxable for the proprietor, who must add it to any other income in calculating her annual federal, state, and/or local income tax liability.

Depreciation is the means by which the costs of long-term (or capitalized) assets are expensed.

Even though they are crucial to the operation of the business, the costs of long-term assets, such as buildings and equipment, are not considered operating expenses. These assets are *capitalized,* and their costs are written off (expensed) over a period of years through a process referred to as **depreciation**. For example, the total cost of a new piece of equipment, including any cost to ship and install the equipment, is recorded as the equipment's **historical** or **capitalized cost**. This value is then reduced by the annual depreciation amount until the asset's book value reaches zero. **Book value** is the value shown on the balance sheet. It equals historical, or capitalized cost less all depreciation taken.

The total cost to purchase and install a piece of equipment or any fixed asset is the asset's **capitalized cost**.

Depreciation helps avoid the large variations in net income that would occur if the total costs of major assets were charged against revenue all at once. Major assets, such as land, buildings, and equipment, are referred to as **capital assets**. In the United States prior to 1954, the costs of capital assets were written off using the straight-line depreciation technique. Under the straight-line method, annual depreciation expense is the total cost of the capital asset less any estimated salvage value, divided by its estimated useful life (in years). For example, the cost of a $1,000 asset with a 10-year life and zero salvage value would be depreciated at the rate of $100 per year.

Beginning in 1954, firms were allowed to use accelerated depreciation methods that sped up the rate at which the costs of assets were expensed. Double-declining balance (DDB) and sum of the years' digits (SYD) were the accelerated depreciation methods in use at that time.[2] Since firms could choose their preferred method, inconsistency existed across firms and even across assets within the same firm. The U.S. Congress enacted the Accelerated Cost Recovery System (ACRS) in 1981, which replaced most prior methods of depreciation.

In 1986, the U.S. Congress approved **MACRS**, which mandates the rate at which assets are depreciated.

ACRS was replaced in 1986 with the *Modified* Accelerated Cost Recovery System, or **MACRS**. As with ACRS, MACRS places long-term assets into classes and specifies the amount of depreciation allowed each year. **MACRS Tables 1 and 2** on the next page are simplified tables based on those presented in the ninth edition of *Financial Management: Theory and Practice*.[3] In our example, we assume Lucy's equipment falls into the MACRS 7-year Class[4], which calls for the total, installed costs of the assets to be depreciated over an eight-year period. Her assets cost a total of $3,100. Using the percentage from MACRS Table 2, her first year depreciation expense would be .14 × $3,100 = $434, for a full year, and $434/12 = $36.16 for one month.

[2] For a complete discussion of depreciation methods, see White, Sondhi, and Fried, *The Analysis and Use of Financial Statements, 2E* (Wiley, 1998), 377–423.

[3] Eugene F. Brigham, Louis C. Gapenski, and Michael C. Ehrhardt, *Financial Management, Theory and Practice, 9E* (The Dryden Press, 1999) 466.

[4] Due to the immaterial cost of the display unit ($250), Lucy could choose to expense it when purchased, rather than capitalize and depreciate it.

MACRS Table 1: Class Lives for Different Types of Property

Class	Type of Property
3-year	Certain special manufacturing tools.
5-year	Automobiles, light-duty trucks, computers, and certain special manufacturing equipment.
7-year	Most industrial equipment, office furniture, and fixtures.
10-year	Certain longer-lived types of equipment.
27.5-year	Residential rental property such as apartment buildings.
39-year	All nonresidential real property, including commercial and industrial buildings.

MACRS Table 2: Annual Depreciation Percentages by Asset Class

Ownership Year	Class of Investment			
	3-Year	5-Year	7-Year	10-Year
1	33%	20%	14%	10%
2	45	32	25	18
3	15	19	17	14
4	7	12	13	12
5		11	9	9
6		6	9	7
7			9	7
8			4	7
9				7
10				6
11				3

Each column totals 100%.

Half-year convention. The percentages above were developed using 200% declining balance depreciation. To avoid complications resulting from when the asset is placed into service its first year, all classes above receive **a half-year's depreciation** the first year. The remaining half-year is taken in the last year making the total years in each category one more than the class.

Residential and commercial real property, 27.5- and 39-year assets, respectively, are depreciated using the straight-line method. Depreciation for the first year is based upon the month the property is placed into service with any remainder taken in the 28th or 40th year, respectively.

Even though **depreciation expense** is not a cash flow, it **reduces** taxable income and company's **income tax liability**. To recognize this tax break as quickly as possible, managers want to speed up the rate of depreciation as much as possible.

Since **interest expense** reduces taxable income, it also reduces income taxes. This reduces the effective cost of borrowed funds.

Unlike interest paid by an individual on credit cards or automobile loans, interest paid by a business is considered a tax-deductible expense. Lucy's interest expense is the total interest paid to her parents for the $5,000 loan. The interest for one month would be the loan principal multiplied by the monthly interest rate, or $5,000 \times .08/12 = \$33.33$.

Deducting COGS, operating expenses, and interest expense from the month's revenue, Lucy's Lemonade shows net income of $1,581 for July. As we will see in the **statement of cash flows,** however, this $1,581 is not all cash.

Balance Sheet

Even though an income statement for a "real life" business can be considerably more complex, Lucy's Lemonade includes many of the more important revenue and expense accounts. However, we have not yet accounted for the assets and liabilities of Lucy's Lemonade. To do this, we must develop a balance sheet.

The balance sheet shows the value of assets, liabilities, and owners' equity at a specific point in time. The two sides of the balance sheet must always be equal. **Assets = Liabilities + Equity**

While the income statement shows operating results over a period of time, the balance sheet reports types and amounts of assets, liabilities, and owners' (stockholders') equity at a specific point in time. An income statement and balance sheet produced at the end of a quarter, combined with the balance sheet from the beginning of the quarter, would show the results of operations as well as changes in asset, liability, and equity accounts over the period.

Recall that Lucy bought inventory, paid two-months' rent and six months' insurance, and installed an icemaker with the initial $10,000 investment. Her assets include inventory and supplies, the ice-making machine, and any cash left over. Since she has prepaid some items, they are also considered assets, as if they were money in the bank. These include prepaid insurance and rent, which are written off one month at a time.

Lucy's Lemonade is a new business, so her suppliers require her to pay half the cost for orders of inventory and supplies when they are delivered/ordered. The balance of these purchases represents a short-term liability, or accounts payable, which is due in thirty days. Her only other liability is the long-term note representing the $5,000 borrowed from her parents. Let's look at the July 1 balance sheet for Lucy's Lemonade in **Exhibit 4:**

Exhibit 4: Opening Day of Mall Business

Lucy's Lemonade
Opening Day Balance Sheet
July 1, 200X

Current Assets:		Current Liabilities:	
Cash	$2,400	Accounts Payable	$ 500
Inventory	500		
Supplies	500	**Long Term Liabilities:**	
Prepaid Rent	2,000	Notes Payable	5,000
Prepaid Insurance	3,600		
Fixed Assets:		**Owners' Equity**	5,000
Equipment	1,500		
		Total Liabilities	
Total Assets	$10,500	**Plus Owners' Equity**	$10,500

Owner's equity equals total assets minus total liabilities. It represents the portion of total assets owned "free and clear" after deducting what is owed to others.

The balance sheet above shows all assets purchased and liabilities incurred. It also shows owner's equity. Owner's equity is considered a "residual" account, because it shows the amount actually owned free and clear after deducting what is owed. In this case, Lucy has a total of $10,500 in assets but owes $5,000 to her parents and $500 to her suppliers. She actually has $5,000 in assets that she can call her own, or her "equity" in the business.

Assets and liabilities are separated into short-term and long-term accounts. Current assets are assets that are expected to be replenished regularly (e.g., inventories and cash). Current liabilities are liabilities that are expected to be paid within one year (e.g., accounts payable and wages payable). Long-term assets and long-term liabilities are those with lives greater than one year. An ice machine, expected to last for several years, is considered a long-term (or fixed) asset. The note is considered a long-term liability since Lucy needs only to make interest payments on the $5,000 note. She can postpone repaying the principal until she feels financially able to do so.

Current or short-term assets and **liabilities** are generally those with expected lives of less than one year.

Before Lucy started writing checks, her only asset was the $10,000 in her cash account. When she wrote checks for insurance, rent, inventory, supplies, and the ice machine, her cash account was reduced for each check written, leaving her with $2,400 in cash and $8,100 in other assets. But why does this total $10,500 rather than $10,000, which was her initial

Long-term assets and **long-term liabilities** are generally those with expected lives greater than one year.

investment? Remember, Lucy ordered and received $1,000 worth of inventory and supplies, but she actually wrote checks for only $500 of this amount. In essence, she borrowed $500 towards her purchases in the form of accounts payable. This is often referred to as **trade credit.**

At the end of the month, the balance sheet is reconstructed to show how the accounts changed over the month. Looking at **Exhibit 5,** we can see that both inventory and supplies have increased.

Exhibit 5: Mall Business, Balance Sheet After One Month

Lucy's Lemonade
Balance Sheet
July 31, 200X

Current Assets:		Current Liabilities:	
Cash	$2,467	Accounts Payable	$ 850
Inventory	1,150		
Supplies	750	**Long Term Liabilities:**	
Prepaid Rent	1,000	Notes Payable	4,000[2]
Prepaid Insurance	3,000		
Total Current Assets	$8,367		
Fixed Assets:		**Total Liabilities**	$4,850
Equipment[1]	3,100		
Less Acc. Depreciation	36		
Net Fixed Assets	3,064	**Owners' Equity**	6,581
Total Assets	$11,431	**Total Liabilities**	
		Plus Owners' Equity	$11,431

[1]Icemaker ($1,500) + Pretzel Oven ($1,350) + Pretzel Display Unit ($250) − Depreciation ($36) = $3,064. Lucy would keep a separate record in the general ledger for each different fixed asset.

[2] Lucy made a $1,000 payment to her parents.

This result is not due solely to new purchases. During the course of business, both of these accounts decreased as product was sold and increased as new purchases were made. As Lucy paid her suppliers, the accounts payable balance decreased, but as she received new orders of inventory and supplies, accounts payable increased. Lucy originally paid two months' rent and six months' insurance, both of which were recorded as prepaid items (assets). Remember, Lucy's rent is $1,000 per month and she pays $7,200 per year for insurance. Since she has "used up" one month's worth of each, prepaid rent is reduced by $1,000, and prepaid insurance by $600. Equipment increased from $1,500 (cost of the icemaker) to $3,100 when Lucy purchased the pretzel oven for $1,350 and the heated display case for $250. All three pieces of equipment fall into the MACRS 7-year class and will be depreciated 14 percent the first year; ($3,100 × .14)/12 = $36.16 the first month.

Prepaid items are expenses, which are paid before they are recognized as operating expenses. The balance of the item, which has not been expensed, is considered a current asset.

Statement of Cash Flows

Cash receipts and cash disbursements over the period are put into three categories: operating, investing, and financing. Operating cash flows are those that result from the operations of the business, in this case, sales of lemonade and pretzels. Investing cash flows are those resulting from the purchase or sale of long-term assets. (Remember, Lucy added to her assets by buying a pretzel oven and a heated display case soon after she opened.) Financing cash flows are those resulting from increased borrowing or reduction of existing debt, such as Lucy's payment to her parents, the issuance or repurchase of shareholder's equity, or the payment of dividends to the company's shareholders. Let's look at **Exhibit 6,** Lucy's statement of cash flows for the month ending July 31.

The statement of cash flows shows changes in the cash account caused by cash flows from operations, investments, or financing.

To determine the true change in cash over the period, cash from operations must be adjusted for **non-cash items, changes in working capital,** and **investing** and **financing** cash flows.

Exhibit 6: Statement of Cash Flows after One Month

Lucy's Lemonade
Statement of Cash Flows
Month Ending July 31, 200X

Operating Activities:	Cash Flow
Net Income	$1,581
Adjustments to NI:	
Non-cash Adjustments:	
Depreciation	36
Reductions in Prepaid Items	1,600
Changes in Working Capital:	
Increase in Accounts Payable	350
Increase in Inventory	(650)
Increase in Supplies	(250)
Net Cash from Operations	$2,667
Investing Activities:	
Acquisition of Assets	($1,600)
Financing Activities:	
Reduction of Long-Term Debt	($1,000)
Summary:	
Net Change in Cash	$ 67
Cash Beginning of July	2,400
Cash End of July	$2,467

It is important to recognize that net income does not necessarily represent cash. This is true because not all revenue and expense items on the income statement represent actual cash flows. Credit sales and credit purchases are examples of non-cash revenues and expenses. The first half of Lucy's statement of cash flows shows the adjustments to net income that are made to determine cash flow from operations.

Recall that Lucy spent most of her $10,000 investment before she opened for business. She paid cash for inventory and supplies, which were expensed accordingly. She also paid cash for an icemaker, two months' rent, and six months' insurance. For these expenses, the cash flows do not "match" the timing of their deductions as expenses.

Consider, for example, the capitalization of the ice machine. When it was purchased, cash was reduced by the amount Lucy paid, and its total cost was entered on the balance sheet as a long-term asset. The cost for the use of this machine is then recognized as a depreciation expense in each year over its MACRS life. Thus, the expense does not match the timing of the cash flow. Since depreciation expense reduces operating income like any other expense but does not represent an actual cash flow, it must be added back to net income in determining cash flow from operations. The effect of prepaid items is very similar.

Lucy also paid the mall $2,000 for two months' rent and she paid her insurance agent $3,600 for six months' insurance. This resulted in a $5,600 decrease in the cash account along with an entry for the two prepaid items under current assets on the balance sheet. When she deducts the $1,000 rent expense and the insurance expense of $600 from July's operating income, the deductions look like any other expense. Since these deductions reduce operating income but are not actual cash flows, we must add their amounts back to operating income to determine cash flow from operations for the month. Cash flows associated with working capital (current assets and current liabilities) are somewhat less obvious.

During the daily course of business, Lucy used up current assets and incurred current liabilities as she sold product and reordered supplies. Consider her inventory of cups and straws. Every time the amount of these items is reduced, it coincides with a sale of lemonade, which is an inflow of cash. To replenish her inventory of cups and straws, Lucy must buy more, which means a decrease in cash. The same holds true for any asset. To increase an asset requires an outflow of cash, while decreasing an asset account results in an inflow.

Increasing accounts payable or other liabilities is the same thing as borrowing. A simple example is notes payable. An increase in notes payable means Lucy has borrowed money, so this represents a source of funds, or a cash inflow. A decrease in notes payable means Lucy has paid cash to reduce the liability.

Another example is wages payable. Assume Lucy pays her employees every two weeks, which means that for a two-week period, she "owes" them their wages. They let Lucy use their money until she actually pays them. When Lucy pays them, the amount of wages payable decreases, so the decrease in the liability accompanies a decrease in cash.

Non-cash expenses on the income statement include prepaid items and depreciation. They are expenses which have no associated cash outflow.

Current assets and liabilities are called **working capital**. Increases (decreases) in asset accounts are outflows (inflows), while increases (decreases) in liability accounts are inflows (outflows) of working capital.

The **statement of cash flows** and the **balance sheet** must agree. The change in cash for the period for the SCF plus the beginning cash balance from the balance sheet must equal the ending cash balance on the balance sheet.

These patterns exist with any asset or liability account. For increases in inventory and supplies, both classified as current assets, we reduce cash from operations. For increases in accounts payable, a current liability, we increase cash from operations. Increases in accounts payable are often associated with the purchase of inventory and supplies on credit, which do not represent an actual outflow of cash—yet. The increase in long-term assets (adding the pretzel equipment) causes a reduction in cash from investing. Reducing the amount of long-term notes payable causes a reduction in cash from financing. The summary line in **Exhibit 6** shows a net change in cash for the month of $67, which brings our current cash balance to $2,467. (This is confirmed on the balance sheet in **Exhibit 5**.)

Statement of Owners' Equity

The statement of owners' equity shows the value of any money (or other capital) the owner has invested in the business.

The statement of owners' equity shows the value of any money (or other capital) the owner has invested in the business. The value of any capital (cash, land, buildings, equipment, fixtures, furniture, etc.) contributed to the business by the owner is considered investment. When Lucy started Lucy's Lemonade, her assets totaled $10,500. Since she owes her parents $5,000 and her suppliers $500, Lucy does not own all the assets "free and clear." After deducting the $5,500 owed to others, Lucy's equity totals $5,000 (her initial investment).

This is similar to the situation facing most homeowners. Say, for example, some homeowners invested $20,000 in their home and took out a mortgage for $70,000. The house is currently worth $100,000. Thus, they now have $30,000 equity (assets minus liabilities) in the home. Notice that in both cases, there is not necessarily a relationship between the value of equity and the amount of cash on hand. Lucy's statement of owners' equity at the end of July is shown in **Exhibit 7**.

Exhibit 7: Positive Net Income and No Owner Withdrawal

Lucy's Lemonade
Statement of Owners' Equity
July 31, 200X

Owners' Equity 7/01/200X	$5,000
Additions:	
Net Income, month ending 7/31/200X	1,581
Withdrawals:	0
Owners' Equity 7/31/200X	$6,581

Net income has been transferred or "closed" to owners' equity (closing entries are discussed in Section 2 of this chapter). As a proprietorship, net income for Lucy's Lemonade belongs to the owner, but Lucy chose not to withdraw any of it during July. Had she done so, her cash and owners' equity accounts would be reduced to reflect the withdrawal.

Now, let's assume that Lucy withdraws $1,500 during July. The balance sheet at the end of July will reflect $1,500 reductions to her cash and owners' equity accounts, and her statement of owners' equity becomes that shown as **Exhibit 8**.

Exhibit 8: Positive Net Income Plus Owner Withdrawal

Lucy's Lemonade
Statement of Owners' Equity
July 31, 200X

Owners' Equity 7/01/200X	$5,000
Additions:	
Net Income, month ending 7/31/200X	1,581
Withdrawals:	(1,500)
Owners' Equity 7/31/200X	$5,081

If instead of withdrawing $1,500, Lucy decides to invest another $1,500 in the business, the investment increases both the cash account and owners' equity account on her balance sheet. Lucy's statement of owners' equity under this scenario, **Exhibit 9,** shows her equity has climbed to $8,081.

Exhibit 9: Positive Net Income Plus Owner Contribution

Lucy's Lemonade
Statement of Owners' Equity
July 31, 200X

Owners' Equity 7/01/200X	$5,000
Additions:	
Net Income, month ending 7/31/200X	1,581
Owner Contributions	1,500
Withdrawals:	0
Owners' Equity 7/31/200X	$8,081

Let's consider our homeowners again. If they still have a $70,000 outstanding mortgage and the value of their house drops below $100,000, their equity in the home will also fall. In the same fashion, if Lucy's Lemonade shows an operating loss (negative net income), her equity in the business declines and could even fall below her initial investment. To illustrate, assume a $2,500 loss for the month of July, along with an additional contribution of $1,500. The combined impact of this situation is shown in Lucy's July 31 statement of owners' equity, **Exhibit 10**. Note that even though Lucy has invested a total of $6,500, her equity in the business is only $4,000 due to the $2,500 operating loss for the month of July. However, at the end of August, if her business shows a profit of $1,500, the end-of-August statement of owners' equity, **Exhibit 11,** would indicate the partial recovery of her lost equity. In this fashion, the value of Lucy's equity is subject to change from month to month.

Exhibit 10: Negative Net Income Plus Owner Contribution

Lucy's Lemonade
Statement of Owners' Equity
July 31, 200X

Owners' Equity 7/01/200X	$5,000
Additions:	
Net Income, month ending 7/31/200X	(2,500)
Owner Contributions	1,500
Withdrawals:	0
Owners' Equity 7/31/200X	$4,000

A point worth remembering is the relationship between successive statements. Notice that the ending balance on the July 31 statement of owners' equity becomes the beginning balance for the next month's statement. Similarly, the ending balance on the August statement becomes the beginning balance on the September statement.

Exhibit 11: Positive Net Income Following a Reduction in Owners' Equity

Lucy's Lemonade
Statement of Owners' Equity
August 31, 200X

Owners' Equity 7/31/200X	$4,000
Additions:	
Net Income, month ending 8/31/200X	1,500
Owner Contributions	0
Withdrawals:	0
Owners' Equity 8/31/200X	$5,500

Although somewhat more complicated, the statement of owners' equity for a **publicly traded corporation** is similar to that for Lucy's Lemonade in many respects. Let's look at **Exhibit 12**, the statement of owners' equity for Lucy's Lemonade assuming she "goes public." You will probably notice first that *owners'* equity is now called *stockholders'* equity. This is because there are now many owners of the business, each of whom has purchased shares of stock on an organized exchange.

Let's change the example considerably and assume that Lucy has incorporated her business and has invested $500,000 of her own capital. She currently holds 100,000 shares of common stock. During its first year in business, assume that her company had net income of $250,000.

Retaining 51 percent ownership in the firm, Lucy sells 49,000 shares at $10.00 per share for a total of $490,000. Each share brought in $10.00, which is divided into common stock at par[5] ($1.00) and additional paid-in capital ($9.00). Lucy also pays dividends of $1.00 per share for a total of $100,000 (she holds 51,000 shares, while the other 49,000 shares are publicly held). Note that withdrawals are now recorded as dividends paid.

An ownership (equity) claim in some companies is obtained by purchasing shares of common stock. These companies, with many outside owners who are not usually involved with business operations, are known as **publicly traded corporations.**

---

[5] The concepts of **par value** and **additional paid-in capital** are discussed in the chapter on Corporate Finance.

Exhibit 12: Statement of Stockholders' Equity after Going Public

Lucy's Lemonade
Statement of Stockholders' Equity
Year Ending December 31, 20X1

Stockholders' Equity 12/31/20X0	$500,000[1]
Additions:	
Sale of Common Stock at Par:	49,000
(100,000 shares authorized; $1.00 Par)[2]	
Additional Paid-In Capital:	
	441,000
Net Income, 20X1:	250,000
Dividends Paid:	(100,000)
Stockholders' Equity 12/31/20X1	$1,140,000

[1] The $500,000 represents Lucy's investment in new newly incorporated business.

[2] Par value does not represent value, in the ordinary sense of the word. It is an arbtrary figure established by management. It represents the amount that must be paid by each stockholder, if the stock is to be considered fully paid when issued. Like bonds, stock can be issued at a discount (below par), at par, or above par (at a premium).

SUMMARY OF SECTION 1

Learning Objective 1: *To understand the form and substance of the four principal financial statements.*

 A. The assets, liabilities, owners' equity, and operations of a business are recorded in the four principal financial statements.

  1. **Assets** are contributed to the business by the owner(s), purchased by the firm, or generated by the business. They can be current (short-term) or fixed (long-term).

   a. **Current assets** are those with lives less than one year and include cash, accounts receivable, and prepaid items.

   b. **Fixed**, or **long-term assets** are those with lives greater than one year and include buildings, equipment, and patents.

  2. **Liabilities** are external claims on the firm's assets by creditors. They can be current (short-term) or long-term.

   a. **Current** or **short-term liabilities** are payable within one year. These include wages payable, accounts payable, and short-term notes payable.

  b. **Long-term liabilities** are those that extend beyond one year. These include long-term notes payable, mortgages payable, etc.

3. **Owners' equity** represents the total value of the ownership claim(s) of the proprietor, partners, or stockholders.

  a. Equity is generated by contributions of the owner(s) (either of cash or assets) or through operations (closing net income to owners' equity).

  b. Equity is a residual account. It is the value of assets owned "free and clear" after deducting total liabilities from total assets.

4. **Operations** are the primary revenue-generating activities of the firm.

  a. Operations can be the production and/or sales of **products**, such as lemonade.

  b. Operations can be sales of **services**, such as accounting or financial advising.

  c. Owners' equity increases with positive net income and decreases with negative net income.

B. The four principal financial statements are the **balance sheet**, the **income statement**, the **statement of cash flows**, and the **statement of owners' equity.**

1. The **balance sheet** shows the values of the firm's assets, liabilities, and owners' equity at a point in time.

  a. The balance sheet is typically generated quarterly and annually.

  b. Looking at two successive balance sheets shows how the asset, liability, and equity accounts changed between the two dates.

  c. The balance sheet must "balance." That is, **Total Assets = Liabilities + Owners' Equity.**

  d. *Owners'* equity on the balance sheet for the proprietorship or partnership is called *stockholders'* equity on the balance sheet for the corporation.

2. The **income statement** shows operating results (net income) over a defined period of time, usually between two balance sheet dates.

  a. **Net Income = Revenues – Expenses.**

  b. **Revenues** are the cash inflows generated by operating the business.

    c. **Expenses,** cash outflows associated with doing business, are divided into COGS, operating expenses, interest expense, and other expenses.

- **COGS** (cost of goods sold) is the total cost of raw inputs; the various components combined into the final product.
- **Operating expenses** are generated in the process of doing business but are not components of the final product. These include wages, utilities, rent, and depreciation.
- **Interest expense** is the interest charged for funds borrowed from creditors. Repayment of principal is not considered an expense.
- **Other expenses** might include pension fund contributions, payments to bond sinking funds,[6] extraordinary items,[7] and research and development.

3. The **statement of cash flows** shows changes in the cash account between two balance sheet dates. Since net income does not necessarily represent cash, it must be adjusted for operating, investing, and financing activities to determine the amount of cash generated.

    a. **Operating activities** are associated with running the business and are divided into cash and non-cash items.

- **Non-cash** operating expenses have no associated cash outflow. These include depreciation expense and reductions in prepaid items.
- **Cash** operating expenses are wages paid, COGS, etc.

    b. **Investing activities** include acquiring or disposing of equipment, buildings, or other long-term assets; and the purchase or sale of bonds or stock in other companies.

    c. **Financing activities** include owner contributions or withdrawals (dividends paid), acquiring or retiring long-term debt, and repurchasing or issuing new equity.

    d. Cash at the end of the period must equal the cash at the beginning of the period plus the change in cash over the period.

---

[6] When firms sell bonds (long-term borrowing), the indenture typically calls for the firm to make annual or semi-annual payments to a "sinking fund." The funds are held by a trustee to assure sufficient cash is available when the bonds mature and must be retired.

[7] Extraordinary items are unusual expenses, which occur occasionally or even rarely. They are not necessarily costs associated with business operations. This might include such items as government expropriation of assets and losses from natural disasters.

4. The **statement of owners' equity** reports the amounts and sources of changes in owners' equity between two balance sheet dates.
   a. Additions to owners' equity are from operations (positive net income) and contributions (investments) by the owners/stockholders.
   b. Reductions in owners' equity are from operations (negative net income), owner withdrawals, and dividends paid.

Learning Objective 2: *To understand the relationships between the four financial statements.*

We saw that values appearing on some statements are carried over to other statements. Here are a few examples:

A. Net income, the "bottom line" on the income statement, is closed to the statement of owners' equity.
B. Net income is entered on the statement of cash flows as the starting point for the cash from operations computation.
C. Reductions in long-term debt, such as notes payable on the balance sheet, are shown as uses of cash on the statement of cash flows (financing).
D. Increases (decreases) in assets on the balance sheet are shown as uses (sources) of cash on the statement of cash flows (investing).
E. Reductions of prepaid assets and depreciation, shown on the balance sheet, are entered as non-cash adjustments in cash from operations.
F. On the statement of cash flows, net change in cash plus beginning cash = ending cash. Beginning (ending) cash is the cash balance on the balance sheet at the beginning (end) of the period.

Learning Objective 3: *To understand the difference between cash and non-cash expenses.*

The difference between cash and non-cash expenses was demonstrated using the income statement and the statement of cash flows.

A. When an expense is paid well into the future, but only written off one month at a time, it is a **prepaid expense**.

B. Prepaid expenses could include rent and insurance that is paid in advance.
   1. You might pay for six months of insurance at one time, while the expense is written off monthly. The amount not expensed is entered as a prepaid asset on the balance sheet.
   2. In the same fashion, if you pay several months' rent but expense rent monthly, the amount not expensed is carried as a prepaid asset on the balance sheet.
C. **Depreciation** is a key non-cash expense. Depreciation represents the charge to income each period for the usage of fixed assets during the period.

Learning Objective 4: *To understand the rationale for capitalizing and depreciating the costs of capital assets instead of expensing them.*

Depreciation represents the expensing of a large asset's cost over its useful life.

A. Since the outflow of cash for the asset occurs when it is purchased, depreciation is another non-cash expense.
B. Writing off the total cost of capital assets at the time of purchase could cause large variations in net income.

Learning Objective 5: *To understand the procedure for classifying cash inflows and cash outflows.*

A. An action that provides an inflow of cash is considered a **source of funds.**
B. An action that causes an outflow of cash is considered a **use of funds.**
C. On the income statement, operating revenues are a source of funds.
D. On the income statement, operating expenses are a use of funds.
E. A change in an asset or liability account on the balance sheet may be a source or use of funds.
   1. A reduction in an asset account is a source of funds.
   2. An increase in an asset account is a use of funds.
   3. A reduction in a liability account is a use of funds.
   4. An increase in a liability account is a source of funds.

SECTION 2: ACCOUNTING PROCEDURES

Financial statements in the U.S. are prepared using guidelines that are determined by the Financial Accounting Standard Board (FASB). These guidelines establish the form and content of financial statements to help keep them standardized across companies and industries. We've looked closely at the four principal financial statements and how they relate to one another. Now it's time to look more closely at individual accounts on the financial statements and various accounting techniques and policies used to keep them consistent, accurate, and reliable.

In this section, your learning objectives are:

1. To become familiar with the "time period principle" and why financial statements are produced on a regular basis.
2. To become familiar with the "matching principle."
3. To understand the difference between accrual basis and cash basis accounting.
4. To become familiar with the "dual entry" system.

Accounting Periods

Reporting of financial accounting data is done at the end of predetermined periods of time (the **time period principle**), and these periods may be of any length. Most companies use the **fiscal year** for their primary external (outside the firm) reporting. They also report results for periods of time less than a year (quarterly, semi-annually) for internal use and for external releases of selected data.

Since a single set of financial statements would only summarize the activities for a single period of time, statements are prepared on a regular basis. Each set of statements begins and ends over the same uniform periods, to allow comparisons over time. For example, we will assume an end-of-quarter income statement and balance sheet are prepared according to the rules indicated above. The results for the quarter could be compared to the results for the same quarter in previous years. This comparison shows whether trends exist in the operating results of the company. For example, has net income improved? Has COGS increased or decreased as a percentage of revenues? Or has inventory increased as a percentage of total assets? This type of comparison, or **trend analysis**, can and should be performed using annual as well as quarterly financial statements (Note that an

A **fiscal year** is any 12-month period, not necessarily beginning January 1.

Trend analysis is performed to detect general patterns in operating results, or other accounting measures, from one period to the next.

upward trend means a general pattern of increases in successive quarters or years. It does not mean every quarter or year has shown an increase).

Trend analysis is a valuable planning tool. For example, after five years of operating Lucy's Lemonade, Lucy can examine her quarterly statements to identify trends and make plans accordingly. During each of the last five years, summers have been her busiest periods. Therefore, she can anticipate hiring more employees during the summer. Winters have been the slowest periods in all five years, and she feels she can also plan on that trend to continue into the future. By understanding these trends in her business, Lucy knows less inventory will be needed in the winter but inventory will need to be increased to handle the increased summer business. She may even decide a short-term loan is necessary to operate the business during the winter; this loan would be repaid in the summer.

Trend analysis is also of value to prospective buyers of the company. Potential buyers may be willing to pay top dollar for a business that shows an upward trend in operating performance, which indicates an efficiently run business that may be capable of even better results in the future. Flat trends, however, typically indicate one of two things: a business that has not been efficiently managed or a business that is in a **mature market**. If a business has been inefficiently managed, new management may be able to increase revenues and profits by making improvements to the business.

According to the **matching principle,** revenues and expenses are matched to each other and the appropriate accounting period.

An extremely important characteristic of accrual based financial statements is the **matching principle**, which requires that revenues and expenses are matched with each other and are matched within the appropriate accounting period. Quarterly or annual comparisons of operating results would be meaningless, unless only summer expenses were counted against summer revenues, fall against fall, winter against winter, and spring against spring. If Lucy wrote off summer expenses (the highest for the year) against winter revenues (the lowest for the year) and vice versa, summer net income might look very good, while net income for winter would likely show a loss. In other words, if she didn't match revenues with expenses, the resulting financial data would not be accurate or reliable or reflect actual operating results.

Basics of Debits and Credits

The basic accounting procedure is to record economic events that occur as the result of financial transactions. This record keeping is done in the **general ledger**. Some accounts in the general ledger are maintained on a daily basis, but several must be updated, or **adjusted**, before their balances can be posted to the financial statements. This assures conformity to the matching principle by charging expenses against revenues during the appropriate period. The necessity to make adjustments stems from the fact that some of the firm's economic activities do not occur as a result of external transactions and thus, remain unrecorded. **Depreciation** and **prepaid insurance** are examples of expenses that do not occur as a result of external transactions during the period in which they are recorded. The full cost of an asset is paid and capitalized at the time the asset is purchased. The total cost is then expensed through depreciation on a periodic basis, so the recognition of the expense does not relate to an external transaction. Insurance is often paid several months at a time but is expensed one month at a time; hence, no external transaction coincides with the expense. As a result, depreciation and insurance expense, along with prepaid insurance and fixed assets, must be adjusted before being entered on the financial statements.

Unearned revenue is another example. In this case, customers have paid in advance, but only a portion of the product has been delivered or a portion of the service performed. According to the **revenue recognition principle**, only that portion of the revenue actually earned can be recognized on the income statement.

Before we look at some actual adjusting entries, it is important to discuss the **dual entry** system, which utilizes **debits** and **credits**. (See **Exhibit 13** below which is a reproduction of **Exhibit 4** in Section 1.) Think of the word debit as meaning *left*, and the word credit meaning *right*. A debit entry is one made on the left, and a credit entry is made on the right.

The **general ledger** is the book "of original entry" in which all accounts are kept and maintained. It usually has a separate page for each account.

The prepaid value of **depreciation** expense is actually the capitalized cost of the asset.

Adjusting entries help match expenses to the appropriate revenues.

According to the **revenue recognition principle**, only the portion of revenue that has actually been earned can be recognized on the income statement.

Remember, **liability** and **equity** accounts represent **claims** on the assets of the business. A liability is a debt claim, while equity is an ownership claim.

Exhibit 13: Opening Day of Mall Business

Lucy's Lemonade
Opening Day Balance Sheet
July 1, 200X

Current Assets:		Current Liabilities:	
Cash	$2,400	Accounts Payable	$ 500
Inventory	500		
Supplies	500	**Long Term Liabilities:**	
Prepaid Rent	2,000	Notes Payable	5,000
Prepaid Insurance	3,600		
Fixed Assets:		**Owners' Equity**	5,000
Equipment	1,500		
		Total Liabilities	
Total Assets	$10,500	**Plus Owners' Equity**	$10,500

Assets are on the left-hand side of the balance sheet and liabilities and owners' equity (claims against the assets) are on the right. A debit entry to an asset account, such as cash or inventory, would be adding value, so a debit increases an asset account. A credit reduces an asset account. Alternately, liabilities are increased by credits and decreased by debits.

Cash Basis and Accrual Basis Accounting

Cash basis accounting recognizes revenues when cash is received and expenses when cash is paid. Net income, under cash basis accounting, is the difference between revenues received in cash and expenses paid with cash during the reporting period.

The recognition of revenues and expenses on a cash basis can cause confusing and misleading financial statements. For instance, assume that Lucy had expensed her equipment at the time of purchase rather than capitalizing and depreciating it. This would probably have caused an operating loss for that period, even though the loss had nothing to do with operations. In the following period, operating income would be artificially inflated due to the lack of depreciation expense.

Accrual basis accounting assigns revenues to the accounting period in which they are earned and matches expenses with the revenues generated by those expenses. The objective of the accrual basis is to report the

Schweser
Study Program

economic effects of revenues and expenses when they are earned or incurred, not when cash is received or paid.

An example is Lucy's payment for insurance. When Lucy paid six months' insurance premiums, she did not record the entire premium payment as an expense. Instead, she recorded a prepaid asset for the amount of the check and expensed it monthly to "match" it to the period it covers.

Another example of the use of accrual-based accounting is accounts receivable (credit sales). If Lucy lets mall employees pay her monthly instead of collecting cash at the time of purchase, accounts receivable are created. Sales are reported on the income statement even though they have not actually been collected, and the amount that is owed to Lucy is included under accounts receivable on the balance sheet. To illustrate the concept of accounts receivable, assume that Lucy's Lemonade has an accounts receivable balance of $1,000. This means that Lucy has sold $1,000 in lemonade and pretzels without collecting the cash. Credit sales of $1,000 would be recorded as follows:

Accounts Recievable	$1,000	
Sales Revenue		$1,000

Now, as Lucy receives payments for her credit sales, they will be recorded as a debit to cash and a credit to accounts receivable as shown below. Unless she has granted new credit, once Lucy has received $1,000 in payments for credit sales the balance of accounts receivable will be zero. Generally, goods are continually sold on account while payments for prior purchases are received. In this way, accounts receivable usually never gets to zero.

Day X:	Cash	$400	
	Accounts Receivable		$400
Day Y:	Cash	$600	
	Accounts Receivable		$600

The accrual basis is more useful for financial analysis because it relates reported financial information to the economic events that generated the results.

- Generally, accrual basis accounting results in a more accurate measurement of net income for the period than cash basis accounting.
- The accrual basis accounting reflects the understanding that the economic effect of revenue generally occurs when it is *earned* and not when cash is received.
- The economic effect of an expense is incurred when the benefit expires or is used up, not when cash is paid.
- Accrual accounting enhances the comparability of income statements and balance sheets from one period to another period.

Adjusting Entries

With a **dual entry system,** for every debit there is a corresponding credit.

Let's start by taking a look at how Lucy recorded her initial investment and the note to her parents. First, we know these transactions increased the cash balance. Second, Lucy's initial investment must be treated as equity, and the amount borrowed from her parents must be treated as a liability. When Lucy received the money from her parents and invested her own money, the following entries were made in the general ledger: (Note that **debits** are on the *left* and **credits** are on the *right*.)

A **debit** entry increases an asset and decreases a liability. A **credit** entry increases a liability and decreases an asset.

Cash (asset)	$10,000	
Note Payable (liability)		$5,000
Owners' Equity (equity)		5,000

There are two important things worth mentioning at this point. First, the entries on the right (credits) always equal those on the left (debits). This is very similar to the concept of a balance sheet. The two sides of the balance sheet always equal. Assets (entries on the left) must equal the total claims against them, liabilities plus equity (entries on the right). Second, cash is increased to $10,000 by a debit, while notes payable is increased by a $5,000 credit. Owners' equity, carried on the right side of the balance sheet, is increased to $5,000 by a credit as if it is a liability. This is because equity, just like a liability, is a claim against the assets of the firm.

Now let's see how the purchase of the icemaker, a fixed (or long-term) asset, was originally recorded in the general ledger. It cost $1,500 and Lucy paid cash. Writing the check is a reduction to cash, so we know cash must be credited. The icemaker is an asset, so fixed assets must be debited as follows:

Fixed Assets	$1,500	
(Accumulated Depreciation)[8]	0	
Cash (asset)		$1,500

Debiting the fixed asset account increases its balance from $0 to $1,500. Crediting cash reduces its balance by $1,500.

In exactly the same fashion, inventory and supplies are debited to indicate an increase to $500 for each of these assets, and cash is credited for $500. Since, as a new business owner, Lucy is required to pay half the cost of inventory and supplies when ordered, we must recognize the creation of accounts payable for the other half. Accounts payable is increased from $0 to $500. These activities are entered in the general ledger as follows:

Supplies (asset)	$500	
Inventory (asset)	500	
Cash (asset)		$500
Accounts Payable (liability)		500

Accumulated depreciation is a contra-asset account. A contra account reduces either an asset or liability on the balance sheet.

Rent expense and insurance expense are somewhat different. When Lucy paid two months' rent and six months' insurance, she actually created assets out of what would eventually be expenses.

Prepaid Rent (asset)	$2,000	
Prepaid Insurance (asset)	3,600	
Cash (asset)		$5,600

Prepaid items are similar to money in the bank. It's as if you set aside cash to pay certain expenses at a later date. Debiting them increases their values, so Lucy had $5,600 "in the bank" to be used for rent and insurance. As shown in the entry above, the $5,600 credit to cash indicates it has been reduced to record the payment of the prepaid expenses.

---

[8] Accumulated depreciation is a contra-asset account. It is reported on the balance sheet and shows the reduction in the value of the assets. The accumulated depreciation account is zero on the day the asset is purchased and grows each period by the amount of depreciation taken on fixed assets.

After these beginning-of-the-month ledger entries, cash has been credited (reduced) a total of $7,600. Since Lucy started with $10,000 and has recorded $7,600 in credits to cash, the balance of her cash account when she opens must be $2,400.

After the first month of operations, Lucy must recognize one month's rent and insurance expense in her balance sheet and income statement. Since cash was credited when the check was originally written, there is no entry for cash at this time. We are now recognizing the expenses, which were paid (prepaid) earlier. Since we recognize the rent expense ($1,000) and insurance expense ($600), we must adjust the balances of prepaid rent and prepaid insurance as follows:

Rent Expense (operating expense)	$1,000	
Insurance Expense (operating expense)	600	
Prepaid Rent (asset)		$1,000
Prepaid Insurance (asset)		600

Expenses are entered using the same rules that we used for assets; they are increased by a debit and reduced by a credit.

Prepaid rent and insurance are assets, so the credit entries reduce their values. The debit entries to rent expense and insurance expense bring their values from $0 to $1,000 and $600, respectively. Even though logic might tell you expenses are more like liabilities, in the dual entry system, they are treated much like assets. A debit increases an expense, while a credit decreases it. Since Lucy paid two months' rent, prepaid rent will have a $0 balance after two months, and rent expense will total $2,000. It will take six months for prepaid insurance to reach $0, at which time insurance expense will total $3,600.

In a similar fashion, the balance of the fixed asset account (icemaker, etc.) must be reduced (adjusted) to recognize the expensing of its cost through depreciation. Depreciation expense is debited for one month's depreciation, and the asset account is reduced by the same amount.

Depreciation Expense	$36	
Accumulated Depreciation		$36

When Lucy prepares her year-end financial statements for external reporting, rent expense will show a total of $12,000, insurance expense will total $7,200, and depreciation expense will be the full 14 percent of \$3,100, or \$434.[9] All three items are then charged against revenue to determine net income, and their balances return to \$0 to begin the accumulation for the next year.[10] This implies that revenue and expense accounts are not *permanent* accounts, like assets and liabilities. The values of assets and liabilities carry forward from year to year. The values for expenses and revenues, however, start each year at \$0, reach the total for the year, and are charged against revenues.

SUMMARY OF SECTION 2

Learning Objective 1: *To become familiar with the "time period principle" and why financial statements are produced on a regular basis.*

A. The **time period principle** states that financial statements are prepared at regular, predetermined intervals.
  1. Firms prepare financial statements annually for external reporting.
  2. Firms prepare quarterly statements for internal evaluation and external release of limited data, such as earnings reports.
  3. Preparing financial statements on a regular, predetermined basis is only useful under the **matching principle,** which requires that revenues and expenses are matched to each other and the period to which they belong.

B. Preparing financial statements on a regular, predetermined basis facilitates **trend analysis.**
  1. A trend is a general tendency toward change in one direction, either up, down, or flat.
  2. Trend analysis can be applied to any financial statement item.
    a. An **upward trend** in operating results means operating income has generally been increasing, not that it has increased every period.
    b. A **downward trend** in operating results means operating income has generally been decreasing, not that it has decreased every year or quarter.

---

[9] There is a small amount of rounding error: $12 \times 36 = \$432$, compared to the \$434 obtained by multiplying $.14 \times 3,100$.

[10] Depreciation expense is closed to calculate net income and goes to zero at the end of each year. Accumulated depreciation continues to grow by the amount of depreciation taken each year until the related assets are sold or otherwise disposed of.

      c. A **flat trend** in operating results means operating income has been more or less constant.

3. If an upward trend is expected to continue, the firm is in an expanding market.
   a. There is room for increased total market sales.
   b. There is room for new competitors.

4. If a downward trend is expected to continue, the firm is being managed inefficiently or is in a declining market. A declining market indicates old, outdated products.

5. A flat trend can be caused by two things:
   a. Inefficient management in an expanding market.
   b. The market is **mature**. A mature market is saturated with competitors. Entry into the market is possible only by purchasing an existing competitor, or by running one out of business.

Learning Objective 2: *To become familiar with the "matching principle."*

A. Under the **matching principle**, revenues and expenses are matched to each other and the period to which they belong.

B. Revenues and expenses are first entered into the **general ledger**.
   1. The general ledger is the book of original entry.
   2. Each revenue, expense, asset, liability, and equity account is usually recorded on a separate page.

C. **Adjusting entries** are made at the end of the term to conform to the matching principle.
   1. **Prepaid items** must be adjusted each month to match the expense to the period covered.
   2. Unadjusted prepaid items are recorded as current assets (prepaid assets).
   3. Prepaid items typically include expenses such as insurance, rent, and depreciation.
      a. **Insurance** can be paid many months ahead.
         - This creates an asset, prepaid insurance, since the cash has been spent but the expense has not been recognized.
         - Each month the asset is credited (reduced) to recognize the charge for one month's insurance expense.
         - This matches the expense to the period and revenues to which it relates.
      b. **Depreciation** represents the expensing of the total cost of fixed assets, such as equipment, buildings, etc.

- Accumulated depreciation is credited the amount of one period's depreciation according to the MACRS system.
- Depreciation expense is debited for the amount.
- This matches the expense to the period and revenues to which it relates.

4. According to the **revenue recognition principle**, only that portion of revenue actually earned should be recognized on the income statement. **Unearned revenue** represents payments by customers for products or services that have not been delivered.

Learning Objective 3: *To understand the difference between accrual basis and cash basis accounting.*

A. **Accrual basis accounting** recognizes revenues in the accounting period in which they are earned and matches expenses with their corresponding revenues.
   1. The objective of accrual accounting is to report revenues and expenses when they are earned or incurred, not when cash is received or paid.
   2. Accrual accounting creates the need for adjusting entries.
B. **Cash basis accounting** recognizes revenues when cash is received and expenses when cash is paid.
   1. Net income is the difference between revenues received in cash and expenses paid with cash.
   2. This can cause confusing and misleading financial statements.
   3. Revenues and expenses are not necessarily matched to each other or to the period to which they relate.

Learning Objective 4: *To become familiar with the "dual entry" system.*

A. In the dual entry system, every debit has a corresponding credit.
   1. **Debits** are made on the left.
      a. Debits increase asset and expense accounts.
      b. Debits decrease revenue, equity, and liability accounts.
   2. **Credits** are made on the right.
      a. Credits increase revenue, equity, and liability accounts.
      b. Credits decrease asset and expense accounts.
B. The general ledger is the book of original entry where all accounts are first debited or credited. Adjusting entries are debits or credits to accounts in the general ledger.

PRACTICE QUESTIONS

1. The more common name for the statement of earnings is the:
    A. balance sheet.
    B. income statement.
    C. bottom line statement.
    D. statement of cash flows.

2. Which of the following shows operating results over a period in time?
    A. The balance sheet.
    B. The income statement.
    C. The statement of cash flows.
    D. The statement of owners' equity.

3. Which of the following shows the values of assets, liabilities, and owners' equity at a point in time?
    A. The balance sheet.
    B. The income statement.
    C. The statement of cash flows.
    D. The statement of owners' equity.

4. Which of the following is **not** one of the four principal financial statements?
    A. The balance sheet.
    B. The income statement.
    C. The statement of cash flows.
    D. The statement of owners' cash flows.

5. When a major asset is placed into service, its total cost is:
    A. entered as a liability on the balance sheet.
    B. capitalized and entered on the balance sheet.
    C. expensed immediately on the income statement.
    D. reduced by any installation and transportation costs and then entered on the balance sheet.

6. Which of the following is included in the total cost of a capital asset?
    A. The invoice price.
    B. The cost to ship it to your location.
    C. The cost to install it at your location.
    D. All of the above are included in the capitalized cost of a depreciable asset.

7. Depreciation:

    A. is a cash expense.

    B. reduces income tax liability.

    C. increases gross operating profits.

    D. is considered a long-term liability.

8. Which of the following is **not** considered a current asset?

    A. Cash.

    B. Inventory.

    C. Accrued wages.

    D. Accounts receivable.

9. The book value of a capital (depreciable) asset is its:

    A. market value, if you wished to sell it.

    B. book value less accumulation depreciation.

    C. invoice price less accumulated depreciation.

    D. total installed cost (historical cost) less accumulated depreciation.

10. Operating expenses do **not** include:

    A. utilities expense.

    B. insurance expense.

    C depreciation expense.

    D. the current tax liability.

11. Which of the following must be added to, or subtracted from, net income when determining a firm's actual cash?

    A. Prepaid insurance.

    B. Unearned revenue.

    C. Depreciation.

    D. All of the above.

12. Prepaid expense items, such as prepaid rent, are usually considered:

    A. capital assets.

    B. current assets.

    C. current liabilities.

    D. long term liabilities.

13. Current assets and liabilities are generally expected to be used or paid within:

    A. the next quarter.
    B. the next 6 months.
    C. the next 12 months.
    D. the next 24 months.

14. Which of the following is considered working capital?

    A. Fixed assets.
    B. Notes payable.
    C. Interest expense.
    D. Accounts receivable.

15. The statement that shows the value of capital invested by the owners is known as the:

    A. balance sheet.
    B. income statement.
    C. statement of cash flows.
    D. statement of owners' equity.

16. A fiscal year is:

    A. any 12-month period.
    B. January 1 through December 31.
    C. any 12-month period beginning no later than January 31.
    D. only used for internal accounting, since it cannot be used for tax purposes.

17. Adjusting entries:

    A. are the result of mistakes.
    B. are the result of the time period principle.
    C. help match expenses to the appropriate revenues.
    D. are voluntary, since they are used only for internal accounting records.

18. Which of the following is **not** correct with regard to the dual entry accounting system?

    A. A debit entry increases an asset.
    B. A credit entry increases a liability.
    C. A credit entry increases a revenue.
    D. A credit entry increases an account receivable.

19. A piece of industrial equipment costs $100,000, and it will cost $20,000 to ship and install. Calculate the annual depreciation expense, accumulated depreciation, and book value at the end of each year, using the MACRS table in Section 1 of this chapter. Assume a seven-year useful life.

20. You sign a note to borrow $10,000 from your banker. The $10,000 will be repaid in one payment in one year. Show the original entries in the general ledger to account for this transaction.

21. With the $10,000 you borrowed in question 20, you purchase $2,000 in inventory, $3,000 in supplies, and leave the rest in the bank. Show the entries associated with these transactions.

22. You have paid six months rent ($1,000 per month) for your building. Show the original payment and the entries at the beginning of the next five months.

23. Given the following information for the Alton Corporation, prepare the company's income statement:

   • Total revenues equal $350,000.
   • $125,000 in inventory and $45,000 in supplies were used to support these sales.
   • Wages totaled $100,000 and rent and utilities totaled $15,000.
   • $30,000 was paid toward a loan, including $5,000 interest.
   • Alton's tax rate is 30 percent.

24. Given the following information, prepare the statement of owners' equity for the Flower Basket.

   • Net income equals $150,000.
   • The proprietors withdrew $50,000.
   • Beginning of period balance in your owners' equity statement was $200,000.

25.   Find the missing values in the following balance sheet:

Balance Sheet
December 31, 20XX

Current Assets:		Current Liabilities:	
Cash	$2,400	Accounts Payable	500
Inventory	500		
Supplies	?	Long Term Liabilities:	
Prepaid Rent	2,000	Notes Payable	?
Prepaid Insurance	3,600		
Fixed Assets:		Owners' Equity	5,000
Equipment	1,500		
		Total Liabilities	
Total Assets	?	Plus Owners' Equity	$10,500

ANSWERS AND SOLUTIONS

1. B. The statement of earnings is sometimes referred to as the income statement.

2. B. The income statement shows operating results (i.e., net income) for a period of time (e.g., a quarter or a year). The balance sheet shows the values of assets, liabilities, and owners' equity at a point in time. The statement of owners' equity shows the value of all owners' equity accounts at a point in time. The statement of cash flows reconciles cash on hand at the end of the period with that at the beginning of the period by adjusting net income for non-cash revenues and expenses. It does not show operating results.

3. A. The balance sheet shows the value of assets, liabilities, and owners' equity at a point in time. The income statement shows operating results (net income) for a period of time. The statement of owners' equity shows the value of all owners' equity accounts at a point in time. The statement of cash flows reconciles cash on hand at the end of the period with that at the beginning of the period by adjusting net income for non-cash revenues and expenses. It does not show operating results.

4. D. There is no financial statement known as "the statement of owners' cash flows."

5. B. The total cost of a capital asset, such as a building or piece of equipment, is capitalized rather than expensed. The capitalized cost is the total of all costs associated with putting the asset in place, which includes the purchase price, shipping costs, installation, special maintenance, and training. This cost is entered on the balance sheet and depreciated at the rate specified by the MACRS tables.

6. D. The invoice price, shipping and installation expenses, and training cost are all capitalized costs associated with capital assets that are depreciated over the asset's MACRS life.

7. B. Although depreciation is a non-cash expense, it reduces taxable income and taxes. It also reduces gross operating profit.

8. C. Current assets are those with lives of one year or less. Although a current item, accrued wages is a current liability.

9. D. The definition of book value is historical (capitalized) cost less accumulated depreciation. Alternatively, if you subtract the recent period's depreciation expense from the book value at the beginning of the period, you will get the current book value.

10. D. Operating expenses are the tax-deductible costs of keeping the business open and producing and selling the final product. The current tax liability is not an operating expense.

11. D. Net income is not necessarily cash. During a reporting period, there may be several non-cash revenue or expense items that affect net income, such as depreciation and unearned revenue (i.e., credit sales). Furthermore, there may be actual cash expenditures that are not fully reflected in net income (e.g., prepaid expenses, purchases of large assets, and principal payments on debt). See the statement of cash flows for other examples.

12. B. Prepaid items are typically expenses that have been paid in advance. A good example is insurance, which may be paid for several months or a year a time, then expensed monthly. The prepaid amount, which has not been expensed, is carried on the balance sheet as a current asset.

13. C. By definition, "current" usually refers to assets that will be used or liabilities that will be paid within a year.

14. D. Technically, any current asset (e.g., accounts receivable) or current liability is working capital. We tend to think of working capital as current assets. Net working capital is current assets minus current liabilities.

15. D. This is the definition of the statement of owners' equity.

16. A. A fiscal year may be any 12-month period, not necessarily beginning January 1st.

17. C. Adjusting entries are used to match revenues with the appropriate expenses. For instance, prepaid items are expensed periodically to recognize them as expenses in the period to which they pertain. Unearned income represents payments received from customers for products and/or services that have not been delivered. As the income is "earned" it is recognized, along with the costs associated with earning them.

18. D. Debits increase asset and expense accounts, and accounts receivable is an asset account. Credits decrease both asset and expense accounts. Liability and revenue accounts are affected in the opposite manner. Debits decrease liabilities and revenues; credits increase them.

19. The total capitalized cost of the equipment is $120,000 (invoice $100,000 plus shipping and installation). Industrial equipment typically falls into the MACRS 7-year category.

Year[a]	MACRS %	×	Capitalized Cost	=	Dep. Expense	Accumulated Depreciation[b]	Book Value[c]
	120,000						
1	14		120,000		16,800	16,800	103,200
2	25		120,000		30,000	46,800	73,200
3	17		120,000		20,400	67,200	52,800
4	13		120,000		15,600	82,800	37,200
5	9		120,000		10,800	93,600	26,400
6	9		120,000		10,800	104,400	15,600
7	9		120,000		10,800	115,200	4,800
8	4		120,000		4,800	120,000	0

[a] The total number of years is one plus the MACRS category due to the half-year convention.

[b] Accumulated depreciation is the total depreciation taken to date.

[c] Book value = capitalized (historical) cost less accumulated depreciation. Also, book value = previous book value less depreciation expense.

20. Signing the note represents both an increase to cash (an asset), as well as an increase to notes payable (a liability).

Cash	$10,000	
Notes Payable		$10,000

21. Inventory and supplies are both asset accounts. You must increase both of them and offset the increases with a decrease in cash.

Inventory	$2,000	
Supplies	3,000	
Cash		$5,000

22.   When you initially pay the six-months' rent, you debit prepaid rent and credit cash. You must simultaneously recognize the first month's rent expense (a debit) and credit (reduce) prepaid rent accordingly.

At the time of payment:

Prepaid Rent	$6,000	
Cash		$6,000

The above entries established the prepaid account and reduce cash.

Rent Expense	$1,000	
Prepaid Rent		$1,000

These entries reduce prepaid rent (credit) and recognize one month's rent expense (debit). The prepaid rent balance is now $5,000.

At the beginning of the next five months, you will make the following entries:

Rent Expense	$1,000	
Prepaid Rent		$1,000

These entries will reduce prepaid rent by $1,000 per month and recognize a $1,000 rent expense per month. After five months, the prepaid rent balance is $0.00 and the entire $6,000 of rent expense has been recognized.

23.

Income Statement
Period Ending XX

Revenues	$350,000
Less:	
Cost of Goods sold:	
Inventory	125,000
Supplies	45,000
Operating Expenses:	
Wages	100,000
Utilities and Rent	15,000
Operating Income:	65,000
Less:	
Interest Expense	5,000*
Earnings before Taxes	60,000
Less Taxes (@ 30 percent)	18,000
Net Income	$42,000

*Note: Only the charge for the use of money, the interest portion of the loan payment, is a deductible expense. The remaining $25,000 represents a partial return of the money owed. It reduces the loan amount on the balance sheet, but it is not considered an expense.

24.

Statement of Owners' Equity
December 31, YY

Owners' Equity 12/31/XX	$200,000
Additions:	
Net Income, Year Ending 12/31/YY	150,000
Less:	
Owner Withdrawals:	50,000
Owners' Equity 12/31/YY	$300,000

25.

Balance Sheet
December 31, 20XX

Current Assets:		Current Liabilities:	
Cash	$2,400	Accounts Payable	500
Inventory	500		
Supplies	**500**	**Long Term Liabilities:**	
Prepaid Rent	2,000	Notes Payable	**5,000**
Prepaid Insurance	3,600		
Fixed Assets:		**Owners' Equity**	5,000
Equipment	1,500		
		Total Liabilities	
Total Assets	**$10,500**	**Plus Owners' Equity**	$10,500

First, we know the total of liabilities plus owners' equity is $10,500, so we can solve for notes payable:

Notes Payable = $10,500 − $500 − $5,000 = $5,000

Next, we know total assets must equal total liabilities plus owners' equity, or $10,500. So, we can solve for supplies as follows:

Supplies = $10,500 − (2,400 + 500 + 2,000 + 3,600 + 1,500) = $500

Quantitative Methods

On the CFA® exam, candidates are asked to solve various types of mathematical problems that deal with probability distributions, confidence intervals, standard deviations, and even Z-scores. This chapter is designed to prepare you for these challenges.

Having a good understanding of the contents of this chapter will help you when you use the Schweser Study Notes® to study for the CFA® exam. In Section 1, you will learn about equations and the necessary tools of algebra. In Section 2, you will learn the meaning and use of many of the most important terms in statistics.

SECTION 1: AN INTRODUCTION TO ALGEBRA

In this section, your learning objectives are:

1. To understand the basic form of an equation.
2. To understand multiplying and dividing both sides of an equation by a constant.
3. To understand adding to and subtracting from a constant from both sides of an equation.
4. To understand the use of parentheses in an equation.
5. To understand equations containing terms with exponents.

6. To understand how to work problems with negative numbers.

7. To be able to solve two equations with two unknowns.

The best place to develop an understanding of quantitative methods is with basic algebra. *Webster's Collegiate Dictionary* defines algebra as "any of various systems or branches of mathematics or logic concerned with the properties and relationships of abstract entities manipulated in symbolic form under operations often analogous to those of arithmetic."[1] This simply means we can use a letter in the place of a number to symbolize an unknown value in an equation.

A variable is a mathematical symbol (letter) in an equation that represents a quantity of something (e.g., cost, size, length). An equation shows the relationship between two or more variables. It is analogous to a perfectly balanced lever with an equal sign acting as the fulcrum. Whatever is on the left of the equal sign is balanced with (i.e., equals) whatever is on the right (e.g., $a = 6$).

Before we actually solve several sample equations, let's look at some mathematical properties that will make algebra easier for us. After stating the rules, we'll use those rules when we solve equations.

Rule 1. *We can multiply or divide all terms on both sides of an equation by the same letter or number without changing the relationship expressed by the equation or the value of the unknown.*

Term is the mathematical expression for an entry in an equation. Equation 1 only has two terms: the letter a on the left side of the equation and the number 6 on the right.

$$a = 6 \qquad\qquad\qquad (1)$$

Let's multiply both sides of Equation 1 by the number 5.

$$5 \times a = 5 \times 6 \quad \Rightarrow \quad 5a = 30 \quad \Rightarrow \quad a = 6$$

Multiplying all terms in an equation by the same number or letter does not change relationship of the equation.

A number in combination with (multiplied by) a letter is referred to as the **coefficient** of the letter. In this case, 5 is the coefficient of a. By multiplying each side of Equation 1 by 5, we did not alter its basic relationship. In fact, we could have multiplied every term in the equation

[1] *Merriam Webster's Collegiate Dictionary, 10E, 2000.*

by any number or any letter without changing the relationship expressed by the equation. In every case, our unknown value, signified by the letter *a*, would still equal 6. We can also *divide* both sides of the equation by a number or letter without altering the relationship expressed by the equation.

$$a = 6 \qquad\qquad (1)$$

This time let's divide both sides by the number 1.

$$\frac{a}{1} = \frac{6}{1} \quad \Rightarrow \quad a = 6$$

Dividing by 1 does not change the relationship expressed in Equation 1 since the value of *a* remains unchanged. To make the example easy, we relied on a very basic rule: Any term (number or letter) multiplied *or* divided by 1 equals the original number or letter.

So, $6 \times 1 = 6$ and $\frac{6}{1} = 6$ or $a \times 1 = a$ and $\frac{a}{1} = a$

Even though we used the number 1 in the example, we could have divided every term in Equation 1 by any number or letter and the result would have been the same. In every case, the letter *a* would have the same value.

Rule 2. *We can add or subtract the same letter or number to or from all terms on both sides of an equation without changing the relationship expressed by the equation or the value of the unknown.*

Let's look again at Equation 1, and this time we will add and subtract a number from both sides.

$$a = 6 \qquad\qquad (1)$$

Adding and subtracting 1,

$$a + 1 = 6 + 1 \ \text{ or } \ a - 1 = 6 - 1$$

The best way to solve an algebraic equation with one unknown is to collect all terms with the unknown on the left of the equal sign (the left side of the equation) and to collect all known values on the right side of the equation.

> **Dividing** all terms in an equation by the same number or letter does not change the value of the unknown term.

> **Adding** the same number or letter to all terms in an equation does not change the value of the unknown.

$$a + 1 = 6 + 1 \quad \Rightarrow \quad a = 6 + 1 - 1 \quad \Rightarrow \quad a = 6$$

$$a - 1 = 6 - 1 \quad \Rightarrow \quad a = 6 - 1 + 1 \quad \Rightarrow \quad a = 6$$

Subtracting the same number or letter from all terms in an equation does not change the value of the unknown.

Think of the equal sign in the equation as a bridge. Every time you move a variable or number from one side of the equation to the other, it crosses the bridge. Whenever a letter or number crosses the bridge, its sign changes.

Notice that in both cases, the 1 on the left side of the equation changed signs when it crossed the bridge. When we added 1 to the left side of the equation and then moved it to the right, it went from positive to negative. When we subtracted 1 from the left side and then moved it to the right, it went from negative to positive. In both cases the positive and negative 1s on the right side of the equation canceled each other out (sum to zero). In fact, if we add any number or letter to, or subtract any number or letter from, both sides of the equation, we observe the same outcome. The additional numbers or letters will cancel each other out on the right side of the equation, and the value of the unknown will remain unchanged.

Now that we have a few rules to make algebra easier for us, we'll proceed to a few examples. Consider the following:

If apples cost $0.25 each, and you have $1.00, how many apples can you buy?

Since each apple costs $0.25, if you multiply that price by the number of apples you buy, the total cannot be greater than $1.00. We will let the letter A represent the number of apples you buy. Assume you buy one apple. That means $A = 1$ and you spend $1 \times \$0.25 = \$0.25$. If you buy two apples, $A = 2$ and you spend $2 \times \$0.25 = \$0.50$. If $A = 3$ you spend $0.75, and if $A = 4$ you spend exactly $1.00. So, the answer is 4. You can buy a maximum of 4 apples with your $1.00, as long as they cost $0.25 each.

Of course, you probably were able to compute the answer in your head as soon as the situation was presented. Did you realize you used algebra to solve the problem? By dividing $1.00 by $0.25 in your head, you actually solved the following algebraic equation:

$$A = \frac{M}{C} = \frac{\$1.00}{\$0.25} = 4 \qquad\qquad (2)$$

where: A = the number of apples you can buy (the unknown)
M = the maximum amount of money you can spend ($1.00)
C = the cost per apple ($0.25)

Notice that we put the unknown variable on the left side of the equation. This is usually the convention that is used. A variable can have more than one value. In this case, the variable A, which represents the number of apples you can buy, will have different values depending upon the money you can spend and the cost per apple.

We could state the problem another way: How much would four apples cost if each apple costs $0.25? If apples cost $0.25 each, four apples will cost $1.00. This modification can be shown by rearranging Equation 2 into Equation 2a:

$$A = \frac{M}{C} \qquad\qquad (2)$$

$$A = \frac{M}{C} \quad \Rightarrow \quad M = 4 \times 0.25 = \$1.00 \qquad (2a)$$

We have taken two very simple liberties here. First, by utilizing **Rule 1** and multiplying each side of Equation 2 by the letter C, we should have gotten:

$$CA = \frac{CM}{C} \quad \Rightarrow \quad CA = M$$

but we rewrote it as $M = AC$

Thus, the top equation reads, *The cost per apple (C) times the number of apples purchased (A) equals the total money spent (M).* But since M is the unknown, it's easier to say, *The total money spent (M) is equal to the number of apples purchased (A) times the cost per apple (C).* The letter M is the unknown and, by convention, we put the unknown variable on the left side of the equation. Of course, the result is exactly the same either way.

The equation is equally valid in either direction, so it really doesn't matter which way we write it. That also holds for the direction we multiply the variables. Notice that we rearranged the combination CA to AC. This is another simple trick, which makes absolutely no difference

The **order** in which letters or numbers are **multiplied** does not change the product.

to the value of M. You may confirm this relationship by multiplying three times two and then multiplying two times three. You'll get six in either case. This property holds, regardless of the numbers or variables used, *as long as you're multiplying*.

Now, let's look at the same problem from another perspective. Let's assume you already purchased eight apples for $2.40. What was the cost per apple? You may make a mental calculation and figure out that the apples cost $0.30 each. Whether you realized it or not, you used algebra to solve this problem. To see this, let's set up Equation 2 exactly as before.

$$A = \frac{M}{C} \qquad\qquad (2)$$

where: A = the number of apples you bought (8)

M = the maximum amount of money you can spend ($2.40)

C = the cost per apple (the unknown)

This time, however, we know how much money you spent ($2.40) and how many apples you bought (8). Again, we substitute values for letters wherever we can.

The result is: $\qquad 8 = \dfrac{\$2.40}{C}$

We face a new challenge. How do you solve for C, when it's in the denominator (i.e., bottom) on the right side of the equation, and you would like it in the numerator (i.e., top) on the left side? To get the C out of the denominator on the right side of the equation, we'll utilize **Rule 1** and multiply each side of the equation by C:

$$C \times 8 = C \times \frac{\$2.40}{C}$$

and the Cs on the right side of the equation cancel each other out. Remember, any number or algebraic letter divided by itself equals *one*, so $\dfrac{C}{C} = 1$.

The equation now reads:

$$8C = \$2.40$$

We're almost there. You have to get the 8 on the left side of the equation over to the right side. When we have to get something out of a numerator, we again utilize **Rule 1** and divide each side of the equation by that number:

$$\frac{8C}{8} = \frac{\$2.40}{8} \quad \Rightarrow \quad C = \frac{\$2.40}{8} = \$0.30$$

You might have noticed we have designated "multiplied by" in two different ways in our example. First we used $C \times 8$ to mean C *times eight*. Then we used $8C$ to mean *8 times C*. Each of these ways is entirely appropriate. In fact, we could also have written $A(C)$ or $(A)(C)$ to indicate A *times C*. So there are at least four ways to write exactly the same thing. Please don't let this confuse or overwhelm you. Just remember that whenever you see two or more letters and/or numbers without a plus or minus sign between them, the operation is multiplication. For example, if you see ac in an equation, this means to multiply a times c. If you see abc in an equation, this means to multiply a times b times c. If you see $ab - c$, this means to multiply a times b and then subtract c from the product.

Here's another algebra example related to apples. You have a total of $5.00 to spend. If the apples cost $0.79 per pound, how many pounds can you buy?

Letting: P = the number of pounds you can buy (unknown)
          C = the cost per pound ($0.79)
          M = the total amount of money you can spend ($5.00)

The amount of money you can spend, M, divided by the price per pound, C, will yield the number of pounds you can purchase, P. Let's set up the equation.

$$P = \frac{M}{C} \quad \Rightarrow \quad P = \frac{\$5.00}{\$0.79} = 6.33 \text{ pounds} \qquad (3)$$

The interpretation of this answer is that with $5.00 you can buy exactly 6.33 pounds.

Now, let's alter this problem to determine the maximum amount of apples you can buy for $5.00. We know you cannot spend more than $5.00, but you certainly can spend less if you prefer. We also know that the number of pounds you buy, P, multiplied by the cost per pound, C, is the total amount you spend. Let's set up that equation:

$$P \times C \leq M \qquad (3a)$$

Equal to or less than sign ($\leq$) means the left side of the equation must be less than or equal to the right side of the equation.

This equation says, *The number of pounds you buy times the cost per pound must be less than or equal to the total money you can spend.* The sign that looks like an underlined arrowhead is actually just another type of equal sign. In this case the sign does not say the left side of the equation *must* equal to the right side. Instead it says the left side must be equal to *or less than* the right side (it may be helpful to think of the arrowhead as pointing at the smaller side of the equation). In this particular situation, we'll treat it like any other equal sign. Let's try it:

$$P \times C \leq M \implies P \times \$0.79 \leq \$5.00$$
$$P \leq \frac{\$5.00}{\$0.79} \implies P \leq \$6.33$$

Notice we get exactly the same *numerical* answer as before. When we solved for *P* the first time, we got exactly 6.33 pounds. This meant you could purchase a maximum of 6.33 pounds. Now, the answer to the equation tells us the amount purchased, *P*, can be a range of values. It can be any value *equal to or less than* 6.33 pounds. In other words, with just $5.00 to spend, you cannot buy more than 6.33 pounds, but you can certainly buy less than 6.33 pounds if you wish.

A word of caution is appropriate here. Even though the $\leq$ sign didn't really change the answer to our problem, it is interpreted quite differently from the $=$ sign. For instance, we used $a = 6$ in the very beginning as an example of an equation. The equal sign is interpreted as saying *a* is equal to 6 and no other value. That is a **strict equality**.

If we substitute $\leq$ for $=$, the meaning of the equation is changed dramatically because the two signs actually ask two different questions. The $=$ sign asks for a specific value. The $\leq$ sign asks for a *range* of values including the maximum value (or upper limit).

The equation $a \leq 6$ is interpreted as saying the letter *a* can have any value as long as it is equal to or less than 6. The unknown, *a*, could have a value that would include all negative values. We could change the $=$ sign in our example to an $\leq$ sign because we wanted to know the absolute maximum we could buy, but we could buy a smaller amount if we wanted.

Parentheses

It's time to add a little more complication. Parentheses are used to group together variables and numbers that should be considered together in the equation. For instance, the equation:

Side notes (left margin):

Solving an equation with an **equal to or less than sign** ($\leq$) gives a **range** of possible values along with a **maximum** value for the unknown.

Solving an equation with an **equal to or greater than sign** ($\geq$) gives a **range** of possible values along with a **minimum** value for the unknown.

$$3(x + 4) = 15 \qquad\qquad (4)$$

says 3 times the quantity $(x + 4)$ is equal to 15. **Quantity** is simply the mathematical expression used to denote the parentheses and everything inside them. We can treat the terms in the parentheses as if they are a single term. That means we can divide both sides of the equation by 3 (using **Rule 1**) and solve for the unknown.

$$\frac{3(x + 4)}{3} = \frac{15}{3} \quad\Rightarrow\quad (x + 4) = 5$$

Once the 3 is no longer outside the parentheses on the left side of the equation, we can simply eliminate the parentheses and solve for the unknown.

$$(x + 4) = 5 \quad\Rightarrow\quad x = 5 - 4 = 1$$

There is another way of solving Equation 4. This time we'll go ahead and multiply everything inside the parentheses by 3 (multiply through by 3) instead of dividing both sides of the equation by 3. You'll note that we get exactly the same answer. This is because we are solving the equation in two different ways without changing the equation in any way.

$$3(x + 4) = 15 \quad\Rightarrow\qquad\qquad\qquad (4)$$

$$3x + 12 = 15 \quad\Rightarrow\quad 3x = 15 - 12 \qquad (4a)$$

$$3x = 3 \qquad\qquad\Rightarrow\quad x = 1$$

Now let's assume you begin with its form in Equation 4a. How would you go about solving it? Try **factoring**. **Factors** are simply numbers that when multiplied together yield the original number (e.g., the numbers 3 and 5 are factors of 15, since $3 \times 5 = 15$). A **prime number** is divisible only by itself and 1 (e.g., the number 3 has no factors other than 1 and 3, so it is considered a prime number). Let's factor out a number common to all the terms on the left side of the equation. To factor the left side of the equation, we'll find the largest number that divides evenly into both $3x$ and 12. The largest number is 3, so we'll factor 3 out of both terms.

$$3x + 12 = 15 \quad\Rightarrow\quad 3(x + 4) = 15$$

When a set of parentheses has no letter or number directly outside, the parentheses can be removed.

When multiplying a number or letter times a quantity inside parentheses, you must multiply the number or letter times each term inside the parentheses.

Dividing both sides of the equation by 3:

$$\frac{3}{3}(x + 4) = \frac{15}{3} \quad \Rightarrow \quad (x + 4) = 5$$

$$x + 4 = 5 \quad \Rightarrow \quad x = 5 - 4 \quad \Rightarrow \quad x = 1$$

It should be clear from the solution above that factoring the left side of the equation did not alter the value of the unknown.

Let's look at a more complex equation:

$$3 = \frac{15}{(x + 4)} \tag{4b}$$

At first this looks difficult, but it's actually just another way of writing Equation 4. We can see this by multiplying both sides of Equation 4b by the quantity $(x + 4)$ as follows:

$$(x + 4) \times 3 = \frac{(x + 4) \times 15}{(x + 4)} \quad \Rightarrow \quad 3(x + 4) = 15 \tag{4}$$

To get the quantity $(x + 4)$ out of the denominator on the right side of the equation, we multiplied both sides of the equation by $(x + 4)$ as if it were a single term. That leaves $3(x + 4)$ on the left side of the equation, and since $\frac{x + 4}{x + 4}$ on the right cancels to *one*, we are left with only the 15 on the right side of the equation. The result is Equation 4, which we solved earlier.

Exponents

Another complication you might see is an equation with an exponent over one or more of the variables as in Equation 5.

$$x^2 = 9 \tag{5}$$

An **exponent** indicates how many times a number or letter or quantity is to be multiplied by itself. An exponent is also referred to as a **power**.

This equation is read as x squared equals 9 (**squaring** a number simply means multiplying it by itself. For instance, 2 squared is $2 \times 2 = 4$). The solution for the value of x is that number which when multiplied by itself (squared) equals 9. You were probably able to determine that the answer is 3, since $3 \times 3 = 9$. Just in case you're confronted with more difficult equations involving exponents, let's see how to solve this one the long way. In order to solve for a variable, the exponent associated with that variable must equal 1. In this example, in order to change the value of the exponent to 1, we can take the square root of both sides of the equation. Since we used easy numbers, the equation is easy to solve as follows:

$$\sqrt{x^2} = \sqrt{9} \qquad \Rightarrow \qquad x = 3$$

Another way to designate square root is with the exponent $1/2$. Let's try solving the equation using that method. Instead of using the square root sign, or radical, we'll use $1/2$ as an exponent.

$$(x^2)^{1/2} = (9)^{1/2}$$

We're trying to find the square root of x^2 and the square root of 9. When you see a term with more than one exponent, you simply multiply them together. In this example, when you multiply the exponents associated with the x variable, you get an exponent of $2 \times \frac{1}{2} = 1$, and because any number raised to the power of 1 equals itself, you are left with x on the left of the equation. Since there is an implied exponent of 1 associated with any number or letter, we can say we actually have $(9^1)^{1/2}$ on the right side of the equation. Again we multiply the exponents and get $1 \times \frac{1}{2} = \frac{1}{2}$, leaving us with $9^{1/2}$ on the right side of the equation:

$$x = 9^{1/2} = 3$$

Since an exponent of $\frac{1}{2}$ indicates square root, we're back to where we started with saying x equals the square root of 9.

Parentheses and Exponents

The logical next step is to solve an equation in which we have a set of parentheses with an exponent. Remember that quantities within parentheses can be treated like a single term. Assume you see the following equation:

$$(x + 5)^3 = 8 \qquad\qquad (6)$$

Keep in mind that in order to solve for a variable, its exponent must equal 1. In this example we can accomplish this by taking the cube root of both sides (the **cube root** of a number is just the number that, multiplied by itself three times, equals the original number. For example, the cube root of 1,000 is 10, since $10 \times 10 \times 10 = 1,000$). Remember, we're going to treat the quantity inside the parentheses just like a single term and multiply the exponents, as we did before.

When a number or letter has **more than one exponent**, the exponents should be multiplied together.

$$((x + 5)^3)^{1/3} = 8^{1/3} \implies x + 5 = 8^{1/3}$$

$$x + 5 = 2 \implies x = -3$$

Negative Numbers

When you subtract any number or letter, you are actually adding the *negative* of that number or letter.

Think of all possible numbers as sitting on a continuous line with zero at the exact center:

-8 -7 -6 -5 -4 -3 -2 -1 0 1 2 3 4 5 6 7 8

If you think of numbers this way, you can see there is a negative number for every possible positive number. And each number and its counterpart are spaced at exactly the same distance from zero, just on opposite sides.

They act sort of like matter and anti-matter. If matter and anti-matter come into contact with one another (are added together) they cancel each other out. So adding 3 and −3 together yields zero. Adding 5 and −5 together yields zero, too. Even adding 1,999,999 and −1,999,999 together yields zero.

Because working with negative numbers can get a little confusing, memorizing a few easy rules is the best solution. Here are some basic rules for working with negative numbers:

Rule 3. *When adding a positive and a negative number, the sign of the sum is the same as the sign of the number with the largest absolute value.*

Absolute value is the value of the number, ignoring the sign (e.g., the absolute value of +3 is 3 and the absolute value of −3 is also 3). To address the problem of adding positive and negative signs, we'll need the aid of our number line again. Let's solve the equation $x = (-4) + (+3)$ using the number line below.

-8 -7 -6 -5 -4 -3 -2 -1 0 1 2 3 4 5 6 7 8

First, look at the positions of the two numbers relative to zero on our number line. If you subtract a value from a number on the line, you count that number of spaces to the left. If you add, you count that number of spaces to the right. So if you subtract 4 from 3, you move 4 spaces to the left of 3 and end up at −1. If you add 3 to −4, you count 3 spaces to the right of −4 and end up at −1. Try it on the number line. You'll see it works. In either case, the answer is −1, and the sign of the sum depends upon the relative sizes of the two numbers (i.e., their absolute values). Since the absolute value of −4 is greater than the absolute value of +3, the sum has a negative sign. The answer to the equation is $x = (−4) + (3) = −1$.

Try applying the rule to the following examples:

    a. $(−1) + (+2) = +1$
    b. $(−3) + (+2) = −1$
    c. $(−3) + (−2) = −5$
    d. $(−5) + (+2) = −3$
    e. $(−125) + (+100) = −25$
    f. $(−125) + (−100) = −225$
    g. $(+125) + (−100) + (−30) + (+25) = +20$

Rule 4. *When subtracting one number from another, the sign of the second number is changed, and the two numbers are added together.*

Subtracting one number from another is like adding the same number with the opposite sign. So if we subtract four from three we get minus one. The equation would be:

    $3 − (+4) = −1$ or $3 + (−4) = −1$

You can see that in the second case, we actually added the opposite of four, or minus four, and we're right back where we were when we were adding positive and negative numbers. Let's try subtracting a negative number.

    $3 − (−4) = ?$

Again, we apply **Rule 4** and reverse the sign of the second number and add it to the first number.

    $3 − (−4) = ?$ $\Rightarrow$ $3 + 4 = 7$

The **absolute value** of a number is its value totally ignoring its sign.

The sum of one or more positive and negative numbers is determined by the **absolute values** of the individual numbers.

Subtraction is really adding the negative of a number.

When subtracting, always change the sign of the second number and add it to the first.

Try applying **Rule 4** to the following examples:

a. $(-1) - (+2) = -3$
b. $(+3) - (+2) = +1$
c. $(-3) - (-2) = -1$
d. $(-5) - (+2) = -7$
e. $(-125) - (+100) = -225$
f. $(+125) - (-100) = +225$
g. $(+125) - (-100) - (-30) - (+25) = +230$

When subtracting, always change the sign of the second number and add it to the first. In the last equation above, we first change the -100 to $+100$ and add it to 125 to get 225. Next we change the -30 to $+30$ and add it to 225 and get 255. Last we change the $+25$ to -25 and add it to 255, and our final answer is $+230$.

Rule 5. *Multiplying an even amount of negative numbers yields a product with a positive sign. Multiplying an odd number of negative numbers yields a product with a negative sign.*

When multiplying two or more positive and negative numbers, the sign of the product is determined by the **number of negative signs**.

Look at some examples:

	# of negative signs
$(-1) \times (-1) = +1$	2
$(-1) \times (-1) \times (-1) = -1$	3
$(-1) \times (-1) \times (-1) \times (-1) = +1$	4
$(-1) \times (-1) \times (-1) \times (-1) \times (-1) = -1$	5
$(-1) \times (-1) \times (-1) \times (-1) \times (-1) \times (-1) = +1$	6
$(-1) \times (+1) \times (-1) \times (+1) \times (-1) \times (+1) = -1$	3
$(-1) \times (+1) \times (+1) \times (+1) \times (-1) \times (+1) = +1$	2

An **even** number of negative signs yields a product with a positive sign. An **odd** number of negative signs yields a product with a negative sign.

Notice the number of negative signs in each equation. You will see that when there is an even number, the product has a positive sign, and when there is an odd number, the product has a negative sign. By the way, this will hold regardless of the actual numbers or letters used [e.g., $(a) \times (-2) = -2a$ and $(a) \times (-2) \times (-3) = 6a$].

Two Equations with Two Unknowns

A somewhat more advanced use for algebra is finding the value of two unknown variable terms. When dealing with two unknowns, we will use two equations (since it is impossible to find the values for two unknowns with less than two equations), and we will solve them "simultaneously." Let's say you are faced with the following two equations:

$$3x + 4y = 20 \qquad \text{and} \qquad x + 3y = -4$$

Even though it might seem like quite a daunting task, solving for these two unknowns, x and y, is actually just a matter of following a very logical series of steps while utilizing some of our algebra rules.

Step 1: Start by setting up the equations as if you were going to add them together like two numbers.

$$3x + 4y = 20$$
$$\underline{+x + 3y = -4}$$

Step 2: Using **Rule 1**, we multiply all the terms in one or both of the equations so that adding or subtracting them will eliminate one of the variables. In our case, we multiply the bottom equation by -3:

$$3x + 4y = 20 \qquad\qquad 3x + 4y = 20$$
$$\underline{-3(x + 3y) = -3(-4)} \quad \Rightarrow \quad \underline{-3x - 9y = 12}$$

Step 3: Add the two equations together by adding the x terms, the y terms, and the numbers.

$$3x + 4y = 20$$
$$\underline{-3x - 9y = 12}$$
$$0x - 5y = 32$$

The reason for multiplying one of the equations by a constant (a number) and then adding them together is getting rid of one of the unknowns. Whether you add or subtract the equations is simply a matter of choice.

Solving for **two unknown variables** requires at least two equations.

To solve two equations simultaneously, add or subtract them to eliminate one of the variables.

Multiplying both sides of the resulting equation by –1 according to **Rule 1**, we get:

$$5y = -32 \qquad \text{and} \qquad y = \frac{-32}{5} = -6.4$$

Step 4: Having determined the value for one of the unknowns, we can insert it back into either of the original equations to solve for the second unknown. Using the first of the two original equations, we have:

$$3x + 4y = 20 \implies 3x + 4(-6.4) = 20 \implies 3x - 25.6 = 20$$

$$3x = 45.6 \qquad \text{and} \qquad x = 15.2$$

Step 5: Plug both values back into the original equations to be sure your answers are correct.

$$3x + 4y \implies 3(15.2) + 4(-6.4) = 20$$

and

$$x + 3y = 15.2 + 3(-6.4) = 15.2 - 19.2 = \underline{-4}$$

Since plugging the values into either equation gives us the same values we began with, our answers for x and y are indeed correct.

SUMMARY OF SECTION 1

Learning Objective 1: *To understand the basic form of an equation.*

An **equation** shows (defines) the relationships among the terms (variables) in the equation.

A. An **equal sign** (=) shows that all the terms on the left side of the equation are equal to all the terms on the right side of the equation. The unknown terms can have only one value.

B. An **equal to or less than sign** (≤) shows that the value of all of the terms on the left side of the equation must be equal to or less than the value of all of the terms on the right side of the equation. The unknown terms in the equation can equal any value as long as it is less than or equal to the maximum defined by the equation.

C. A **greater than or equal to sign** ($\geq$) shows that the value of all the terms on the left side of the equation must be equal to or greater than the value of all of the terms on the right side of the equation. The unknown terms in the equation can equal any value as long as it is greater than or equal to the minimum defined by the equation.

D. When a term moves from one side of the equation to the other, its sign changes, either from negative to positive, or from positive to negative.

Learning Objective 2: *To understand multiplying and dividing both sides of an equation by a constant.*

Multiplying or dividing all terms in an equation by the same number or letter does not change the structure of the equation or the value of the unknown.

A. The multiplicand (i.e., the multiplied value) acts as a scalar.
  1. All terms are increased or decreased by the same proportion.
  2. The value of the unknown term(s) is unaffected.
B. The divisor (i.e., the divided value) acts as a scalar.
  1. All terms are increased or decreased by the same proportion.
  2. The value of the unknown is unaffected.
C. Division is the inverse of multiplication.
  1. The inverse of a number is one divided by that number; e.g., the inverse of three is 1/3.
  2. Dividing by three is the same as multiplying by 1/3.

Learning Objective 3: *To understand adding and subtracting a constant from both sides of an equation.*

When the same letter or number or letter is added to or subtracted from all terms in an equation, neither the structure of the equation nor the value of the unknown term(s) changes.

A. Multiplying or dividing by 1 does not affect the value of a number or letter.
  1. Any number or letter divided by 1 equals the number or letter.
  2. Any number or letter multiplied by 1 equals the number or letter.

B. Changing the order in which terms are multiplied does not affect the equation or the value of the unknown terms (i.e., the product of $a \times b$ is the same as the product of $b \times a$).

C. Changing the order of the equation does not affect the equation or the value of the unknown term(s).

1. The values of x and y in the equation $3x + 4 = 9y + 1$ are the same as the values of x and y in the equation $9y + 1 = 3x + 4$.

2. The order of the variables on either side can be rearranged without affecting the equation or the value of the unknown term(s).

Learning Objective 4: *To understand the use of parentheses in an equation.*

A. A set of parentheses and all terms within them are referred to as a **quantity**; e.g., $(x + 4)$ is referred to as the quantity $x + 4$.

B. The parentheses and their contents can be treated as a single term; e.g., $x(y + 1) = 4$ is the same as $(y + 1) = \frac{4}{x}$.

C. When multiplying a number or letter times a quantity inside a parentheses, you must multiply the number or letter times each term inside the parentheses; e.g., $3(x + 4) = 25$ means $3x + 12 = 25$.

D. A quantity within a set of parentheses can be the result of factoring.

1. Start with an equation such as $35x + 7 = 23$.

2. Look for the largest number that goes evenly into both the number (coefficient) 35 and the number 7.

   a. 35 is divisible by 1, 5, 7, and 35.

   b. 7 is divisible by 1 and 7 (7 is a prime number).

   c. The largest common factor is the number 7.

3. Factor 7 out of the coefficient 35 and the number 7 and place parentheses around the remaining numbers and letters as follows: $7(5x + 1) = 23$.

Learning Objective 5: *To understand equations containing terms with exponents.*

A. An exponent of a number or letter is referred to as a **power**; (e.g., x^3 says x cubed or x to the third power).

B. The power refers to the times the letter or number is multiplied by itself.

1. 5^3 means five times five times five (three times).

2. y^3 means y times y times y (three times).

C. An exponent can be any value i. In order to solve for an unknown variable that has an exponent, the exponent of that variable must be removed; (i.e., made equal to 1).
1. To remove an exponent, multiply it by its root.
    a. The ith root is denoted with a radical, $\sqrt[i]{}$, or the fraction $\frac{1}{i}$.
    b. The fourth root of 4 is denoted as either $\sqrt[4]{x}$ or $x^{\frac{1}{4}}$.
2. To remove a square (exponent of 2), take the square root
    [i.e., $(x^2)^{\frac{1}{2}} = x$ or $\sqrt[2]{x^2} = x$].
3. To remove a cube (exponent of 3), take the cube root
    [i.e., $(x^3)^{\frac{1}{3}} = x$ or $\sqrt[3]{x^3} = x$].
4. To remove any exponent i, take the ith root
    [i.e., $(x^i)^{\frac{1}{i}} = x$ or $\sqrt[i]{x^i} = x$].
D. Quantities within parentheses can have exponents; e.g.$(x + 1)^2$, means $(x + 1)(x + 1)$.

Learning Objective 6: *To understand how to work with negative numbers.*

A. The sign of the sum of a positive number and a negative number is determined by the absolute values of the two numbers.
1. $(-5) + (+3) = -2$
2. $(+168) + (-53) = 115$
B. When subtracting two numbers, change the sign of the second number and add the two.
1. $(45) - (-33) = 45 + 33 = 78$
2. $(32) - (+14) = 32 + (-14) = 18$
C. When multiplying negative numbers, the sign of the product depends upon the number of negative numbers.
1. An even number of negative signs means a positive product; e.g., $(-3) \times (-3) = 9$.
2. An odd number of negative signs means a negative product; e.g., $(-3) \times (-3) \times (-3) = -27$.

Learning Objective 7: *To understand how to solve two equations with two unknown variables.*

There must be at least two equations in order to solve for the values of two unknown variables; e.g., $2x + 3y = 19$, and $3x - 3y = 1$.

A. Set up the two equations as if you are adding them.
$$2x + 3y = 19$$
$$4x - 2y = 5$$

B. Multiply one of the equations by a number, which will enable you to eliminate one of the unknowns.

$\boxed{-2}$ $\quad 2x + 3y = 19 \quad \Rightarrow \quad -4x - 6y = -38$
$\qquad\quad 4x - 2y = 5 \quad \Rightarrow \quad 4x - 2y = 5$

C. Add the two equations together by adding the x terms, the y terms, and the numbers.

$$-4x - 6y = -38$$
$$\underline{\;\; 4x - 2y = 5 \;\;}$$

$0x - 8y = -33 \quad \Rightarrow \quad -8y = -33$

D. Solve for the remaining unknown variable.
$$8y = 33 \quad \Rightarrow \quad y = \frac{33}{8} = 4.125$$

E. Plug the value for the first unknown variable into one of the original equations and solve for the second unknown variable.
$$4x - 2y = 5 \qquad \Rightarrow \qquad 4x - 2(4.125) = 5$$
$$4x - 8.25 = 5 \qquad \Rightarrow \qquad 4x = 5 + 8.25$$
$$4x = 13.25 \qquad \Rightarrow \qquad x = \frac{13.25}{4} = 3.3125$$

F. Plug both values back into both of the original equations to check your answers.
$$2x + 3y = 19 \qquad \Rightarrow \qquad 2(3.3125) + 3(4.125) = 19$$
$$4x - 2y = 5 \qquad \Rightarrow \qquad 4(3.3125) - 2(4.125) = 5$$

SECTION 2: AN INTRODUCTION TO STATISTICS

In this section, your learning objectives are:

1. To distinguish between populations and samples.
2. To distinguish between qualitative and quantitative variables.
3. To calculate measures of central tendency.
4. To calculate measures of dispersion.

Now that you have learned many of the tricks of algebra, it's time to move on to statistics. *Webster's Collegiate Dictionary* defines statistics as "a branch of mathematics dealing with the collection, analysis, interpretation, and presentation of numerical data."[2] When we are trying to determine certain characteristics about a large population, we take a sample from that population. We then use that sample to derive some statistics and make inferences about the population. In order to understand what this means, it is useful to become familiar with some of the more valuable statistics vocabulary.

> A **statistic** is a piece of information; it is a characteristic of a sample.

Statistic

A statistic is a piece of information that can be agonizingly trivial and totally uninteresting, or extremely controversial and provocative. A statistic can describe, measure, or define. An example of a statistic is that 51 percent of Americans are female.

Population

Population is the collection of all possible individuals, objects, measurements, or other items; e.g., the population of the U.S. is all people who call the United States their home country. If you found a huge tank filled to the top with millions of colored balls, the population of colored balls would include all the balls in the tank. The population of carp in the world is not just those that live in beautifully maintained and landscaped pools in Japan; the carp population would include every single carp, no matter where it lives.

> A **population** is the collection of all possible individuals, objects, or other items.

---

[2] *Merriam Webster's Collegiate Dictionary, 10E, 2000.*

An important characteristic of a population is its size. For instance, the population of the U.S. is over 240 million people. That means there are over 240 million members of that particular population. If you wanted to estimate the average height of an American, you would not want to go around to every single person and measure his or her height. Even if you could afford the extreme cost in both time and money, it would be a logistical nightmare. The field of statistics allows us to estimate these values without actually measuring each member of the population.

Sample

A **sample** is a portion of a population that is used to estimate characteristics of (i.e., make inferences about) the population. If we were interested in the average height of a U.S. citizen, we could select people from all over the United States (a sample of people), measure them, and find the average height. The average height of the individuals in the sample is then used to infer the average height of all people in the U.S.

To estimate the percentages of balls in the tank that are red, green, or blue, we could draw a sample of balls (actually draw several samples) and count the number of balls of each color in each sample. From these samples we would make an inference about the actual percentages of each color in the population.

There are a few characteristics of samples that are very important. One is **randomness**. A random sample has no detectable plan or pattern. Observations are drawn in a random manner with no preference given to any particular value, size, or location. You don't want to force the sample to yield statistics that are **biased**[3] because of the way the sample is taken. For example, if you are trying to estimate the percentage of people in the U.S. who are over age 65, you would not take your sample observations[4] from a retirement community. If you did that, you may well estimate that nearly 100 percent of the U.S population is over 65! An appropriate sample would be drawn from many different areas across the country, in a completely random or unbiased way.

A **sample** is a portion of a population that is used to estimate characteristics of (make inferences about) the population.

To avoid a **biased** statistic, the sample should be **random**.

[3] In this case, a biased sample statistic is one whose value is forced to be higher or lower than the true population measure simply by the way the sample is drawn.

[4] An observation is one member of a sample. A sample of size 30 has 30 observations.

Another characteristic important to the sample is **size**. When an extremely large sample is drawn, the costs can be very high, and the inferences not significantly stronger than those of a somewhat smaller sample. However, if the sample is too small, the inferences drawn from the sample may not be trustworthy. Even though we will not pursue ideal sample size in this chapter, it is important to remember that sample size is very important to the value (the confidence) you can place on the inferences you make about a population.

Variables

Recall that a variable is an unknown quantity (measurement) that can have different values. If you were estimating average height and measured every person in your sample, the first value of the variable "height" would be the height of the first person measured. The second value would be the height of the second person, the third value would be the height of the third person, and so on. The variable "height" would have as many values (observations) as there are people in your sample.

There are two main categories of variables, **qualitative** and **quantitative**. A qualitative variable measures attributes. These could include gender, religious preference, eye color, type of running shoe preferred, or state of birth. In other words, qualitative variables do not use numbers.

Conversely, **quantitative** variables are expressed numerically. These could include the average number of children in the typical household, the average height of American females, the percentage of people in the population with false teeth, or the average number of computers sold daily.

Quantitative variables can be divided into **discrete** and **continuous**. Think of discrete as meaning that the variable can only have a countable number of easily identified values. If the variable can only take on a whole number value from 1 to 10, it would be considered discrete. Its only possible values are 1, 2, 3, 4, 5, 6, 7, 8, 9, and 10. You'll notice that you can easily count each possible value. Also, whether you realize it or not, there are fairly large distances between the possible values.

Now, let's say the variable can have any incremental value between 1 and 10. In this case, the variable can assume an infinite number of possible values and is called a **continuous** variable. When the variable was

Qualitative variables describe attributes of the sample. **Quantitative** variables measure numerical values of the sample.

A **discrete** variable can only have a countable number of easily identified values.

A **continuous** variable can have an infinite number of outcomes.

discrete, two of its possible values were 3 and 4, and it could not have a value between 3 and 4. As a continuous variable, it can have the values 3 and 4, but it can also take on any of the infinite values between 3 and 4.

To illustrate, consider a continuous variable that is measured in inches. If the value of the first measurement is 3.0 inches, the next possible value would be so close to 3.0 that we have no instrument capable of measuring the distance. Consider the maximum number of zeros you can place between the decimal point after the 3 and a 1. An example would be 3.00001, but of course you can place many more than four zeros between the decimal and the 1. In fact, the number of zeros you could place between the decimal point and the 1 is infinite.

Data

Let's turn our attention to the terminology that is used to describe data. When we wanted to estimate the average height of a large group of people, we measured a sample of them and wrote down each measurement. Let's assume we collected the following measurements:

Person[5]	Height in Inches
1	70
2	71
3	73
4	66
5	62
6	70

The term **data** is plural. It is used to mean all the sample observations taken together.

Data point is used to mean a single observation.

These measurements are referred to collectively as the sample **data** (plural) while each individual measurement or observation is a **data point**. One observation would be the value 70 inches. Another would be 66 inches. Once we have collected our data, we will look for ways of describing them as a whole; i.e., we will describe the data **distribution**.

The **distribution** is the way the individual data points or observations are scattered or distributed. There will be a center to the scatter of data

---

[5] We are assuming a very small sample size to make the example easier. In reality, you would measure anywhere from several dozen to several thousand people, depending upon the size of the population.

with the observations in some sort of pattern around that center. Think of dropping a handful of marbles. They will fall to the ground, bounce, roll a little, and stop in some sort of a pattern. The pattern can be closely grouped, widely spread out, or anywhere in between. We could say the pattern is the way the marbles are *distributed* on the ground. Let's look at some ways to describe the distribution.

Central tendency is used to refer to any measure of the center or middle of the sample or population.

Measures of Central Tendency

To describe the data, we will want to find the center point of the data. This is known as **central tendency**. Once we have done that, we will want a measure of how the data are scattered or distributed around the center point.

Mean.   Mean is just another word for *average*, or the center of the data. For instance, when we previously mentioned estimating the average height, we could have used the expression "mean height." Unfortunately, there are actually two types of means with which you should be familiar. The most common one is the **arithmetic mean**.

The **arithmetic mean** is the sum of all the observations divided by the number of observations.

The arithmetic mean is denoted by:

$$\bar{x} = \frac{\Sigma x}{n} \qquad\qquad (7)$$

or
$$\mu = \frac{\Sigma x}{N} \qquad\qquad (8)$$

Equation 7 finds the **sample mean** and Equation 8 is used to calculate the **population mean**. The Greek letter sigma, Σ, simply denotes a sum. In Equation 7, we add up (sum) the individual observations, denoted by x, and divide by the number of observations in the sample, n. This gives us the sample mean, $\bar{x}$.

Equation 8 is used to calculate the mean of the entire population, denoted by μ. Again we sum the observations, but this time we divide by the number of observations in the entire population, N.

Earlier, to estimate the average height of the U.S. population, we took a sample of people and measured their heights. By substituting the data (measurements) into the equation to find the sample mean, we get:

$$\bar{x} = \frac{\Sigma x}{n} \quad \Rightarrow \quad \frac{70 + 71 + 73 + 66 + 62 + 70}{6} = 68.7 \text{ inches}$$

Geometric mean is used for interest rates and growth rates. It is a multiplicative mean.

The **geometric mean** is a little more complicated and is used with ratios, percentages, and growth rates. The geometric mean is found using the following equation:

$$GM = \sqrt[n]{(1 + x_1)(1 + x_2)(1 + x_3) \dots (1 + x_n)} - 1.0 \qquad (9)$$

where GM = the geometric mean

x_i = the ith measurement (the first, second, third, etc.)

n = the number of data points (observations)

We add 1.0 to each observation's value, which is a percentage expressed as a decimal, multiply all the observations together, find the nth root of the product, and then subtract the 1.0 (nth refers to the number of observations. If there were two observations, you would find the square root. With 20 observations, you find the 20th root).

Perhaps a simple example will show that this isn't as bad as it looks. Let's assume you have had your money in a mutual fund.[6] Over the last five years the fund has shown returns of 15 percent, 12 percent, 14 percent, 16 percent, and 6 percent. What were the arithmetic and geometric returns for the fund?

First, the arithmetic mean, $\bar{x}$ is:

$$\bar{x} = \frac{\Sigma x}{n} \Rightarrow \frac{0.15 + 0.12 + 0.14 + 0.16 + 0.06}{5} = 0.126 = \boxed{12.6\%}$$

Next, the geometric return, GM is:

$$GM = \sqrt[n]{(1 + x_1)(1 + x_2)(1 + x_3) \dots (1 + x_n)} - 1.0$$

$$GM = \sqrt[5]{(1 + .15) \times (1 + .12) \times (1 + .14) \times (1 + .16) \times (1 + .06)} - 1.0$$

$$= \sqrt[5]{(1.15)(1.12)(1.14)(1.16)(1.06)} - 1.0$$

$$= \sqrt[5]{1.80544} - 1.0 = 0.125, \text{ So } GM = \boxed{12.5\%}$$

[6] A mutual fund is an investment company that gathers together the investments of many individuals and invests the total amount for them. This provides professional management and greater diversification of individual investments. Diversification will be discussed in a later chapter.

So, what's the difference between the arithmetic mean and the geometric mean? You will notice that, although they are close, the geometric mean is smaller than the arithmetic mean. In fact, the geometric will always be less than or equal to the arithmetic mean. In this example, the arithmetic mean is the average annual return for the investment. If you were interested in estimating the return for the following year, you would probably want to use the average annual return. So you would estimate your mutual fund will have a 12.5 percent return next year.

The geometric mean shows the average annual growth in your cumulative investment for the five years, assuming no funds are withdrawn. In other words, the geometric mean assumes compounding. In fact, when evaluating investment returns, the geometric mean is often referred to as the **compound mean**.

Let's consider an example of this compounding idea. Assume you put $1,000 in a savings account that pays 5 percent. What is the amount you will have at the end of two years?

At the end of the first year, you will have the initial $1,000 plus 5 percent interest on the $1,000. You'll have:

$$V_1 = \$1,000 + (\$1,000 \times i) = \$1,000 + (\$1,000 \times .05)$$
$$= \$1,000 + \$50 = \$1,050$$

At the end of the second year you'll have:

$$V_2 = \$1,050 + (\$1,050 \times i) = \$1,050 + (\$1,050 \times 0.05)$$
$$= \$1,050 + \$52.50 = \$1,102.5$$

Notice that in the second year you earned interest on the interest you earned in the first year (as long as you did not withdraw it). This is the phenomenon known as compound interest, or simply "compounding." In other words, you are earning interest on interest.

Let's play around for a moment using the tools that we have learned. Look at the first part of the solution above and you'll see $1,000 + (i \times 1,000) = $1,050. Now, factor $1,000 out of the left side of the equation. [7]

$$V_1 = \$1,000(1 + i) = \$1,050 \qquad (9a)$$

This shows that the amount in the savings account after one year is the amount at the beginning of the year times the quantity $(1 + i)$, where i is the rate of interest. Now, look at the equation we used to find the amount in the savings account at the end of the second year.

$$V_2 = \$1,050 + (\$1,050 \times i) = \$1,102.50$$

Again, we will remove a common factor from the left side of the equation, and we are left with:

$$V_2 = \$1,050(1 + i) = \$1,102.50 \qquad (9b)$$

So, the amount in the savings account at the end of the second year is the amount at the beginning of the second year multiplied by the quantity $(1 + i)$. Let's put both of the new equations together and see if anything jumps out at us.

$$V_1 = \$1,000(1 + i) = \$1,050 \qquad (9a)$$

$$V_2 = \$1,050(1 + i) = \$1,102.50 \qquad (9b)$$

If you look closely, you'll see that Equation 9a actually defines the first term ($1,050) of Equation 9b. Since Equation 9a tells us that $1,000 $(1 + i) = $1,050, we can substitute the left side of the equation for $1,050 in Equation 9b to get:

$$V_2 = \$1,000(1 + i)(1 + i) = \$1,102.50$$

$$V_2 = \$1,000(1 + i)^2 = \$1,102.50 \qquad (9c)$$

---

[7] By factoring, we find a number that is common to both terms. Remember, a factor is simply one of two or more numbers that, when multiplied together, yield the original number. If you multiply the terms in the parentheses by $1,000, you'll be back to the original two terms.

If we were to calculate the amount we would have after three years (at the end of year three), we would multiply the amount after two years, $1,102.50, by $(1 + i)$. This would give us:

$$V_3 = \$1,102.50(1 + i) = \$1,102.50(1.05) = \$1,157.62$$

If we substitute the left side of Equation 9c for $1,102.50 in the above equation, a definite pattern begins to appear.

$$V_3 = \$1,000(1 + i)^2(1 + i) = \$1,157.62$$

$$V_3 = \$1,000(1 + i)^3 = \$1,157.62$$

To find the amount in the savings account after one year, we multiplied the initial amount (deposit) by $(1 + i)$. To find the amount at the end of two years, we multiplied the original deposit by $(1 + i)^2$, and to find the amount after three years we multiplied by $(1 + i)^3$. In fact, as long as the interest rate, i, does not change, the exponent of the quantity $(1 + i)$ will always be equal to the number of years, or more precisely, it will equal the number of compounding periods.

Range, Median, and Mode. Earlier, in our attempt to estimate the average height of a large population of people, we took the following sample observations:

Person	Height in Inches
1	70
2	71
3	73
4	66
5	62
6	70

The **range** of a sample is the distance between the largest and the smallest observations.

We found the average height of an individual in our sample to be 68.7" or 1.74498 meters. To gain a little more insight into the population, we want to calculate more descriptive statistics, such as the **range**. The range is simply the distance between the lowest and the highest observation for height. In our case we say the observations *ranged* from 62" to 73". The range shows us how dispersed the sample observations are.

There are eleven inches between the largest observation and the smallest. The larger the range, the greater the dispersion of observations, and the smaller the range, the less dispersed (more tightly grouped) the observations.

The **median** is the middle observation. If we ranked our height observations from the smallest to the largest, the same number of observations will fall above and below the median value. Our observations are 62, 66, 70, 70, 71, and 73. The median of the six observations falls between the third and fourth ranked observations. Thus, the simple average of the third and fourth observations, 70, represents the median of our sample. There are two observations greater than 70 (71 and 73), and two observations less than 70 (62 and 66).

The **mode** is the observation that appears most often. In our case both the median and the mode are 70. The mean, median, and mode are all measures of **central tendency**. They all locate the center of the observations or population.

The range, along with the measures of central tendency, describe what is known as the **distribution** of the values or observations. In our case, we can sum up the distribution of the observations as follows:

> n = 6 observations
> Mean = 68.7 inches
> Median = 70 inches
> Mode = 70 inches
> Range = 11 inches (62 inches to 73 inches)

We can look at these statistics and learn much about the sample. For instance, we see its center is around 70 inches, and there is a range of 11 inches between the smallest and largest observations in the sample.

A note is necessary at this point. You probably questioned why the mean and median, both measures of the center of the distribution, are different. In fact, you might even be asking yourself, "Why do we need so many measures of the center of the distribution in the first place?"

This question deserves some attention. The **median** finds the center of the distribution by number of observations. There are an equal **number**

The **median** of a sample has the same number of observations above and below it.

The **mode** of the sample observations is the value that appears most often.

of observations above and below the median, regardless of their values. The **mean**, on the other hand, actually adds all the observations together and divides by the number of observations to find the **mathematical cente**r. You probably noticed that the mean of the sample observations, 68.7, isn't even one of the observations. This is quite frequently the case.

More Measures of Dispersion

Mean Deviation and Standard Deviation. The **mean (average) deviation** is a measure of the dispersion of the sample observations around the center of the distribution. It measures the average deviation from the mathematical mean. A deviation is measured as the distance from the mean to each observation.

With a mean of 68.7", the deviations for our sample are:

70" − 68.7"

71" − 68.7"

73" − 68.7"

66" − 68.7"

62" − 68.7"

70" − 68.7"

and the mean deviation, *MD* is:

$$MD = \frac{\Sigma|x - \bar{x}|}{n} \qquad (10)$$

where: x = the value of each observation

$\bar{x}$ = the arithmetic mean of the observations

n = the number of observations

$|x - \bar{x}|$ = the absolute value of each deviation[8]

and

$$MD = \frac{|70 - 68.7| + |71 - 68.7| + |73 - 68.7| + |66 - 68.7| + |62 - 68.7| + |70 - 68.7|}{6}$$

$$MD = \frac{1.3 + 2.3 + 4.3 + 2.7 + 6.7 + 1.3}{6} = 3.1$$

---

[8] Since summing the negative and positive deviations would tend to cancel them out, we have to ignore their signs and sum their absolute values.

The **mean deviation** is the average of the absolute values of the distances between each observation and the mean.

So the average or mean deviation for our sample is 3.1 inches. This means that, on average, the sample observations fall 3.1 inches from the mean. If the mean deviation had been 1.0 inch, the observations would be much more closely grouped around the mean, or much less dispersed. Had the mean deviation been 6 inches, the observations would be more spread out or dispersed.

Another way to measure the dispersion of our sample is with the **standard deviation**. As you can probably guess, we must *standardize* the deviations. When you standardize numbers, you typically divide them by some common value. This puts all the numbers in terms of some common or *standard* measure, like pounds per square inch or parts per million.

For example, assume you are trying to determine whether the people in a certain area tend to be overweight, and you weigh as many of them as possible. You would probably want to standardize the observations (weights) by dividing the weight of each person by his or her height to find the average pounds per foot of height.

Why, you might ask, would you want to do that? A simple answer is that on a 6' 6" person, 250 pounds might not be considered heavy. For a person 5 feet tall, however, the conclusion regarding a 250-pound observation is considerably different.

The **variance** of a sample must be found before the standard deviation can be found.

Standardizing the deviations of our height sample, however, is somewhat more complicated than this example. In our case, we need to square each deviation and sum them before we divide to find the average. This might seem quite different from the mean deviation, and indeed it is. Look at the equation below, which gives us the population variance.

$$\sigma^2 = \frac{\Sigma(X - \mu)^2}{N} \qquad (11)$$

In this equation:

The **standard deviation** is the mean of the squared deviations from the mean.

σ^2 = the population variance (the arithmetic mean of the squared deviations from the population mean)

μ = the mean of the population

X = an individual member of the population

N = the number of observations in the population

When calculating variance, we square the deviations instead of using their absolute values as we did with the mean deviation. After we calculate the variance for the population, we find the standard deviation. The standard deviation, σ, is simply the square root of the variance, σ^2.

$\sigma = \sqrt{\sigma^2}$ or

$$\sigma = \sqrt{\frac{\Sigma(X - \mu)^2}{N}} \qquad (12)$$

> The **standard deviation** is the square root of the variance.

The equations for variance and standard deviation of the sample are slightly different. Since the sample is smaller than the population, finding the arithmetic mean of the squared deviations tends to underestimate the true value. We have to adjust the formula slightly to account for this. The standard deviation for a sample is as follows:

$$s^2 = \frac{\Sigma(x - \bar{x})^2}{n - 1} \qquad (13)$$

where: s^2 = the sample variance

          x = an individual observation in the sample

          $\bar{x}$ = the sample mean

    $(n - 1)$ = the number of sample observations minus 1

Notice we divided by $(n - 1)$ rather than n. This is the modification for the size of the sample compared to the population. As with the population, the standard deviation of the sample is the square root of its variance:

> To avoid under-estimating the sample variance, we divide by $n - 1$ rather than n.

$s = \sqrt{s^2}$ or

$$s = \sqrt{\frac{\Sigma(x - \bar{x})^2}{n - 1}} \qquad (14)$$

For our previous example related to estimating the average height of a large population of people, we calculate the standard deviation below:

$$s = \sqrt{\frac{(70 - 68.7)^2 + (71 - 68.7)^2 + (73 - 68.7)^2 + (66 - 68.7)^2 + (62 - 68.7)^2 + (70 - 68.7)^2}{6 - 1}}$$

$$s = \sqrt{\frac{1.69 + 5.29 + 18.49 + 7.29 + 44.89 + 1.69}{5}} = \sqrt{15.87} = 3.98$$

Thus, the standard deviation of our sample is 3.98 inches. As with the mean deviation: the larger the standard deviation, the greater the dispersion of the observations about the mean. This means that the observations are relatively spread out. This is often referred to as a "loose" distribution. The smaller the standard deviation, the more the observations are grouped around the mean. The observations are less spread out. We would describe this as a "tight" distribution.

SUMMARY OF SECTION 2

Learning Objective 1: *To distinguish between populations and samples.*

A. A **population** is the collection of all possible individuals, objects, or other items (e.g., all the people in a country).
B. A **sample** is a portion of the population that is used to estimate characteristics of the population.
   1. A sample should be representative of the population (i.e., sample observations should be selected at random from the population).
   2. The sample should be unbiased (i.e., a random sample will not favor any particular size, age, weight, length, color, or other measure).
   3. Characteristics of the sample are known as **statistics** and they are used to estimate characteristics of the population.

Learning Objective 2: *To distinguish between qualitative and quantitative variables.*

A. **Qualitative variables** measure attributes (e.g., color, gender, size, height).
B. **Quantitative variables** are expressed numerically (e.g., the number of children per household).
C. Quantitative variables can be **discrete** or **continuous**.
   1. **Discrete quantitative variables** are easily counted. The variable x can have any whole number value from 1 to 10, where x can have the value 1, 2, 3, 4, 5, 6, 7, 8, 9, or 10.
   2. **Continuous quantitative variables** have an infinite number of possible values.
      a. The variable x can have any value from 1 to 10.
      b. Considering all fractional or decimal values, there are an infinite number of values from 1 to 10.

Learning Objective 3: *To calculate measures of central tendency.*

A. The **mean** of the sample is the arithmetic or geometric average value.
   1. **Arithmetic mean** is the simple average of the values (i.e., the sum of the values divided by the number of values).

$$\bar{x} = \frac{\Sigma x}{n} \qquad \text{(sample mean)} \qquad (7)$$

$$\text{or} \quad \mu = \frac{\Sigma x}{N} \quad \text{(population mean)} \qquad (8)$$

   2. **Geometric mean** is the multiplicative average of the values. It is used with percentages such as interest rates and growth rates.

$$GM = \sqrt[n]{(1 + x_1)(1 + x_2)(1 + x_3) \ldots (1 + x_n)} - 1.0 \qquad (9)$$

Learning Objective 4: *To calculate measures of dispersion.*

A. Dispersion around the mean is known as the **distribution** of the data.
B **Mean deviation** is the arithmetic average deviation from the mean.

$$MD = \frac{\Sigma |x - \bar{x}|}{n} \qquad (10)$$

C. The **standard deviation** is the "standardized" deviation from the mean.
   1. Standard deviation is the square root of the variance.
   2. Variance is the arithmetic mean of the squared deviations from the mean.

$$\sigma^2 = \sqrt{\sigma^2} \qquad \text{or}$$

$$\sigma^2 = \sqrt{\frac{\Sigma(X - \mu)^2}{N}} \qquad \text{(population)} \qquad (12)$$

$$s = \sqrt{s^2} \qquad \text{or}$$

$$s = \sqrt{\frac{\Sigma(x - \bar{x})^2)}{n - 1}} \qquad \text{(sample)} \qquad (14)$$

PRACTICE QUESTIONS

1. If $a + 6 = 44$, which of the following represents the value of a?
   A. 9.
   B. 26.
   C. 38.
   D. 50.

2. If $\frac{a}{4} = 2$, which of the following represents the value of a?
   A. 2.
   B. 3.
   C. 6.
   D. 8.

3. A student has $25,000 in her bank account and the university charges a total of $500 per credit hour. How many credit hours can she purchase before she must borrow money?
   A. 5.
   B. 12.
   C. 50.
   D. 150.

4. If $\frac{15}{c} = 3$, which of the following represents the value of c?
   A. 3.
   B. 5.
   C. 15.
   D. 45.

5. If $p \leq \frac{25}{5}$, which of the following represents the value of p?
   A. Less than or equal to 5.
   B. Greater than or equal to 5.
   C. Equal to 5.
   D. Equal to 25.

6. In the equation $3(x + 5) = 45$, which of the following represents the value of x?

   A. 10.
   B. 15.
   C. 20.
   D. 25.

7. In the relationship $(x + 5)^{1/3} = (y - 5)^{1/3}$, which of the following **correctly** represents the relationship between x and y?

   A. $x = y$.
   B. $x = y^3$.
   C. $x = y - 10$.
   D. $x = y + 10$.

8. If $4x + 4y = 24$ and $2x + 3y = 24$, which of the following statements is **correct**?

   A. $x = 6$.
   B. $x = 12$.
   C. $y = 6$.
   D. $y = 12$.

9. If $x = 3$ and $y = 6$, which of the following represents the value of $3x + 4y$?

   A. 3.3.
   B. 6.
   C. 14.
   D. 33.

10. Which of the following statements is **incorrect**?

    A. $5(x + 3) = 5x + 15$.
    B. $(6x + 3) = 3(2x + 1)$.
    C. $3(x + 3) = 3x + 3$.
    D. $(32x - 8y) = 8(4x - y)$.

11. Which of the following represents the **correct** way to calculate the arithmetic mean of 6 numbers? The sum of:

    A. the numbers divided by 6.
    B. the numbers after raising each to the 6th power.
    C. the numbers multiplied by 6.
    D. 1 plus each number divided by 6.

12. If $x = 2 - y$ and $y = x - 4$, which of the following relationships is **correct**?

    A. $x = 3$.
    B. $x = 6$.
    C. $y = 1$.
    D. $y = 14$.

13. Which of the following values represents the arithmetic mean of 25, 30, and 20?

    A. 18.
    B. 25.
    C. 30.
    D. 35.

14. If returns for the last five years are 2 percent, 15 percent, 17 percent, 19 percent, and 23 percent, which of the following represents their geometric mean?

    A. 12.39%.
    B. 14.97%.
    C. 15.21%.
    D. 18.03%.

Below are the monthly salaries for 6 people. Use the data for problems 15 through 20. Round all answers to the nearest whole number.

Person	1	2	3	4	5	6
Salary/Month ($)	5,000	3,000	3,500	4,000	4,250	4,300

15. Which of the following represents the arithmetic mean salary for the **population**?

    A. 4,000.
    B. 4,008.
    C. 4,200.
    D. 5,280.

16. Which of the following represents the mean deviation of the salaries for the **population**?

    A. 508.
    B. 793.
    C. 1,492.
    D. 4,008.

17. Which of the following represents the variance of the salaries for the **population**?

    A. 400,347.
    B. 716,480.
    C. 741,680.
    D. 768,410.

18. Which of the following represents the standard deviation of the salaries for the **population**?

    A. 525.16.
    B. 632.73.
    C. 816.20.
    D. 861.20.

19. Which of the following represents the variance of the salaries, if the data represent a **sample**?

    A. 400,347.
    B. 480,417.
    C. 890,016.
    D. 891,600.

20. Which of the following represents the standard deviation of the salaries, if the data represent a **sample**?

    A. 632.
    B. 693.
    C. 934.
    D. 940.

ANSWERS AND SOLUTIONS

1. C. Subtracting 6 from both sides of the equation, we are left with $a = 38$.

2. D. Multiplying both sides of the equation by 4, we are left with $a = 8$.

3. C. Let n represent the number of credit hours (the unknown). We know that the number of hours multiplied by the cost per hour, \$500, yields the total spent, which cannot be more than \$25,000. We represent this in equation form as:

   $$500n = \$25,000$$

   and

   $$n = \frac{\$25,000}{\$500} = 50$$

4. B. Multiplying both sides of the equation by c, we are left with:

   $$15 = 3c$$

   and

   $$c = \frac{15}{3} = 5$$

5. A. Dividing 25 by 5, we are left with $p \leq 5$. The $\leq$ sign indicates "less than or equal to," so the interpretation of the equation is p is less than or equal to 5.

6. A. First we multiply through the parentheses by 3 and are left with $3x + 15 = 45$. We then subtract 15 from both sides and get $3x = 30$. Dividing both sides leaves us with $x = 10$.

7. C. First, by cubing both sides we have $x + 5 = y - 5$. Subtracting 5 from both sides leaves us with $x = y - 5 - 5$, and finally $x = y - 10$.

8. D. First, set up the equations as simultaneous equations:

   Equation 1: $4x + 4y = 24$
   Equation 2: $2x + 3y = 24$

   Next, multiply both sides of equation 2 by -2 and add the two equations:

   $$
   \begin{array}{r}
   4x + 4y = 24 \\
   \underline{-4x - 6y = -48} \\
   -2y = -24
   \end{array}
   $$

Dividing both sides of the result by –2 leaves us with $y = 12$. Substituting this value of y into our first equation, gives us $4x + 4(12) = 24$. Subtracting 48 from both sides and dividing by 4 leaves us with $x = -6$.

9. D. Substitute the values for x and y in the equation leaves:

$$3(3) + 4(6) = 9 + 24 = 33$$

10. C. Multiplying through the parentheses in answer C gives us $3x + 9$, not $3x + 3$.

11. A. Note: Dividing after summing the numbers or before will not change the value of the arithmetic mean.

12. A. First set up the simultaneous equations:

$$x = 2 - y$$
$$y = x - 4$$

Now get all the variables on the left and all the numbers on the right.

(Remember, a number or variable changes signs when it "crosses the bridge.")

$x + y = 2$
$y - x = -4$ Adding the two together:

$2y = -2$ and substituting -1 for y in the first equation, $x = 2 - (-1) = 3$.
$y = -1$

13. B. The arithmetic mean is the sum of the numbers divided by the number of numbers, 3.

$$\frac{25 + 30 + 20}{3} = \frac{75}{3} = 25.$$

14. B. The geometric mean, GM is

$$GM = \sqrt[n]{(1 + x_1)(1 + x_2)(1 + x_3) \ldots (1 + x_n)} - 1.0$$

$$GM = \sqrt[5]{(1 + .02) \times (1 + .15) \times (1 + .17) \times (1 + .19) \times (1 + .23)} - 1.0$$

$$= \sqrt[5]{(1.02)(1.15)(1.17)(1.19)(1.23)} - 1.0$$

$$= \sqrt[5]{2.0088} - 1.0 = 1.1497 - 1.0 = .1497 = 14.97\%$$

15. B. $\dfrac{5,000 + 3,000 + 3,500 + 4,000 + 4,250 + 4,300}{6} = 4,008.3$

16. A. The mean deviation, MD is:

$$MD = \frac{\Sigma|x - \bar{x}|}{n}$$

where x = the value of each observation

$\bar{x}$ = the arithmetic mean of the observations

n = the number of observations

$|x - \bar{x}|$ = the absolute value of each deviation

$$MD = \frac{|5,000 - 4,008| + |3,000 - 4,008| + |3,500 - 4,008| + |4,000 - 4,008| + |4,250 - 4,008||4,300 - 4,008|}{6}$$

$$MD = \frac{992 + 1,008 + 508 + 8 + 242 + 292}{6} = \frac{3,050}{6} = 508.3$$

17. A. The variance of a population is found using:

$$\sigma^2 = \frac{\Sigma(X - \mu)^2}{N}, \text{ where}$$

μ = the mean of the population

X = an individual member of the population

N = the number of observations in the population

$$\sigma^2 = \frac{(5,000 - 4,008)^2 + (3,000 - 4,008)^2 + (3,500 - 4,008)^2 + (4,000 - 4,008)^2 + (4,250 - 4,008)^2 + (4,300 - 4,008)^2}{6}$$

$$\sigma^2 = \frac{(992)^2 + (-1,008)^2 + (-508)^2 + (-8)^2 + (242)^2 + (292)^2}{6}$$

$$\sigma^2 = \frac{984,064 + 1,016,064 + 258,064 + 64 + 58,564 + 85,264}{6} = \frac{2,402,084}{6} = 400,347$$

18. B. The standard deviation is the square root of the variance, so:

$$\sigma = \sqrt{400,347} = 632.73$$

19. B.   The variance of a sample is found using:

$$s^2 = \frac{\Sigma(x - \bar{x})^2}{n - 1}, \text{ where}$$

s^2 = the sample variance

x = an individual observation in the sample

$\bar{x}$ = the sample mean

$(n - 1)$ = the number of sample observations minus 1

Since the numerator is exactly the same as the numerator in problem 17, we need only change the denominator to find the variance of the sample:

$$s^2 = \frac{984,064 + 1,016,064 + 258,064 + 64 + 58,564 + 85,264}{5} = \frac{2,402,084}{5} = 480,417$$

20. B.   Again, the standard deviation is the square root of the variance, so:

$$s = \sqrt{480,417} = 693.12$$

Corporate Finance

The field of finance is actually three interrelated areas: (1) financial institutions and capital markets; (2) investments; and (3) corporate finance. The financial institutions and capital markets area deals with financial institutions, such as banks, and the markets thorough which long and short-term debt and equity securities are sold and traded by investors. The investments area focuses on valuing investment opportunities and making investment decisions. Corporate finance, also called financial management, is the most extensive area.

Corporate finance is the study of how corporations raise and use capital, how corporate financial managers evaluate possible capital investments, and how investors value corporations. Unlike a proprietorship or partnership, the corporation is a separate, legal, tax-paying entity. Typically the owners, known as **stockholders**, are numerous and scattered literally anywhere in the world. They rely upon managers, who may or may not be owners, to make all the operating decisions.

Due to this separation of corporate management and ownership, some interesting conflicts arise. The owners of the firm may or may not be interested in daily operations, but they are very interested in the value of their investment in the company (the stock they hold). Alternatively, management is very interested in daily operations, particularly as they relate to salary and job security. The implication is that not every decision a corporate manager makes is necessarily in the owners' best interests.

Section 1 of this chapter discusses the three primary forms of business: the proprietorship, the partnership, and the corporation. Section 2 presents the three most common forms of publicly traded securities: common stock, preferred stock, and bonds. Section 3 presents the concepts of risk and return, agency costs, and corporate capital structure.

SECTION 1: FORMS OF BUSINESS

In this section, your learning objectives are the following:

1. To understand the three basic business forms: the proprietorship, the partnership, and the corporation.
2. To distinguish between the three business forms.

When humans first walked the Earth, they probably foraged for food like any other living creature trying to survive. Individuals probably didn't give much thought to the welfare of others outside of their group. Those who could fend for themselves the best got sufficient food, animal skins for clothing, and decent shelter. Individuals who could hunt well, but didn't like to forage for food, ended up with more animal skins than they needed and only occasional fruits and vegetables to eat. Those who were too slow or weak to hunt animals probably ate fruit and vegetables but had little clothing and ate little meat.

Some industrious nonhunting individual no doubt got the idea of gathering more fruit than he needed, so he could trade the extra for a better place to sleep, a better skin to wear, or even another type of food. Hunters started trading their extra skins for fruit or a better place to sleep. Soon all the people in the group began similar trading and business had begun. This form of business is known as **barter**. In a barter system, people trade items that have equivalent value.[1] Of course, this isn't exactly what we study in corporate finance, but the barter system is alive and well in many parts of the world.

Whether or not this is how it began, business, in one form or another, has become an integral part of every culture. Whenever an opportunity has arisen, someone has taken advantage of it and the myriad types

Barter system: A market system where items are traded rather than bought or sold with currency.

---

[1] Value in this context is different from the word we use today. Today, we tend to think in terms of monetary value. Value to the caveman was no doubt related more to satisfaction or fulfilling his needs than to selling the item to others.

and sizes of businesses we see today are the result. Of course, without the necessary funding along the way, the business world would not have developed to its current status.

Let's turn our attention to the financial aspects of the development of business. Jack owns and operates a portable hot dog kiosk in a large city. Since his business is flourishing, he purchases another inexpensive hot dog stand for cash and hires Jill to manage the new stand.

Because of the growth of business, Jill approaches Jack with the suggestion that they rent a small building she has found. The location is excellent, and rent is inexpensive. Since sales are increasing and customer loyalty is high, Jack feels renting the building is something he should pursue. However, Jack will need $100,000 to purchase new equipment and to make repairs and alterations to the building. Jack has $20,000 that he can invest in the business, and the bank will loan him $60,000. Jill offers to invest the other $20,000 but only in exchange for half ownership. Under this arrangement, they both own the business, and they share equally in the profits.

Eventually, Jack and Jill own and operate several hot dog shops and hire a team of managers for each of the shops. With the number of locations and increasing obligations and liabilities, Jack and Jill's attorney, John, recommends that they incorporate as J&J Dogs. Incorporation will allow J&J Dogs to continue operations as usual while freeing Jack and Jill from some of the liabilities of business ownership and the hassle associated with the limited life of a partnership.[2]

John indicates to Jack and Jill that by forming a corporation, they effectively create a separate entity. The corporation has a life of its own, separate from those of Jack and Jill. The life of their original partnership is tied directly to the lives of the partners. If either one of them dies, the partnership ceases to exist. However, if they choose to incorporate, J&J Dogs could continue indefinitely regardless of whether or not Jack and Jill survive. In addition, by forming a corporation Jack and Jill insulate themselves from some of the liabilities of operating a business.

---

[2] There are other reasons to incorporate, including limiting personal tax obligations, which are discussed later in the chapter.

Let's look at a simple example of how liabilities can arise. Jack and Jill cannot possibly ensure that all sanitary and safety precautions are being followed all the time at all their shops. For example, a careless employee could leave hot dogs out of refrigeration too long before cooking them. From this seemingly minor oversight, a customer contracts a rare disease, which usually limits itself to pigs.

Under their current arrangement as a partnership, Jack and Jill could be held personally liable for the victim's illness. An ensuing lawsuit could take all the assets of J&J Dogs, as well as those of Jack and Jill. However, if J&J Dogs is incorporated, Jack and Jill's losses are limited to what they have invested in J&J Dogs. The lawsuit could take the business assets, but none of their personal assets are at risk.[3] After hearing this potential horror story, Jack and Jill agree to form a corporation.

After incorporation, their business flourishes and they have people from all over the country clamoring to learn the secrets of their success. While Jack and Jill will not give away their secret recipes, they will let others lease the rights to use them by offering franchises locally. Soon, they're on their way to real success as J&J Dogs rapidly becomes a household name. Jack and Jill consider establishing a national franchise of their business. Of course, this requires a substantial investment.

The best way they can come up with the millions of dollars needed to "go national" with their franchises is to go public. **Going public** is the act of selling a portion of the company (shares) to outside investors; these shares then trade on organized exchanges. After the **initial public offering** (**IPO**) of shares, there are thousands of owners of J&J Dogs.

An **initial public offering** (**IPO**) is when a firm first sells shares publicly.

Although totally fabricated, the story makes a very important point. Business as we know it could not have developed without finance. When Jack first expanded his operation from one to two kiosks, it was his own savings that made this possible. *He* financed the expansion. However, expansion into a fixed location was beyond his means. He needed the infusion of capital a partner could provide.

Forming a corporation provided Jack and Jill with limited liability and protected the company from the death of either partner. However, it

---

[3] There are many iterations of this scenario in which Jack and Jill could be held personally liable. Nonetheless, two of the primary benefits to incorporation are limited personal liability and unlimited corporate life.

ultimately could not provide the necessary capital for national expansion. Jack and Jill had to sell a portion of their company to the public through an IPO. This provided a major infusion of capital as well as future access to capital markets.

Let's look at what we know about the various business forms in which Jack was involved:

Proprietorship

The least complicated form of business to establish is the proprietorship. When Jack had only one hot dog kiosk, his business was a proprietorship. Legally, the business and Jack were indistinguishable. When his kiosk earned a profit, it belonged exclusively to Jack, and he paid income taxes on it. If the business showed a loss for the period, Jack could use that loss to offset profits from other sources of personal income. He alone had total claim to all profits and had to accept all losses.

Any liability incurred by the business was also directly tied to Jack. If the business could not pay a liability (e.g., a note to a bank or debt to a supplier), Jack could be forced to pay the debt from his personal assets. If Jack couldn't pay the liability, creditors could seize the business, which would include all of Jack's personal assets. This is because in a proprietorship, liability to the owner is unlimited. If someone sues the business, all personal and business assets are considered to be in a single entity. The lawsuit could seize any or all of Jack's assets, including those in the business. In addition, the life of a proprietorship is limited to the proprietor's life. If the proprietor dies, the business effectively dies also. It becomes another asset in the proprietor's estate.

> A **proprietorship** is a business owned by a single individual. Legally, the business and the owner are indistinguishable.

One of the most frequently given reasons for starting and maintaining a proprietorship is freedom to make decisions. Jack made all the business decisions. He decided where to locate the kiosk, the types of hot dogs he would sell, the price he would charge, and the hours of operation for the business. Jack is an entrepreneur. An **entrepreneur** is someone willing to accept the risks associated with starting a business from scratch with their own ideas and money. He is typically willing to risk all his personal assets to finance the business and to stay a proprietorship.

Partnership

A partnership is a more complicated form of business. It is a legal contract between two or more individuals that explains the ownership interests in a business. The business in our example is J&J Dogs, and the partnership agreement specifies that Jack and Jill each own 50 percent of the business. While J&J Dogs was being operated as a partnership, the partnership agreement defined how ownership in J&J Dogs was divided between Jack and Jill.

> A **partnership** is a business with two or more owners. Legally, a partnership is very similar to a proprietorship.

Legally, a partnership is very similar to a proprietorship. As with a proprietorship, we say profits and losses "flow through" to the owners. That is, the partnership itself does not pay income taxes. Jack and Jill divided any profits and losses equally and reported them on their personal income tax returns.

Also, like a proprietorship, partnership debts "flow through" to the owners according to their proportional ownership. Since Jack and Jill each owned 50 percent of the business, they each were liable for 50 percent of any debts or other claims against the business. If J&J Dogs went out of business with large debts, Jack and Jill would each be liable for 50 percent of the debt. Creditors would seize business and personal money and/or assets from both the partners to satisfy the claims.

From Jack's perspective, the primary benefit from forming the partnership was getting the capital necessary to expand the business. Expansion required additional equity capital,[4] which he did not have and Jill could provide. There were other benefits (e.g., sharing management responsibilities and division of the liability exposure), but financing was paramount to the expansion and ultimate success of the business.

While he gained assistance in running the business, Jack was no longer free to make decisions on his own. There was the distinct possibility that Jill might not agree with him on the types of food to purchase, the hours of operation, prices to pay for inputs and prices to charge, along with many other daily business decisions. In our example, Jack never had problems with his partner, but disagreements among partners is one of the primary reasons for the dissolution of partnership agreements and some business failures.

---

[4] **Equity** means ownership. **Equity capital** is the owners' contribution to the business in the form of money or other assets.

Corporation

A corporation is a business entity that is legally separated from the owners. This separateness affords the corporate form three specific advantages over the proprietorship and partnership forms of business:

(1) **Unlimited Life.** Since the corporation is a legal entity totally separated from the owners, its life is not tied to the owners. If both Jack and Jill died, their ownership shares in the corporation, not the assets of the corporation, would become part of their respective estates.

(2) **Limited Liability.** In a proprietorship or partnership, all profits, losses, debts, and other liabilities "flow through" to the owner(s). In the case of a corporation, the owners are only liable for the amount they have invested in the corporation. For instance, a large lawsuit could easily claim more than the available assets of J&J Dogs, Inc. Since Jack and Jill are considered legally separate from the corporation, the suit cannot take their personal assets. They can only lose their time, effort, and monetary investments in the business.

(3) **Ease of Ownership Transfer.** Publicly traded corporations are known as a Subchapter C Corporations (the "C" pertains to the chapter in the IRS code that describes taxation of this form of corporation). These would include firms such as Microsoft, IBM, McDonald's, and Exxon. Ownership interest in these firms, which are usually large, is obtained by purchasing their **common stock**. If the common stock of the firm is registered with the SEC, it can be traded publicly. Common stock is sold in shares with each share indicating a percentage ownership in the firm. If you hold 10 percent of all the common stock of a firm, you own 10 percent of that firm. Ownership interest permits holders of common stock to vote at stockholder meetings. Stockholders usually have one vote per share of stock they own. Votes are cast on major questions faced by the corporation, such as the election of the Board of Directors.

Large corporations typically have millions of shares of stock outstanding and have thousands of owners. Since some owners would have to travel hundreds or even thousands of miles to attend the stockholder meeting to cast their votes, management will send out what are known as proxies. A **proxy** is nothing more than an absentee ballot. On the proxy, the stockholder indicates his choice for members of the **Board**

A **corporation** is a legal entity separate from its owners.

A corporation has an **unlimited life**.

Owners of corporations enjoy **limited liability**.

Common stock signifies ownership of a corporation.

The **common stock** of large C corporations can be bought or sold quickly and easily.

The firm's **Board of Directors** decides if and when **dividends** will be paid.

Dividends are the portion of net income paid out to the owners, the stockholders.

Dividends are distributed after the firm pays incomes taxes. **Double taxation** occurs when the stock-holder pays income taxes on the dividends received.

To help alleviate triple taxation, Congress enacted the **dividends received deduction**.

of Directors (the Board) or votes yes or no on other questions. If a stockholder fails to return the proxy by the indicated date, management typically has the right to cast that stockholder's votes.

As mentioned previously, a shareholder meeting is held to elect new members to the Board. The charge of the Board is to elect, advise, and oversee the president of the corporation. They are paid an honorarium and are expected to meet regularly, usually quarterly. The only prerequisite to being a member of the Board is interest and valuable expertise.

At the end of the year, when financial statements are drawn up and taxable income for the year is determined, the corporation itself pays income taxes. In this regard, corporations are different from proprietorships and partnerships, where taxable income flows through to the owners. The corporation's taxable income minus taxes equals net income, or income after taxes.

A very important decision made by the Board is when to pay **dividends** and how much to pay. Dividends are cash that corporations pay to their stockholders; dividends can also be in the form of additional common stock. Stock and cash dividends will be discussed later. Dividends are typically only a small portion of the total return on investing in common stock. The larger portion of the return normally comes from increases in the price of the stock (or capital appreciation). Since dividends are paid out of net income, the income that generated the dividends has already been taxed. Stockholders then pay income taxes on the dividends they receive, creating **double taxation**. Note that stockholders are only required to pay income taxes on the portion of net income they actually receive, the dividends.

Corporations also purchase the common stock of other corporations. Corporation B is considered the investor when it buys the common stock of corporation A. When corporation A pays dividends to its stockholders (both common and preferred), corporation B pays taxes just as any other investor would. Corporation B pays dividends to its stockholders, also. The income used to generate those dividends includes the now double-taxed dividends from corporation A. When corporation B's stockholders pay taxes on the dividends they receive, this implies the dividends from corporation A have been taxed *three* times.

The U.S. Congress has enacted the **dividends received deduction** to help alleviate this *triple taxation*. According to this provision of the tax code, corporate owners of equity securities may deduct between 70 and 100 percent of dividends received before calculating taxable income.

The profits of any firm (e.g., net income) belong to the owners of the firm. Rather than pay out all of net income to the stockholders, the Board will "retain" a portion for future investment. This means that net income is divided into two parts. The first is the portion paid to stockholders in the form of dividends, and the second is the portion reinvested by management for the stockholders. This portion is called **retained earnings** on the firm's balance sheet.

> **Retained earnings** is the portion of net income retained for investment.

Since it was part of net income, retained earnings represents profits generated by the firm that have not been paid to the stockholders. By retaining part of the firm's earnings,[5] management is implicitly promising to use it to maintain or replace equipment or to invest it in profitable projects or expansion. Notice that the owners of the firm, the stockholders, do not determine what percentage of net income will be retained, how much will be paid out as dividends, or even when or if dividends are paid. As a general rule, firms with many investment opportunities tend to pay smaller dividends, while firms with fewer investment opportunities, such as public utilities, tend to pay larger dividends.

The above discussion pertains to the (typically) larger form of corporation, the C corporation. This is the form of corporation whose stock is listed on the New York Stock Exchange, the American Stock Exchange, regional exchanges, and NASDAQ. These securities have been pre-approved for public sale by the Securities and Exchange Commission (SEC). Approval by the SEC means only that management has disclosed all relevant information and followed all guidelines for selling securities publicly. It does not guarantee the quality of the securities. This point will be discussed in more depth in the Capital Markets chapter.

> **C corporations** can have several thousand investors and their securities can be publicly traded.

Although definitely not a requirement, the first corporation formed by Jack and Jill might have been a Subchapter S Corporation. Similar to a C corporation, incorporation gives the owners (stockholders) limited

> **S corporations** are legally very similar to partnerships and have a limited number of owners. Their securities cannot be publicly traded.

---

[5] Please note that retained earnings does not represent cash. This is a very important concept, which is explained in the Financial Statement Analysis chapter.

liability, but taxation and some other legal requirements operate more like a partnership. There is a limit to the number of stockholders, and shares in S corporations are not publicly traded.

SUMMARY OF SECTION 1

Learning Objective: *To understand and distinguish between the three basic business forms: the proprietorship, the partnership, and the corporation.*

A. **Proprietorship**
1. A proprietorship is the easiest and least expensive way to start a business.
2. One owner is free to make all decisions.
3. The business and the owner are indistinguishable, with all profits and losses "flowing through" to the owner.
4. It can be difficult to get necessary operating capital or capital for expansion, as collateral for loans is limited to assets in the business and assets held by the owner.
5. The owner has unlimited liability.
   a. The owner is personally responsible for any debts incurred by the business.
   b. If business assets are insufficient to satisfy business or legal claims, the owner's assets can be seized.
6. The life of the proprietorship is linked to the life of the proprietor.
7. Ownership is fairly difficult to sell (i.e., the owner must find buyers).

B. **Partnership**
1. A partnership is easy to form and is only slightly more expensive to form than a proprietorship.
2. There can be two or more partners.
   a. There must be legal documentation that clearly specifies the proportional ownerships.
   b. Decisions are generally made jointly.
      • There may be operating partners and silent partners.
      • Silent partners buy a portion of the partnership but do not help operate the business.

3. The business and the owners are one.
   a. Legally, the business and the owners are indistinguishable.
   b. All profits and losses "flow through" to the owners according to their proportional ownership.
4. Operating and expansion capital are somewhat easier to obtain for a partnership than for a proprietorship.
   a. Collateral for loans is limited to assets in the business and the personal assets of the partners.
   b. A partnership generally has more collateral than a proprietorship.
5. The owners have unlimited liability.
   a. The owners are personally responsible for any debts incurred by the business.
   b. If the business is sued, the owners are personally responsible for any settlements according to their proportional ownership.[6]
   c. If business assets are insufficient to satisfy business or legal claims, the owners' assets can be seized.
6. The life of the partnership is linked to each of the lives of the partners.
   a. If any partner dies, the partnership dies also.
   b. The proportional interest in the business assets becomes part of the partner's estate.

C. **Corporation**
   1. A corporation is the most complex and expensive form of business ownership. There are two basic forms of corporations.
   2. **S Corporation**
      a. These are operationally very similar to partnerships.
      b. While there can be more than one owner, the number of owners is usually small.
      c. The corporation itself does not pay income taxes.
      d. Profits and losses "flow through" to the owners according to their proportional ownership.
      e. Unlike a partnership, the owners have limited liability.
      f. The stock is not publicly traded, so selling ownership may be difficult.

---

[6] Under certain circumstances, a partner may be responsible for the entire settlement if other partners' assets are insufficient to settle their portion of the claim.

3. **C Corporation**
   a. C corporations can have one or more owners (usually a large number of owners).
   b. Regardless of the number of owners, all owners have limited liability.
   c. All forms of corporations have unlimited life (i.e., if an owner dies, his or her stock becomes part of the estate).
   d. The ease of raising capital depends upon the size of the corporation.
      - Very small C corporations have as much difficulty raising capital as a proprietorship does.
      - It is usually much easier for very large C corporations to raise capital.
   e. Common stock of a corporation may pay dividends.
      - Dividends are usually paid quarterly.
      - Dividends are paid out of net income (after taxes).
      - Stockholders pay taxes on dividends received, creating double taxation.
      - Congress enacted the dividends received deduction to help corporate investors.

SECTION 2: HOW CORPORATIONS RAISE CAPITAL

In this section, your learning objective is the following:

- To understand and distinguish the characteristics of three of the most familiar publicly traded corporate securities: common stock, bonds, and preferred stock.

In this section, we focus on a very important and popular characteristic of large C corporations, a characteristic that distinguishes them from all other business forms.[7] That characteristic is the ability to raise capital by selling securities that are **publicly traded**—meaning the securities can be purchased and sold by the general public. The three most commonly used securities are common stock, bonds, and preferred stock.

---

[7] S corporations and small C corporations can certainly use these securities, but S corporations cannot sell them publicly and small Cs don't use them because of the costs involved. The discussion in this section is limited to the securities of large C corporations.

Common Stock

When corporations issue common stock, they are selling **ownership** in the firm. And, like the corporation itself, common stock has no **maturity**. When a security has a maturity date, it has a limited life (there is a date on which it must be surrendered to the firm for final payment, and it is no longer outstanding).

The typical large corporation may have millions or even hundreds of millions of shares of common stock outstanding. Once issued by the firm, these shares are traded among investors on an organized exchange (e.g., the New York Stock Exchange) or on the over-the-counter market (e.g., NASDAQ). It is not uncommon for over a million shares of the common stock of large corporations like IBM to change hands in a single day on the New York Stock exchange.[8]

Before being issued (sold), the firm must register its securities with the state in which the incorporation takes place and the Securities and Exchange Commission (SEC). Referred to as "Blue Sky Laws," state regulations ensure the company and its securities are legitimate. The Securities Exchange Act of 1934 established the SEC, which regulates all interstate offerings in amounts exceeding $1.5 million.[9]

Registration with the SEC is accomplished by constructing what is known as a **prospectus**. The prospectus contains information on the size (amount) of the issue, the type of security being issued, the offering price of the security, and the investment banks that are licensed to sell the issue and their portion of the underwriting,[10] as well as information about the firm and its officers. This information is intended to aid the investor in making an educated purchase decision. It is neither a guarantee of nor a statement regarding the quality of the investment.

> When a corporation issues common stock, it is selling **ownership** in the firm.

> To sell securities publicly, the firm must first get the **prospectus** approved by the SEC.

---

[8] Firms may list their stock on several exchanges. When the New York Stock Exchange reports the number of shares traded for a particular stock, the number includes all that firm's shares sold on all exchanges on which the stock is listed.

[9] The $1.5 million refers to the value of securities sold in one issue. For instance, if the firm raises $1.0 million by selling securities or does not sell them across state lines, the SEC has no jurisdiction. The state in which the firm sells the securities retains its jurisdiction regardless of the issue size.

[10] When underwriting a security offering, an investment bank is effectively guaranteeing sale of all or part of the issue.

Approval by the SEC means only that the proper information has been provided in the prospectus.

The **preemptive right** means current stockholders must be given the right to purchase new shares in proportion to their current ownership before they are offered to the general public.

Voting rights are typically attached to the common stock of the firm (one share = one vote). This enables the owners of the firm, the holders of the firm's common stock, to help make major corporate decisions by casting their ballots during shareholder meetings. Major corporate decisions would include election of board members or the decision to accept or reject a merger with another company. Proxy ballots are used for those shareholders who cannot attend the meetings to cast their votes in person.

However, firms will sometimes issue common stock without voting rights. Typically this stock is associated with a subsidiary rather than the corporation as a whole. In the past, General Motors Corporation had more than five "classes" of common stock outstanding, only one of which included the right to vote.

Common stock usually will also include a **preemptive right**. If this characteristic is included, each stockholder has the right to maintain her percentage ownership in the company. This can be important when the firm issues new common stock. Without this protection, large shareholders could have their percentage ownership and voting power seriously reduced by the issuance of additional shares to new shareholders.

Not all corporations pay dividends. The firm's Board of Directors decides if and when dividends will be paid. Once dividends are announced, all current stockholders have the right to receive them. The following timeline shows the series of events associated with declaring and paying dividends.

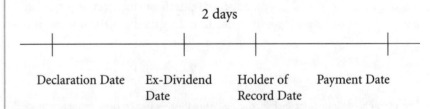

The Board of Directors declares the payment of dividends at their quarterly meeting. This date is known as the **declaration date**. Since common stock may be frequently traded, to avoid confusion between legal ownership of the stock and the dividend recipient, the declaration includes the **holder of record date**. Whoever is listed as the official owner of the shares on that date will receive the dividend payment. To allow time for notification of the change of ownership to reach the firm, the stock will actually trade **ex-dividend** on the announced **ex-dividend date**. Anyone who purchases the stock on or after that date is not entitled to receive the announced dividend. Dividends are paid on the **payment date**. To partially alleviate the effects of double taxation, corporate holders of common stock are allowed to deduct from 70 to 100 percent of dividends received before calculating state and federal taxable income, depending upon the percentage ownership.

Common stock is a residual ownership. What does this mean? Let's look at an analogous relationship. Assume you sold your home, which had a mortgage[11] associated with it. Your equity in the home is the amount left from the sale after paying off the mortgage. This is the same idea as the ownership or equity claim of common stock. In times of bankruptcy, the common stockholders are the last to be paid. They receive what is left over (i.e., the residual), which is almost always zero. In addition, common stockholders are the last to be paid during normal operations. For instance, interest payments to bondholders and dividends to preferred stockholders must be paid before dividends can be paid to holders of common stock.

Even though it might seem as though common stockholders bear all the risk associated with the company, there is a very important advantage to owning common stock. Only common stockholders benefit from an increase in the value of the firm. If the firm's assets increase in value, the increased value goes entirely to the common stockholders. The bondholders and preferred stockholders do not share it. Whereas bondholders and preferred stockholders receive a somewhat more certain series of cash flows, the stockholders have the possibility of large capital gains. It is the hope of these increases in stock price that motivates investors to purchase common stock.

---

[11] A mortgage indicates you have borrowed money to help pay for the home. The mortgage is the legal document that gives the details about the debt: the lender, the borrower, the amount of the loan, the interest rate, the amount and timing of repayment, etc.

When a firm sells **bonds**, it is borrowing. The firm must pay annual or semiannual interest to the bondholders as well as return the amount borrowed, the principal, when the bond matures.

Fixed income securities require the firm to pay specified cash flows on specified dates.

All the firm's outstanding bonds are ranked by seniority. **Seniority** specifies the order in which bondholders will be paid in case of bankruptcy.

A **debenture** is a bond with no collateral.

Bonds

When corporations issue (sell) bonds, they are *borrowing*. The typical corporate bond has a **face value** of $1,000,[12] which represents the amount borrowed or the **principal**. Unlike common stock, bonds almost always have a maturity, which can range anywhere from five to thirty years. On this **maturity date**, the firm repays the original $1,000 borrowed to the bondholder.

Unlike a home mortgage or car loan, which are fully **amortized**,[13] corporate bonds tend to be interest-only securities. The firm typically makes semiannual interest-only payments until the bond matures (semiannual interest payments are common in the U.S., whereas annual interest payments are the norm in Europe). The payments are called **coupon payments**. The **coupon rate**, stated as a percentage of par or face value, determines the interest payment. The coupon payments and the principal are automatically sent to the registered owner of the bond.

All securities are affected to a degree by changes in interest rates. Their prices tend to move in the opposite direction of interest rates (i.e., increases in rates will lower prices, and decreases in rates will raise prices). However, **fixed income securities** (e.g., bonds) are particularly sensitive to changes in interest rates. Generally, the longer the maturity of the bond, the more sensitive it is to changes in interest rates. We will explore this concept further when we discuss security valuation.

As with individual borrowing, bonds can be backed by (guaranteed by) collateral. These are called **mortgage** (or **senior**) **bonds**, and the collateral could be equipment, buildings, or any other fixed asset. **Debentures** are bonds that are not backed by collateral. They are guaranteed only by the firm's promise of repayment, and they are **subordinated** to the mortgage bonds.

In bankruptcy, bonds are repaid according to their rank from the most **senior issues** to the most subordinated issues. The implications for risk are obvious, and the coupon rate on the bonds will reflect their rank. Bonds with the lowest level of seniority will have higher coupon rates than more senior issues, and mortgage bonds will have the lowest rates.

[12] Although not a requirement, virtually all U.S. corporate bonds are issued with $1,000 face (par) values.

[13] Monthly home mortgage and car payments contain interest and principal. See the Time Value of Money section in the Security Valuation chapter for an example.

When corporate bonds are **callable**,[14] management has the right to retire them early (i.e., before their maturity date). To force the early retirement of the bonds management announces the call publicly, and whoever owns the bonds must surrender them. Since calling the bonds means paying off the debt early, management typically won't do it unless there is a benefit. The benefit lies in being able to take advantage of lower interest rates by replacing an issue with another issue at a lower coupon rate.

> A **callable bond** may be retired early to take advantage of falling interest rates.

To guarantee bondholders at least a certain amount of time at the high coupon rate, U.S. corporate bonds are not usually callable for the first five years. This is known as **call protection**, because during this period management is legally prohibited from calling the bonds. During the next five years, the bonds are callable at face value plus a **call premium**. The premium usually starts at one year's interest in year six and decreases in equal annual increments to zero by year ten. For example a $1,000, 8 percent bond would be callable at $1,080 in year six, $1,060 in year seven, $1,040 in year eight, and so on.

> The **conversion ratio** specifies the number of shares received at the time of conversion.

When a corporate bond is **convertible**, the owner of the bond may exchange it for another type of security, usually common or preferred stock. The bond will be convertible into a set number of shares, determined by the **conversion ratio**. For example, if the bond has a conversion ratio of 25:1, this means it is exchangeable for 25 shares of stock at anytime at the discretion of the owner. If the bond sells for $1,000 this implies a **conversion price** of $1,000/25 or $40.00. If the owner converted immediately after purchasing the bond, he would effectively pay $40.00 per share of stock.

> A **convertible bond** may be exchanged for common or preferred stock of the issuing firm.

Since the ability to convert to common or preferred stock is usually considered a valuable option, convertible bondholders are willing to accept a lower rate of interest. The coupon rate on convertible bonds averages about two-thirds of the coupon rate on an otherwise identical nonconvertible bond.

All the features of corporate bonds that we have discussed will be contained in the issue's **indenture**. The indenture is the written contract between the firm and the bondholders. It will contain all the features

> The **indenture** is the legal contract between the firm and the bondholders. It contains all the provisions of the issue.

[14] Firms typically issue callable bonds during times of historically high interest rates. As interest rates fall, fewer bonds are issued with call features. Because of historically low rates and other factors, fewer callable bonds are being issued.

The **trustee** looks after the provisions of the bond issue for the bondholders.

of the bond, including its face value, coupon rate, maturity date, interest payment dates, any collateral, its rank with respect to other bonds previously issued by the firm, whether it is callable, whether it is convertible, and the name of the **trustee** and the procedures followed in case of bankruptcy. Since there are many owners (often tens of thousands), the trustee is the individual or institution which looks after the issue and ensures the firm follows all the prescribed conditions in the indenture. In addition to the features listed above, indentures will also contain bond covenants. These can be **negative covenants** that prescribe what management cannot do, including restrictions on incurring additional debt without meeting certain conditions or the approval of the current bondholders. They can also be **affirmative covenants** that prescribe what management must do, including maintaining certain levels of financial ratios, maintaining the firm's equipment in good working condition, and providing the trustee with periodic reports.

A **sinking fund** provides assurance that sufficient funds will be available to retire the bond issue as specified.

Bond indentures often contain a **sinking fund** provision. Under this provision, management makes annual deposits with the trustee to ensure funds are available to retire the issue upon its final maturity. Bonds can sometimes be issued as **serial bonds**, which are retired in portions according to their serial numbers (their registration numbers). For example, if 20 percent of the bonds are retired every four years, the entire issue will be retired in 20 years. A sinking fund can also be used to retire all the bonds in the issue at once. If a sinking fund is used, the firm makes annual deposits with the trustee, but the account grows until used at the maturity date to retire the issue. In either case, a sinking fund makes investing in bonds less risky, because it helps ensure timely retirement of the debt.

Although **preferred stock** is technically an equity security, it has both debt and equity characteristics.

Preferred Stock

Technically an equity security, preferred stock is a **hybrid security**. It is called a hybrid because it has characteristics of both equity and debt (i.e., stocks and bonds). These characteristics are discussed below:

Preferred stock usually has a maturity date. It can have a sinking fund and it can be callable.

Equity-Like Characteristics:

1.   Preferred stockholders receive dividends. There is a major difference between interest and dividends. Interest is a tax-deductible expense, while dividends are paid from net income.

2. The claims of preferred stockholders are subordinated to the claims of bondholders. In case of bankruptcy, bondholder obligations must be satisfied before preferred stockholders receive anything. Also, preferred dividends are paid after bond interest payments.

3. Preferred stock can be perpetual. Like common stock, it can have an infinite life.

4. Like common stock, preferred stock has a par value. Unlike common stock, the firm must pay this par value to preferred shareholders in the case of bankruptcy.

5. Although an uncommon occurrence, preferred stock can have voting rights.

6. A rare but possible provision of preferred stock is participation in the firm's earnings. In this case, increases in common dividends correspond with increases in preferred dividends.

Bond–Like Characteristics:

1. Like interest on the firm's bonds, preferred dividends must be paid before the firm pays common dividends. This is the **cumulative dividend** provision of preferred stock. If the firm should miss a preferred dividend payment, it cannot pay common dividends until all missed as well as current preferred dividends are paid.

2. Like bonds, the dividend on preferred stock is stated as a percentage of its face or par value. Although coupon payments are usually paid semi-annually, preferred dividends are typically paid quarterly.

3. Like bonds, most preferred stock has either a stated or implied maturity as well as a sinking fund.

4. Like bonds, preferred stock is considered a fixed income security. The preferred stockholder receives a stream of fixed dividends and then the par or face value at maturity.

5. Like bonds, preferred stock can be callable and/or convertible. The call and convertibility provisions are very similar to those associated with bonds.

6. Like bonds, preferred stockholders usually do not have voting rights.

As with common stock, **perpetual preferred stock** has no maturity.

Most preferred stock is **cumulative**. This means all preferred dividends must be paid before the firm can pay common dividends.

From an accounting standpoint, preferred stock is an equity security. It pays dividends[15] and is carried in the stockholders' equity section of the balance sheet. Financial analysts, however, always consider preferred dividends when measuring the firm's credit rating and its ability to meet its fixed obligations. This is fairly strong evidence that investors tend to consider preferred stock as a debt security.

Because of its cumulative provision, the risk of preferred stock is very similar to that of the issuing firm's bonds. The dividend paid to preferred stock is usually lower than the coupon (interest) paid on the firm's bonds. This makes investing in preferred stock questionable for anyone not receiving the "dividends received" deduction (see Section 1 for more information).

Let's look at an example for a corporation receiving an 80 percent dividends received deduction:

The interest rate (i.e., coupon rate) on Company X's bonds is 9 percent and the face value of one bond is $100. The dividend on their preferred stock is 6 percent of the stock's par value, which is also $100. This means the bonds pay $9.00 per year in interest and the preferred pays $6.00 per year in dividends. Using a corporate federal-plus-state marginal tax rate of 40 percent, the after-tax interest payment on the bonds is $9.00 − .40($9.00) = $5.40. The after-tax dividend from the preferred is $6.00 − .40(.20)($6.00) = $5.52.[16] For a corporate investor, the after-tax cash flow and the percentage return (5.52% vs. 5.4%) for the preferred stock are greater than that for the bond, even though the bond pays a higher rate.

Now, let's assume an individual, non-incorporated investor. This person receives $9.00 in interest from the bond and $6.00 in dividends from the preferred, and he pays full taxes on both interest and dividends. The after-tax cash flows and yields, assuming a 28 percent tax rate, are $6.48 or 6.48 percent on the bond and $4.32 or 4.32 percent on the preferred. For the individual, the bonds are clearly a better investment.

---

[15] Remember the very important distinction between dividends and interest payments. Interest payments are a tax-deductible expense for the firm, while dividends are paid out after calculation of net income (after taxes). Also corporate investors pay full taxes on interest received but can deduct a portion of dividends received before calculating taxable income.

[16] Since the corporation can deduct 80% of the dividend before calculating taxes, it has to pay 40% taxes on only 20% of the dividend.

SUMMARY OF SECTION 2

Learning Objective: *To understand and distinguish the characteristics of three of the most familiar publicly traded corporate securities: common stock, bonds, and preferred stock.*

A. **Common stock** is an equity security, which represents ownership in the issuing firm.
  1. Common stock has no maturity.
  2. Common stockholders typically have one vote for every share they hold.
     a. Votes are cast at stockholder meetings.
     b. Votes are for election of board members and for other major corporate decisions.
     c. Proxy ballots are used if the stockholder cannot attend the meeting.
  3. Common stock is publicly traded, with new issues requiring registration with the SEC by filing a **prospectus**.

B. **Bonds** are debt securities, which represent borrowing by the issuing firm.
  1. Bonds typically have maturities ranging from 5 to 30 years.
  2. Bonds usually pay interest semiannually. At maturity, the **par** or **face value** is repaid to the holder of the bond. The par value of the bond represents the amount of funds borrowed, the **principal**.
  3. Holders of bonds are not entitled to vote on corporate matters.
  4. **Callable** bonds give the firm the opportunity to retire the bond issue early and replace it with another issue at a lower rate of interest.
  5. **Convertible** bonds can be exchanged at the discretion of the holder for common stock. The conversion ratio describes how many shares of common stock can be obtained by surrendering the bond.
  6. Bonds are ranked for payoff in case of bankruptcy.
     a. Bonds are ranked by order of seniority (i.e., earlier issues have seniority over newer issues).
     b. Bonds are ranked by collateral (i.e., mortgage bonds have seniority over debentures).
  7. All characteristics of the bond are contained in its **indenture** (i.e., the legal contract between the firm and the bondholders).

a. The indenture may also contain covenants.
- Affirmative covenants dictate what management must do, such as file periodic reports with the trustee.
- Negative covenants describe what management cannot do, such as issue more debt without approval of the trustee.

b. The trustee monitors the actions of the firm to ensure adherence to all the conditions of the indenture.

8. Bonds sometimes have a sinking fund. This refers to the annual deposits the firm must make with the trustee to ensure sufficient funds to retire the issue as scheduled.

C. Preferred stock is a hybrid security, which has both debt-like and equity-like characteristics.

1. Equity-like characteristics are those that make preferred stock similar to common stock.

a. Preferred stock dividends are paid out of net income.

b. Preferred stockholder claims are subordinated to the bond claims.

c. Preferred stock can be perpetual (i.e., has no maturity).

d. Preferred stock is carried in the owners' equity portion of the balance sheet.

e. Although rare, preferred stock can be participating (i.e., if common stock dividends are increased, preferred dividends must be also).

f. Although rare, preferred stock can have voting privileges.

2. Debt-like characteristics are those that make preferred stock like bonds.

a. Preferred stock holders receive a fixed dividend.
- The dividend is stated as a percentage of par or face value.
- Preferred stock is usually not participating.
- Preferred stockholders do not usually share in the firm's gains as common stockholders do.

b. Preferred dividends are usually cumulative. As with interest on bonds, preferred dividends must be paid or management cannot pay common dividends.

c. Preferred stock can have a maturity, complete with sinking fund (i.e., at maturity the face or par value is repaid).

d. Preferred stock can be callable or convertible.

e. Preferred stockholders usually do not have a vote.

f. Financial analysts treat preferred stock like any fixed obligation.

SECTION 3: RISK AND RETURN

In this section, your learning objective is the following:

- To understand the connection between risk and return, agency costs, and capital structure.

Risk

In the chapter on economics, we discussed how all of our personal decisions are made in terms of costs and benefits. Corporate finance is not immune from this concept. When a corporate manager makes a decision to purchase a certain piece of equipment, expand operations, or start a new product line, the manager must consider both the costs and the benefits of the decision.

In this section, we will study costs and benefits in the framework of **risk** and **return**, what is often referred to as the two "R's" of finance. Decisions made by the corporate financial manager will usually involve money, since money is both the cost and the benefit of most financial decisions. Risk is quite important when virtually no financial decision is immune from uncertainty.

We will use the word *uncertainty* as a synonym for risk. In finance, whenever you are uncertain about an outcome, that outcome is considered risky. Let's assume today is the day your best friend Chris promised to pay back the $20 he borrowed from you last week. Are you certain Chris will pay you the $20 today as promised? If Chris gives you the money today, you will have received the payment exactly as you expected. If you receive the money tomorrow or the next day, you will not have received it when expected.

Let's define risk as *the possibility of an unfavorable event*. Is receiving the $20 late an unfavorable event? What if you needed the money today to repay a friend who loaned you $20? It doesn't matter if you receive the money late or even if you don't receive it at all. Either outcome would be considered quite unfavorable.

Risk is the possibility of an unfavorable event (i.e., the possibility the return on the investment will be lower than expected).

Uncertainty is a synonym for risk. Whenever the future return is not known with certainty, the investment is risky.

Usually the further in the future the cash flow is expected, the less likely the case flow will be recognized. Therefore, **risk tends to increase with time**.

Since most financial decisions result in receiving (or paying) a cash flow[17] in the future, and, since the future is always uncertain, there is obviously risk associated with any future cash flow. In fact, as the cash flow will occur farther and farther into the future, that cash flow will tend to be riskier. Remember, risk refers to an unexpected event, regardless of the cause. It doesn't matter what causes the cash payment to be missed or paid late.

Given enough time, just about anything can happen. That means that the longer the time before you expect a cash flow, the higher the possibility that something will happen to affect the way it's received or even if it's received at all. Since no one can predict the future, we must accept that some amount risk is inevitable.

What Causes Risk?

Risk is caused by microeconomic and macroeconomic factors.

Risk, as it is applied to common stock, is defined exactly the same as it is for any other investment. It is the possibility of an unfavorable event. From the investor's perspective, the most disastrous unfavorable event is a decline in the price of the stock. We can define the unfavorable event for a common stock as a decline in price, but what causes stock prices to fall?

Macroeconomic factors, such as inflation, unemployment, or government spending affect all stock prices.

The forces that can affect stock prices can be separated into two general categories: macroeconomic and microeconomic. **Macroeconomic** variables (e.g., inflation, the national unemployment rate, government policies) are economy-wide in nature and affect all stock prices to varying degrees. For instance, inflation causes overall price increases, resulting in decreased demand and reduced profits. As the unemployment rate increases, economy-wide consumption declines, also resulting in reduced profits. We will see later in the book that macroeconomic factors such as these can be the most troublesome for investors.[18]

Microeconomic (Firm-Specific) Variables

Microeconomic factors are associated with the firm or the issue itself.

Microeconomic variables are those that are specific to each firm. They are the characteristics of the firm: its management, employees, products, and financing choices. Let's take a little time to discuss some of the microeconomic forces that affect stock prices.

---

[17] **Cash flow** refers to the movement of money. Cash moves in or out of the corporation. It has also come to mean the cash itself, as in "The *cash flows* from that product should cover . . . ."

[18] We will concentrate our discussion here on microeconomic (firm-specific) risk factors. Macroeconomic (systematic) risk factors are discussed in detail in the Portfolio Theory chapter.

Business Risk. From the chapter on Financial Statement Analysis we know there are several factors that can affect income from operations, also known as **operating income** or **earnings before interest and taxes (EBIT)**. Let's look at the top portion of Exhibit 1, Lucy's Lemonade Income Statement, from chapter 2, Financial Statement Analysis.

EBIT is $1,614, and the values of many factors have been deducted from revenue to yield that particular value. A change in the value of any one of those factors, including revenue, will change EBIT. From chapter 3, Quantitative Methods, we know that a factor with many different possible values has a distribution of possible values. A change in any of the factors leading to EBIT (revenue or expense) will yield a different value from the distribution of possible values for EBIT. In other words, EBIT is variable.

Income from operations is also known as **EBIT** (earning before interest and taxes).

Exhibit 1: Lemonade Business in the Shopping Mall

Lucy's Lemonade
Income Statement
Month Ending July 31, 200X

Revenue	$8,500
Less:	
Cost of Goods Sold:	
Mix: Lemonade	975
Mix: Pretzel	350
Paper Goods	625
Operating Expenses:	
Wages	2,500
Utilities	800
Rent	1,000
Insurance	600
Depreciation	36
Income From Operations	1,614

We will define **business risk** as the uncertainty in EBIT or the forces that cause this uncertainty (as with many other terms in finance, there are other definitions for business risk, but this definition will fulfill our needs in this chapter). Whenever a factor has a distribution of possible values, we say the true value of that factor is uncertain. Remember, we are using uncertainty as a synonym for risk, so an uncertain factor is risky in a corporate finance context.

Business risk is the uncertainty in EBIT or the forces that cause EBIT uncertainty.

Of course, risk doesn't apply to Exhibit 1 because this level of EBIT has already been realized. We encounter risk when we're trying to predict a future value. Whenever the true value of a future cash flow is not known with certainty, we call it an unknown. We might have a pretty good idea about the range of values it could have, but we can't predict it with certainty.

This section is concerned with the causes of uncertainty, the causes of risk. Defining business risk as uncertainty in EBIT, let's explore some of the better-known causes of business risk.

Variability in Revenue. If the firm's future revenues are highly variable (subject to extreme changes), future EBIT will be highly uncertain. Anything that causes sales variability is considered a source of business risk. This would include demand for the product or service and the price at which it sells.

If demand for the firm's output is subject to seasonal swings or if the product has many substitutes, sales will be very hard to predict. Also, if the product market is subject to severe price variability, as with the market for computer chips, there will be variability in sales revenues.

Cost and Price Structure. Some firms face uncertainty in the costs of their inputs. This variability in input costs will obviously cause variability in EBIT. This is also the case if the firm is not able to adjust selling price quickly to compensate for changing input prices.

Competition and New Product Development. Some firms' revenues are very difficult to predict because competitors, domestic or international, may enter the market at any time with a competing or improved product. This will obviously affect the firm's revenues. The degree to which competing products affect revenues will depend upon how quickly and inexpensively the firm can develop another product.

Operating Leverage. Operating leverage depends upon the proportion of the firm's costs that are fixed. In the short run, the higher the proportion of fixed costs, the less flexibility management has in lowering costs. In the long run, management can change the entire cost structure.

Operating leverage is measured as the percentage change in EBIT that results from a given percentage change in revenues. With no fixed

Operating leverage is caused by the use of fixed assets. It is the percentage change in EBIT given a percentage change in revenues.

costs, the change in EBIT is the same as the change in revenues (assuming variable costs are a fixed percentage of sales revenue). For example, if revenues increase or decrease 10 percent, EBIT will also increase or decrease 10 percent. Fixed costs act as a lever and cause the percentage change in EBIT to be greater than the percentage change in revenues. A high proportion of fixed costs could cause the percentage change in EBIT to be three or four times the percentage change in revenue. In this case, a 10 percent increase or decrease in revenues would lead to a 30 or 40 percent increase or decrease in EBIT. EBIT has been leveraged; its distribution of possible values has been widened. Business risk has increased.

You might have guessed that business risk is more dependent upon the industry than upon management decisions. For example, the auto and steel industries have many large fixed assets, and labor is usually unionized. Because fixed assets lead to fixed operating costs such as depreciation, maintenance, and replacement, and union contracts typically dictate the number of workers and their wages over long periods of time, these industries can do little about their fixed cost structure. Alternatively, real estate development companies tend to own very few assets and utilize subcontracted labor.

Financial Risk. Whereas business risk is mostly a result of the firm's assets and its revenue and cost structure, financial risk is the risk of the firm due to *management's choice* to use debt financing. The effects of debt financing are shown on the income statement below EBIT in the form of interest expense. Interest expense has the effect of levering[19] net income up or down, depending upon the movement in revenue. This levering of net income effectively increases or widens the distribution of its possible values, and increases risk.

> **Financial risk** is the added risk borne by the stockholders due to management's use of debt.

Financial Leverage. Financial leverage is the percentage change in net income (NI), resulting from a given percentage change in EBIT. With no interest charges, the change in NI is the same as the change in EBIT (assuming taxes are a fixed percentage of taxable income). For example, if EBIT increase or decrease 10 percent, NI will also increase or decrease 10 percent. Interest acts as a lever and makes the percentage change in NI greater than the percentage change in EBIT. A greater

> **Financial leverage** is the percentage change in Net Income given a percentage change in EBIT.

---

[19] We refer to debt as *leverage*, because it increases (levers) the change in net income due to changes in revenues.

dependence upon debt financing could cause the percentage change in NI to be three or four times the percentage change in EBIT. In this case a 10 percent increase or decrease in EBIT would lead to a 30 or 40 percent increase or decrease in NI. NI has been leveraged; its distribution of possible values has been widened, and financial risk has increased.

Characteristics of the Firm's Securities

Type of Security. Different securities issued by the same firm will have different risk. It is quite easy to see one source of the difference by looking at the firm's income statement. Recall that interest is paid before management can pay dividends, and preferred dividends are paid before common dividends.

We defined risk as the possibility of an unfavorable event. From the perspective of the holder of a corporate security, an unfavorable event is not receiving an expected payment, whether it's interest on a bond or a dividend on common or preferred stock.

When faced with adverse situations, firms will look for ways to conserve cash. Since defaulting[20] on an interest payment will cause a reduction in the firm's credit rating and can even cause bankruptcy, management will be extremely reluctant to miss an interest payment. The implication is that interest payments to bondholders are held of utmost importance and missed only under the most serious circumstances. The dividend to preferred stockholders is not as sacred,[21] but missing them means management cannot pay common dividends. The bottom line is that common dividends are the first to get cut. Only after such a cut will management consider omitting preferred dividends, with a cut in interest payments only as a last resort.[22]

Based on the information above, we know that bonds are considered the firm's least risky security and common stock the most risky.

---

[20] A technical default is missing, delaying, or partially paying a required payment as with the interest obligation on corporate bonds. Since banks and trustees (bondholders) are not usually interested in running a firm, more often than not the firm must miss several interest payments or show insolvency before the trustee will file suit. Even then, management and the trustee will usually try to work out a new payment schedule.

[21] In some circumstances, default on preferred dividends can cause serious legal repercussions ranging from suspension of common dividends to seizure of the firm.

[22] We are assuming management has exhausted all possible avenues for obtaining outside capital, both debt and equity.

Preferred stock will fall somewhere between the two, according to its specific characteristics.

Maturity of the Security. The prices of fixed income securities (e.g., bonds and preferred stock) are sensitive to changes in interest rates. Also, the longer the maturity of the security, the more its price will change when interest rates change. For example, the price of a 20-year bond will fall more than the price of a 5-year bond with the same coupon rate for a given change in interest rates. To compensate for this added risk, bonds with longer maturity will tend to have higher coupon rates.

Nature of the Return. The return to any security can take only two forms, cash flow and price appreciation. In general, the greater the percentage of total return that comes from cash flow, the less risky the security. Assume you are considering two bonds issued by the same company, and the bonds have exactly the same number of years remaining to maturity. If the bonds have different coupon rates, the price of the bond with the lower coupon rate will be more sensitive to changes in interest rates. In fact the lower the coupon rate, the more sensitive the price of any bond to changes in interest rates.

The United States Treasury borrows funds using three different securities. **Treasury bills** have maturities up to one year; **Treasury notes** are issued with maturities from one to ten years; and **Treasury bonds** are issued with maturities from ten to thirty years. Treasury bills, simply called **T-bills**, are pure discount instruments. They pay no coupon payments over their lifetimes. Instead they are issued at a discount from face value and pay the face value at maturity.

For example, a $10,000, 6 percent[23] 364-day T-bill would cost you $9,393.33 at issue. One year later, when the T-bill matures, you would receive the $10,000 face value for a return of 6.48 percent. Notice that this return is completely a function of price appreciation. Since the T-bill pays no coupons, you would expect its price to be sensitive to changes in interest rates. The only thing that keeps their prices from changing dramatically as interest rates change is their very short maturities. Remember, the sensitivity of the security's price depends upon both the form of its return and its maturity.

Treasury bills, notes, and bonds represent borrowing by the U.S. government. The Treasury pays semiannual interest payments on notes and bonds. Holders of Treasury bills do not pay interest payments.

[23] 6 percent is the ask discount for the T-Bill. Pricing and return calculations for T-bills appear in section four of the Capital Markets chapter.

Stand-alone risk is the total risk of the investment.

Systematic risk is caused by macroeconomic factors. It is also known as nondiversifiable risk.

Firm-specific risk is also known as unsystematic risk or diversifiable risk.

Stand-Alone Risk. If a particular security is the only investment you hold, you are subject to that security's **stand-alone risk**. You can think of stand-alone risk as the security's total risk. Total risk is the sum of the security's risk caused by microeconomic forces and the risk caused by macroeconomic forces. We call the risk caused by microeconomic forces the **firm-specific risk** or **unsystematic (diversifiable) risk**. This is the risk caused by characteristics of the firm and the security. We call the risk caused by macroeconomic forces the **systematic risk**. This is the risk caused by the whole economy or "system." Thus:

Total Risk = Systematic Risk + Unsystematic Risk

Stand-alone risk (i.e., total risk) is the sum of systematic risk and unsystematic risk, so if the security is your only investment, you are subject to that security's total risk. If, for instance, you hold only Microsoft ™ stock you are subject to Microsoft's total, or stand-alone, risk. If Bill Gates were to suddenly sell his Microsoft stock, that event would most likely cause Microsoft stock to fall in price. Would this cause all stocks to fall? Absolutely not (in fact, some of Microsoft's competitors' stocks might actually rise, if investors feel those companies might capture some of Microsoft's market share). This is an unsystematic or firm-specific event. If Microsoft had a major fire in one of its larger locations, this would probably have a similar impact but not quite as great. Both of these events are specific to Microsoft alone. They are firm-specific events and part of Microsoft's firm-specific risk.

What if the drop in Microsoft's stock price was caused by changing interest rates or some other economy-wide or systematic event? If Microsoft is your only investment, you don't really care what made the stock price fall. Your total investment suffers regardless of the cause. Since Microsoft is your only investment, your wealth is totally dependent upon the price of Microsoft stock. Since Microsoft is subject to wide variations in stock price, both increases and decreases, your wealth is subject to those same wide swings in value.

What is the point of this discussion? It is not wise to invest all your money into only one investment. Since your total worth is dependent upon the successes or failures of that one investment, it would make better sense to hold it as part of a larger portfolio.

Portfolio Risk

Portfolio is the name given to your total collection of investments.[24] When several investments are held in a portfolio, their price changes will tend to offset one another. Some of these price changes are caused by systematic factors and some are caused by unsystematic factors. Systematic factors affect all of your investments, but usually the individual prices will react to differing degrees. For example, recall that for a given a rise in interest rates, prices of long-term bonds fall more than the prices of short-term bonds. Also, changes in inflation will typically hurt bonds more than common stocks.

It would be quite unusual for all of your securities to suffer similar unsystematic events at the same time. Above we mentioned a scenario in which Bill Gates were to unexpectedly leave Microsoft, leaving investors uncertain about the company's future. Perhaps one of your firms would have unusually hard labor negotiations causing a prolonged strike or another might suffer severe building or equipment damage during a storm. On the other hand, one of the companies might announce that its researchers have discovered a cure for the common cold, and the company's stock will rise significantly.

The point is that all companies have periods of hardship as well as periods of success. However, the randomness of these events means that at any point some firms might experience unexpected gains when others experience unexpected losses.[25] Since these events are random, they tend to offset each other and protect the total portfolio value from large swings.

The result of combining many investments into a portfolio is that part of the risk of each investment has been reduced. The total risk of the portfolio is less than the sum of the total risk of the individual investments. This is because of a statistical phenomenon known as **diversification**.

Without going into the mathematics of diversification, we will simply say that diversification is due to lack of **perfect correlation** between the returns on the investments in your portfolio. **Correlation,** ρ, refers

> Because of **diversification**, the unsystematic risk of a portfolio can be reduced or even eliminated.

> Diversification is possible due to lack of an exact relationship between the returns on investments.

---

[24] A portfolio can be as few as one or two investments, but when we refer to a portfolio, we will assume many different investments.

[25] This example refers to above or below normal returns. We will see how risk and return are valued later.

to the degree to which investment returns move together and it must have a value from -1 to $+1$, so

$$-1 \leq \rho \leq +1 \tag{1}$$

A trick to remembering what correlation means is to determine how well you know what one investment is doing just by looking at another. For instance, a correlation of $+1$ between two investments means their returns always move in the same direction and the two securities are **perfectly positively correlated**. You need only look at one security to know how the other security performed.

In a similar fashion, **perfect negative correlation** (correlation of -1), means that two securities always move in opposite directions, and a correlation of 0.0 means there is no statistically identifiable relationship between the returns on the two investments. If one of them went up, the other could have gone up or down or not moved at all.

Correlation is actually an alternative way to measure co-movement. **Covariance** is another measure of the degree to which two investments' returns "co-vary." The term covariance may remind you of the term variance from the Quantitative Methods chapter. For a share of common stock, its variance depends upon how much its return changes from period to period as well as how quickly it changes. Equation 2 shows how we would find the variance of the returns for a share of a common stock.

$$\sigma^2 = \sum_{i=1}^{N} \frac{(R_i - \bar{R})^2}{N} \tag{2}$$

where R is the stock return on day i.[26]
$\bar{R}$ is the average daily return over the time period.
N is the number of daily returns in the time period.

The covariance of the returns on two common stocks, $\sigma_{a,b}$, is measured using:

$$\sigma_{a,b} = \sum_{i=1}^{N} \frac{(R_{a,i} - \bar{R}_a)(R_{b,i} - \bar{R}_b)}{N} \tag{3}$$

[26] This formula measures the variance for the stock returns using daily returns over a time period. There is argument about how variance should be measured, however. Some analysts use weekly returns and some use monthly returns.

where the variables are defined the same way as in Equation 2 but there are now two different stocks in the equation, a and b. We use corresponding observations (e.g. daily returns) for each stock over the exact same time period. You will notice that covariance is measured in very much the same way as variance.

An alternative formula exists for us to express covariance, and it is actually more beneficial to our discussion. That formula is:

$$COV_{a,b} = \sigma_a \sigma_b \rho_{a,b} \qquad (4)$$

where $COV_{a,b}$ is the covariance of stocks a and b.

        σ_a is the standard deviation of stock a.[27]

        σ_b is the standard deviation of stock b.

        $\rho_{a,b}$ is the correlation of the two stocks.

If we rearrange the formula to solve for the correlation of the two stocks, we see that correlation is actually the **standardized covariance**:

$$\rho_{a,b} = \frac{COV_{ab}}{\sigma_a \sigma_b} \qquad (5)$$

We see in Equation 5 that the correlation between two stocks is just their covariance divided by (standardized by) the product of their standard deviations. This makes the value of correlation as described in Equation 1 much easier to understand than variance and covariance.

Correlation is the tendency for the returns on investments to move in the same direction.

Let's return to our discussion of correlation. Correlations of −1, 0, and +1 are extremes, and you will only see them for very short periods of time. For example, you might see two stocks move in the same direction for a week or two, but over a statistically valid period of time (e.g., six months), their true correlation will emerge.

Correlations between any two common stocks will typically have a positive, but not perfect, correlation. It is this lack of perfect positive

---

[27] Frequently we speak of the correlation of two stocks or the standard deviation of a stock. When you hear this, the speaker is actually referring to the standard deviation of the stock's returns or the correlation between the returns on the two stocks.

correlation that produces diversification. Almost all common stocks tend to move in the same direction over long periods of time, but they are also likely to move in opposite directions periodically. The implication is that you can randomly select a group of stocks and combine them in a portfolio, and the portfolio will have less total risk than the sum of the total risks of the individual stocks.

Remember it is the unsystematic or firm-specific risk of stocks that is uncorrelated. It is the unsystematic portion of a stock's risk that is greatly reduced or even eliminated if the stock is included in a large portfolio. For a large portfolio, total risk is only that risk produced by economy-wide factors. The only risk that remains in a well-diversified portfolio is **systematic risk**.

This raises an interesting question. If unsystematic risk is reduced or even eliminated in a portfolio, where does it go? Here's a little saying that might help: A stock doesn't know it's in a portfolio. As far as the stock is concerned, its performance is independent of whether it is in a portfolio or not.

When you combine investments, you actually create a totally new asset (i.e., a portfolio). Any investment is described in terms of risk and return, and this is true for the portfolio, too. It is the risk of the portfolio, not the risk of the individual stocks in the portfolio, which does not contain unsystematic risk. In other words, the total risk for a large, well-diversified portfolio is systematic risk only, because the unsystematic risk has been diversified away. All the individual stocks still contain their individual systematic and unsystematic risk characteristics, but the effects of diversification have greatly reduced or even eliminated the unsystematic risk of the portfolio.

We are interested in the risk we are exposed to, not the risk we can eliminate. When you hold a stock by itself, you are exposed to its total risk, systematic as well as unsystematic. When you hold the stock in a portfolio, you are exposed only to its systematic risk. The conclusion is that you can reduce risk by holding investments in a large, well-diversified portfolio.

In order to achieve complete diversification in a portfolio, a portfolio may require more than 100 stocks. To purchase this number of different stocks may be cost prohibitive. However, you can achieve excellent diversification benefits by investing in **mutual funds**. Mutual funds are very large investment companies, which combine the funds of small investors to purchase the stocks of many different corporations. Investors in the mutual fund own shares of the mutual fund, not the individual companies. The publicly traded securities of other companies are the mutual fund's assets.

Many of today's mutual funds have several billion dollars in capital under management for their investors. The secret is that hundreds of thousands of investors send their money to the typical large mutual fund. Combining their money, the professional fund manager can invest millions of dollars in each of hundreds of different stocks, achieving maximum diversification. A feat obviously beyond the grasp of the typical investor!

Return

The return on an investment can be stated in dollars or as a percent. As a convention, however, we usually state return as **annualized percentage return**. This is because stating the return in dollars neglects the size of the investment, and stating the percentage return for any time period would not standardize it.

For example, let's assume you have made two investments. You put $150 in Investment A and $100 in Investment B, which can be renewed. At the end of the first year, B pays you $115 (your $100 plus a return of $15). You repeat Investment B with the entire $115 and receive $132.25 at the end of the second year (your $115 plus a return of $17.25). For the $150 you invested in A you receive $190 in two years (your $150 plus a $40 return). Which of your two investments performed better?

Investment B paid 15 percent each year, while the two-year return for Investment A was 26.67 percent. The cash return on A was $40 while the total cash return for B was only $30. In both categories, A seems to be the better investment. Let's take another look.

Remember, we said that dollar return ignores the size of the initial investment. Although the cash flow to A was larger, it cost much more than Investment B, although at first you might not think that is the

For accuracy in investment comparisons, investment returns should be stated as an annual percentage.

case. You earned $32.25 on Investment B, and it appears you had to invest a total of $215 to get that, $100 at the beginning of year one and $115 at the beginning of year two. But that is not so.

Looking closely, we see you never had more than $100 of your own money in Investment B, the $100 you originally invested. The $115 you invested over the second year was actually your original $100 plus the $15 return from the first year. Now the cash flow to B looks much better, but it still seems inferior to A because the total cash received was only $32.25. By comparing the two investments on cash return alone, A still looks better. However, if we standardize each dollar return by dividing it by the amount invested, we see A paid $40 for a $150 investment or 26.67 percent while B paid $32.25 on a $100 investment or 32.25 percent. Having calculated two-year returns for both investments, B looks better.

Comparing the two investments based on annual percentage return proves that B is the better investment. If we standardize both percentage returns and restate them in annual terms, the percentage return for B is still 15 percent but the annual return for A is only 12.55 percent.

In summary, when comparing investments it is always best to compare them on the basis of **annualized percentage return**.

Return and Risk: The Two Rs of Finance

From our discussions above and in the Quantitative Methods chapter, we know to measure risk, the dispersion or range of possible returns, using the investment's standard deviation. We also stated that the larger the standard deviation, the wider the dispersion of possible returns and the greater the uncertainty associated with the actual outcome. Since uncertainty is a synonym for risk, the greater the standard deviation, the greater the risk.

To compare investments, one must always compare both risk and return.

Consider the following two investments:

Stock	Expected Return	Standard Deviation
A	15%	.25
B	15%	.58

If you had to choose between these two stocks, which would you choose? You probably answered stock A. Although both stocks have the same expected return, the risk (i.e., standard deviation) for B, the measure of its risk, is much greater than the standard deviation of A. Look at another example:

Stock	Expected Return	Standard Deviation
A	10%	.25
B	15%	.25

In this case you would select stock B. Both stocks have the same risk, but the expected return for B is greater than that for A.

You will notice that we chose between the two stocks by considering both their risk and their (expected) return, the two R's. If you chose stock A in the first scenario and stock B in the second, you are what we call a **rational investor**. A rational investor is one who will always minimize risk for a given level of return or maximize return for a given level of risk.

What does this discussion of investing in common stocks have to do with corporate finance? First, as an investor, you are interested in valuing the securities issued by corporations. To do that, you will need to know how to estimate expected returns as well as the risk associated with them. More relevant to our corporate finance discussion, however, is that management's goal in running a corporation is maximizing shareholder wealth. This is accomplished by maximizing the price of the firm's common stock.

This last concept is beyond the scope of this chapter. However, the value of any asset, including stocks, bonds, or even the firms that issue them, is based upon the asset's expected cash flows (returns) and its risk. Simply put, the manager will attempt to maximize the firm's cash flows while simultaneously minimizing risk, resulting in a higher stock price. So the relationship between risk and return and management's responsibility to the stockholders becomes clear.

You will see in the Security Valuation chapter that the price of any asset is the present value of future cash flows. The present value of the cash flows is determined by discounting them at their required return, and the required return is determined by the risk of the investment (the

> When choosing investments, a **rational investor** will minimize risk for a given level of return or maximize return for a given level of risk.

volatility of the cash flows). For firms, as well as their securities and any other cash-flow-producing asset, maximizing cash flows and simultaneously minimizing risk will maximize value.

Agency Costs

In Section 2, we assumed management would strive to maximize stockholder wealth by maximizing the firm's stock price. However, this assumes that management and the stockholders always have the same personal goals. This is not necessarily the case.

> The manager acts as an agent for the absentee owners, representing them in the daily operations of the firm.

The problem of agency costs arises from the separation of corporate ownership and management. Since the owners are numerous and scattered all over the country, managers must act as their agent and run the firm for them. Every operating and investment decision the manager makes is actually made for the owners. It's very similar to the relationship of homeowners and a real estate agent. The agent represents them to potential buyers of their home, and the homeowners must depend upon the agent to act in their best interest.

There are two agency relationships in large corporations: between the firm's stockholders and its managers, and between the firm's stockholders and the firm's bondholders. Before we discuss these, however, let's be sure you completely understand the relationship between stockholders and bondholders and the sources of risk in a large corporation.

> Agency costs are the actual or implied costs associated with the separation of ownership and management. They arise from the separation of ownership and management.

From the discussion on causes of investment risk, you will recall that characteristics of the issuing firm contribute a large portion of the risk of its securities. We divide these characteristics into two categories: financial risk and business risk. Financial risk comes from the way management finances the firm's assets and growth. Using common equity stabilizes the firm's cash flows, while using debt causes leverage or volatility in the firm's cash flows (i.e., using debt makes the firm riskier.) There is also a certain amount of volatility in the firm's earnings due to business risks. This is generally due to the type of industry, but management can still make asset choices that will increase or decrease business risk.

Stockholders are primarily concerned with the price of their stock. They want management to make decisions that will cause the price to increase, regardless of the risk involved. Bondholders, on the other hand, are far more interested in the firm's (management's) ability to pay the coupons and repay principal when due. The ability to make interest payments as part of the normal operations of the firm depends upon management's ability to consistently generate sufficient operating income or EBIT.

This is one source of disagreement between stockholders and bond-holders. Stockholders want management to undertake risky projects and increase the amount of debt to increase their expected returns even though these practices also increase risk. This is because a large portion of this increased volatility is due to unsystematic factors, which can be diversified away by holding the stock as part of a large portfolio. They are left with higher expected returns without the associated higher risk.

Bondholders would prefer that management be cautious running the firm. They prefer less risky projects in an effort to keep EBIT as stable as possible. Also, debt acts like a double-edged sword. Not only does debt create variability, it also comes with a fixed interest payment. The more debt employed by management, the riskier the firm and the higher the interest payments. Both of these are contrary to the wishes of the bondholders.

Because the conflict between stockholders and bondholders exists, stockholders will tolerate additional risk with its accompanying increased expected returns. Bondholders want stability with its lower, more consistent returns. If stockholders get their wish, they, in effect, steal value form the bondholders. The increased risk reduces the value of the debt claims on the firm while simultaneously increasing the value of the equity claims. If the bondholders get their way, their value is maintained, but the value of the equity claims is not maximized. With whom do you think management will side?

Management is well aware that the stockholders own the firm and have voting privileges that could affect their future. They must consider the wishes of the stockholders, but this doesn't mean they will let stockholder desires influence all their decisions. Consistently making the decision the stockholders want will make the firm's bottom line more uncertain. Since managers are ultimately responsible for the bottom line, they must decide between increasing the firm's risk in order to possibly increase its returns to the stockholders, or keeping the firm's earnings more predictable to preserve their position with the company. Obviously, the manager will not make the firm as risky as possible to please the stockholders, so the stock price will never reach its theoretical maximum. This loss of (possible) value is a form of agency cost to the stockholder. Another source is management's extravagant use of perquisites or activities and decisions of which the stockholders would not approve.

The only way to ensure managers will always make the desired decision from the viewpoint of the stockholders is to hire someone to oversee everything they do, which would be quite expensive as well as confining for the manager. The value saved through this overseer's actions might not be as great as the cost. Once again, a tradeoff is required. Stockholders must reach the point where managers are free to make everyday decisions without someone looking over their shoulders. However, managers must be monitored to prevent a complete abuse of the stockholders' investment. This is usually accomplished through the annual audits performed by large independent accounting firms.

Capital Structure

Capital structure refers to how the owners paid for the firm. **Exhibit 2**, Lucy's Lemonade Balance Sheet, reproduced below from the Financial Statement Analysis chapter, will demonstrate what is meant by capital structure. The left side of the balance sheet shows the assets of the firm including current and fixed assets. The right side is divided into liability and owners' equity accounts. These accounts represent the sources of capital utilized to pay for the assets.

Capital structure gives information about the firm's long-term or permanent sources of capital. In the statement below, we see the relationship between the long-term liabilities and the equity accounts.

Exhibit 2: Mall Business, Balance Sheet After One Month

Lucy's Lemonade
Balance Sheet
July 31, 200X

Current Assets:		Current Liabilities:	
Cash	$2,467	Accounts Payable	$ 850
Inventory	1,150		
Supplies	750	**Long Term Liabilities:**	
Prepaid Rent	1,000	Notes Payable	4,000[2]
Prepaid Insurance	3,000		
Total Current Assets	$8,367		
Fixed Assets:		**Total Liabilities**	$4,850
Equipment[1]	3,100		
Less Acc. Depreciation	36		
Net Fixed Assets	3,064	**Owners' Equity**	6,581
Total Assets	$11,431	**Total Liabilities**	
		Plus Owners' Equity	$11,431

[1]Icemaker ($1,500) + Pretzel Oven ($1,350) + Pretzel Display Unit ($250) − Depreciation ($36) = $3,064. Lucy would keep a separate record in the general ledger for each different fixed asset.

[2] Lucy made a $1,000 payment to her parents.

The typical large corporation has several different issues of long-term debt (bonds) outstanding as well as a great deal of common stock. It is the relative proportions of these that represent the capital structure of the firm.[28]

If a firm with $1,000,000 in total assets is "financed" with $500,000 long-term debt (usually simply referred to as debt) and $500,000 common equity, we say the firm's debt ratio is 50 percent (i.e., $500,000/$1,000,000 = .50). Notice its equity ratio, the ratio of equity to total assets, is also 50 percent and its debt-equity ratio is $500,000/$500,000 = 1.0.

---

[28] Some argue the firm's capital structure includes all forms of permanent capital. This would include common stock, preferred stock, bonds, and any short-term sources that remain at a more or less constant level on the balance sheet. One short-term source could be a large note payable that is continually rolled-over (refinanced).

We will discuss the firm's **cost of capital** in the Security Valuation chapter. However, capital structure will affect the rate at which the firm can borrow as well as the rate required by its equity holders. Management's choices for funding can affect not only the firm's cost of capital but the value of the firm as well.

SUMMARY OF SECTION 3

Learning Objective: *To understand the connection between risk and return, agency costs, and capital structure.*

A. **Risk** is the possibility of an unfavorable event (usually a lower than expected return on the investment).
   1. Receiving a cash flow later than expected.
   2. Not receiving an expected cash flow.
B. Risk implies a range (distribution) of possible returns.
   1. The distribution of possible returns is measured using the standard deviation.
   2. The greater the standard deviation, the wider the range of possible returns, and the greater the risk associated with the investment.
C. Risk in publicly traded securities is caused by microeconomic and macroeconomic factors.
   1. **Microeconomic factors** are characteristics of the issuing firm and the security itself. These cause the unsystematic or diversifiable risk of the security.
   2. **Macroeconomic factors** are economy-wide forces such as inflation. These cause the systematic or non-diversifiable risk of the security.
D. **Firm-specific factors** consist of business risk and financial risk.
   1. **Business risk** is due to characteristics of the industry, the type of business in which the firm operates.
      a. Firms in the industry might be subject to variable revenues.
      b. The firm's cost and pricing structures might not be flexible.
      c. New product development might be slow.
      d. Management may have little flexibility in the choice of assets utilized.
         • Use of fixed assets causes operating leverage.
         • The greater the amount of fixed assets, the higher the operating leverage.

- Operating leverage is measured as the percentage change in EBIT given a percentage change in revenues.
2. **Financial risk** is due to the utilization of fixed-obligation sources of financing, primarily bonds. Using debt causes **financial leverage**.
   a. The more debt used and the greater the fixed obligation, the higher the financial leverage.
   b. Financial leverage is measured as the percentage change in net income given a percentage change in EBIT.
E. Characteristics of the securities themselves can cause risk.
   1. The type of security affects its risk.
      a. Debt is senior to (i.e., paid before) equity.
      b. Preferred stock is senior to common stock.
   2. The maturity of the security affects its risk. The prices of long-term bonds are more sensitive to changes in interest rates than the prices of short-term bonds.
   3. The nature of the security's return affects its risk.
      a. There are only two possible means of achieving a return: **cash flows** (interest payments) and **capital gains** (increases in value).
      b. Generally, the greater the cash flow portion of the return, the less sensitive the security is to changes in interest rates.
F. Security risk can be measured in two categories.
   1. **Stand-alone risk** is the total risk of the security.
      a. Its systematic risk plus its unsystematic risk.
      b. You are exposed to its total risk if you hold a security by itself.
   2. **Portfolio risk** refers to the risk of the security when it is held in a portfolio of investments. **Diversification** causes reduction of the unsystematic risk of the portfolio.
   3. Lack of correlation between securities results in diversification benefits, where correlation is designated by ρ, where $-1 \leq \rho \leq +1$.
      a. Perfect positive correlation, $+1$, means two securities' returns always move together in the same direction.
      b. Perfect negative correlation, -1, means two securities' returns always move in opposite directions.
      c. A correlation of 0.0 means there is no detectable statistical relationship between the movements of the two securities' returns.

      d. When two securities' returns are not perfectly positively correlated, holding them together in a portfolio produces diversification.

  4. Return should be standardized. The return on an investment should be stated as an **annualized percentage return.**

  5. An investment's required return is the return investors require for holding the investment.

      a. Required return is based upon the risk of the investment.

      b. The greater the risk associated with an investment, the higher the required return.

  6. **Rational investors** will always consider both risk and return in evaluating investments.

      a. They will minimize risk for a given level of return.

      b. They will maximize return for a given level of risk.

G. **Agency costs** are the actual or implied costs associated with the separation of ownership and management.

  1. Managers are the owners' agents. They operate the firm in the absence of the owners.

  2. The goals of the managers might not agree with those of the owners.

      a. Owners want management to take risky projects to increase the expected return on the firm's stock.

      b. Owners can diversify away the unsystematic risk by holding the firm's stock in a portfolio.

  3. Managers are concerned with the owners' wishes, but are probably more concerned with maintaining their employment.

      a. Excess risk causes more volatility (uncertainty) in the firm's cash flows.

      b. If the firm does well, management and owners do well.

      c. If the firm does poorly, the owners are partially protected by diversification but management loses their jobs.

  4. Managers will tend to be defensive in their decisions.

      a. Not always make the value maximizing decision.

      b. The firm's stock price will never reach its theoretical maximum.

      c. The loss of value is due to agency, which is an implicit agency cost.

  5. The owners can hire overseers to ensure their wishes are met, which can be expensive and is an explicit agency cost.

6. Excess paperwork reduces the manager's ability to make timely decisions for everyday operations (an implicit agency cost).

H. There is also an agency relationship between stockholders and bondholders.

1. Bondholders receive fixed interest payments and the face value of the bonds at maturity.

2. Bondholders want the firm to maintain a low level of risk.

a. High firm risk increases stock prices but reduces bond prices.

b. Bondholders are concerned management will increase the firm's risk once they have purchased the bonds. The value lost by the bondholders is captured by the stockholders.

I. **Capital structure** refers to the way management has paid for the firm's assets.

1. Any long-term form of capital is considered. Usually this means common stock, preferred stock, and bonds.

2. Any permanent form of capital should be considered. Short-term sources of capital should be considered if they are maintained at a more or less constant significant level. If they represent a minute portion of the firm's total capital, permanent short-term sources can be ignored.

J. The firm's capital structure affects the firm's **cost of capital**, which is a weighted average of the costs (returns required by investors) of the firm's sources of capital: common stock, long-term debt, and preferred stock.

PRACTICE QUESTIONS

1. An owner has the greatest amount of control involving business decisions under which of the following forms of business?

    A. Proprietorship.
    B. Partnership.
    C. S corporation.
    D. C corporation.

2. Which of the following statements about partnerships is incorrect?

    A. A partnership is easy to form.
    B. Taxable income flows through to the partners, who must report it for the calculation of their personal income taxes.
    C. The partners have limited liability.
    D. The life of a partnership is linked to the lives of the partners.

3. Which of the following is the most complicated type of business to form?

    A. Proprietorship.
    B. Partnership.
    C. Corporation.
    D. Small business.

4. Which of the following is **not** a characteristic of an S corporation?

    A. An S corporation is similar to a partnership.
    B. An S corporation pays income taxes.
    C. An S corporation's stockholders have limited liability.
    D. An S corporation's stock is not publicly traded.

5. Which of the following terms represent a current stockholder's right to purchase new shares before they are offered to the general public?

    A. Prospectus right.
    B. First right.
    C. Legal right.
    D. Preemptive right.

6. Which of the following statements is **incorrect**?

   A. A corporation is not legally required to pay dividends.
   B. Dividends are mailed to the investor who is registered as the owner of the stock on the holder of record date.
   C. Anyone who purchases common stock on or after the ex-dividend date is entitled to the announced dividend.
   D. The Board of Directors declares dividends.

7. When corporate bonds are callable, which of the following statements would be **true**?

   A. They may be converted to common stock at the holder's discretion.
   B. They may be exchanged for another bond at the owner's discretion.
   C. They can be retired early by management.
   D. They cannot be held until maturity.

8. Which of the following terms describes the legal contract between the firm and the bondholders?

   A. Debenture.
   B. Indenture.
   C. Prospectus.
   D. Covenants.

9. Which of the following statements about preferred stock is **incorrect**?

   A. Preferred stock can be callable and/or convertible.
   B. Preferred stock pays dividends.
   C. Preferred stock dividends are typically cumulative.
   D. Preferred stock is never associated with voting privileges.

10. Which of the following is **not** a microeconomic factor that can affect the risk of a common stock?

   A. Inflation.
   B. A change in the firm's management.
   C. The firm's assets.
   D. The firm's cost and price structures.

11. Which of the following is **not** an example of business risk?

    A. Variability of the firm's revenue.
    B. Inability to adjust output prices in response to increased costs.
    C. Inability to respond quickly to a new product introduced by a competitor.
    D. Rapidly changing inflation.

12. Which of the following is **not** an example of financial risk?

    A. The additional risk to the stockholders from management's use of debt financing.
    B. A result of the firm's asset structure.
    C. Uncertainty in the firm's operating income, EBIT.
    D   A function of the firm's operating leverage.

13. Which of the following security classes is considered as the most risky for investors?

    A. Common stock.
    B. Treasury securities.
    C. Bond.
    D. Preferred stock.

14. The risk caused by microeconomic factors is known as:

    A. systematic risk.
    B. firm-specific or unsystematic risk.
    C. stand alone risk.
    D. total risk.

15. The unsystematic risk of a portfolio:

    A. can be reduced or even eliminated.
    B. cannot be eliminated.
    C. must be greater than the portfolio's systematic risk.
    D. is the portfolio's stand alone risk.

16. If the returns on two stocks always move in opposite directions, the correlation between them is:

    A. +1 (perfect positive correlation).
    B. -1 (perfect negative correlation).
    C. +2 (positive correlation).
    D.   0 (no correlation).

17. A rational (i.e., risk averse) investor would choose which of the following investments?

Investment	Expected Return	Standard Deviation
A	10%	.25
B	10%	.50

   A. A.
   B. B.
   C. Both A and B.
   D. Either A or B.

18. Agency costs:

   A. are due to conflicts of interest between owners and managers.
   B. are due to the separation of ownership and management.
   C. are due to conflicts of interest between stockholders and bondholders.
   D. All the above are characteristic of agency costs.

19. Capital structure refers to:

   A. the ratio of the firm's current to long-term liabilities.
   B. the ratio of the firm's current to long-term assets.
   C. the assets of the firm.
   D. how management has raised capital to pay for the firm's assets.

ANSWERS AND SOLUTIONS

1. A. In a proprietorship, there is a sole owner. This individual has complete control over all decisions. In all the others there are multiple owners.

2. C. In a partnership, the owner's liability is proportional to his or her percentage ownership in the business.

3. C. Corporations must be registered with the Secretary of State and require more external reporting.

4. B. One of the primary advantages of the corporate form of business is limited liability. However, in an S Corporation, the owners pay taxes as if they were partners. That is, taxable income flows through to the owners according to their percentage ownership.

5. D. The preemptive right is the right of common stockholders to maintain their percentage ownership in the corporation. This gives them the right to purchase new shares before they are offered to the public.

6. C. Paying dividends is more a tradition than an absolute requirement for corporations. When a corporation pays dividends, the Board of Directors declares them, and they are payable to the investors registered as owners on the holder of record date.

7. C. Callable bonds do not have to be called. When they are, the holders of the bonds **must** surrender them to the firm. Management typically calls bonds when interest rates have fallen, and the bonds can be replaced with a new issue with a lower coupon rate.

8. B. The legal contract between the firm and the bondholders is known as the indenture. A debenture is a non-collateralized bond.

9. D. Preferred stock pays dividends, which are usually cumulative. Preferred stock can be callable and/or convertible. Although preferred stocks may possess voting privileges, they usually do not.

10. A. Microeconomic factors include within-firm factors. Inflation is a macroeconomic (system-wide) factor.

11. D. Business risk is caused by the industry within which the firm operates and the assets the firm employs.

12. A. This is the definition of financial risk.

13. A. The financial claims of common stockholders are subordinated to all other claimants.

14 B.   Unsystematic risk or firm-specific risk is the risk caused by microeconomic forces.

15. A.   Systematic risk cannot be eliminated, but unsystematic risk can be reduced or even eliminated through diversification in a portfolio.

16. B.   When two stocks move in exactly the opposite direction, they are said to be perfectly negatively correlated.

17. A.   The expected return is the same for the investments. Since a rational investor will always minimize risk for a given level of return, the rational investor will choose investment A.

18. D.   The origin of agency costs is the separation of ownership and management. The goals of the stockholders, bondholders, and management are sometimes at odds.

19. D.   Capital structure refers to the proportions of debt and equity financing used to pay for the firm's assets.

Capital Markets

Markets provide the means for buyers and sellers to exchange goods and services. Exchange can be for money or for other goods and services (as in a barter system). Markets can have physical locations, where buyers and sellers actually meet, or they can be channels through which goods and services flow. In the latter case it is possible that neither the buyer nor the seller knows who is on the other end of the transaction.

A form of market that should be very familiar to you is a marketplace for food, where vendors sell their various products for cash or on credit. Buyers make their selections from piles of fruits and vegetables as well as shelf after shelf of variously packaged goods. These marketplaces range from very large supermarkets to very small stores specializing in imported products or naturally grown foods, and even include vending machines in which you deposit coins and receive a canned drink or other product.

Capital markets provide individuals, businesses, and governments a way to get the capital they need for operating and expanding.

There are also markets for money, which provide the means for transferring funds from those with an excess of money to those with a shortage. These **capital markets** provide individuals, businesses, and governments with a way to get the capital they need for operating and expanding.

Section 1 of this chapter discusses the different forms of markets. Sections 2 and 3 cover primary and secondary capital markets, respectively. Section 4 focuses on the money markets.

In this chapter, your learning objectives are the following:

1. To understand the differences between direct, broker, and dealer markets and between spot, forward, and futures markets.
2. To understand primary markets and the role of the investment banker.
3. To understand secondary markets and the securities traded there.
4. To understand the most active markets in the world, the money markets, and some of the instruments traded in them.

SECTION 1: MARKETS

There are actually three basic types of markets. First there is the **direct market**, in which the buyer and seller must actually contact one another directly. When you visit a farmer's market, you are participating in a direct market. You see the items you want, and you purchase them. The obvious benefit with direct markets is the ability to inspect the item before you purchase it. Of course, this also presents a potentially large problem for both you and the vendor: You must be able to travel to the market and the vendor can sell only to those who make the trip.

> In a **direct market**, the buyer and seller must actually contact one another.

The second type of market is the **broker market**. In this case, a broker facilitates the transaction by bringing the buyer and seller together. Consider a real estate transaction. You may choose to sell your home by yourself (i.e., "by owner"), which would be a case of direct marketing. In order for you to be successful, you must be able to actively market your property, meet prospects at your home, and negotiate the sale terms. You can advertise your house in newspapers or other publications, but that can be expensive.

> A **broker** helps bring the buyer and seller together.

If you have a real estate broker handling the sale for you, she will advertise the sale through specialized real estate networks. The broker will help you establish a fair offering price, give you ideas on how to improve the appearance of the house, show the house to prospects, and even act as the go between during negotiations. In other words, the broker acts as your agent in presenting the home to a very wide range of prospective buyers, in exchange for commission on the sale of the home.

Notice that the real estate broker does not actually take ownership in the home being sold. Rather, the function of the broker is to bring the buyer and seller together.[1] In a **dealer market**, the dealer buys goods and then sells them. The dealer actually takes *ownership* of the product before reselling it to the final user. The dealer can sell his products at a central location, such as a grocery store, or he can sell them through a network or even over the Internet.

A **dealer** actually takes ownership before reselling the product.

All three forms of markets exist today. You've seen cars by the side of the road or in parking lots with "For Sale" signs in the windows. You've seen apartments for rent or houses for sale by owner. These are common examples of the direct market at work. Next door to the "For Sale By Owner" sign in one front yard, you might have seen a yard with a real estate company sign, an example of the broker market. And you have visited a grocery store or any of thousands of other retail stores, which are examples of the dealer market.

Money markets and capital markets[2] are very similar in many respects to the markets we have discussed above. The goal is to facilitate the transaction between the buyer (the borrower) and the seller (the lender). A major difference does exist between product markets and capital markets. In product markets, the buyer actually takes ownership of the product. In capital markets, you only *rent* the capital. Someone with excess capital (the lender) charges a fee (interest) for the use of their capital for a period of time, after which the borrower must return the original capital borrowed, the **principal**.

Capital markets can also be discussed within the three market forms discussed above. In a direct capital market, the individual or firm with a need for capital must contact the supplier (lender) directly. The lender holds the borrower's securities (equity or debt), which denote a claim by the lender on the money and other assets of the borrower. Note there is no broker or dealer involved in the transaction.

In a brokered capital market, an investment banker, acting as a broker, brings the borrower together with the lender(s). This is what we call a **private placement**.

[1] Although technically a form of direct market, it could be argued that the Internet acts as a broker in bringing the buyer and seller together.

[2] **Money markets** deal with short-term borrowing and investing and **capital markets** with long-term.

A **financial intermediary** borrows money from a saver or investor and lends it to others.

In the third type of market, the dealer market, a bank or other **financial intermediary** takes "ownership" of the capital then lends it to others. In the process, two different types of securities are created. When you "buy" a Certificate of Deposit (CD) at a bank, you are actually loaning money to the bank. In return, you receive a certificate stating the amount you loaned the bank (the face value of the CD), the rate of interest you are earning (the rate the bank is paying to borrow your money), and the date the certificate matures (the date the bank must repay you).

What happens to the money you loaned to the bank? The bank, in turn, loans the money to others. Let's assume that you "loan" the bank $10,000 through the purchase of a CD. Furthermore, let's assume that a small-business owner wants to borrow $10,000 from the bank to buy equipment. The bank takes the $10,000 from the CD you "purchased" and loans the money to the business owner. In return, the bank receives a mortgage on the equipment in an amount equal to the funds borrowed. The illustration below shows how the mortgage is transformed by a financial intermediary into a CD.

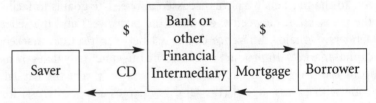

Spot, Forward, and Futures Markets

A **spot market** is where securities, commodities, and other goods are traded for immediate delivery.

A **spot market** is where securities, commodities, and other goods are traded for immediate delivery. The price you receive in a spot market is the current market value determined by the supply of and demand for the product. The most common spot market is the retail store (e.g., shoe store or a grocery store), where the customer selects the desired product and takes it directly home (known as "cash and carry").

In financial spot markets, investors buy currencies, securities, and commodities for "immediate" delivery of two to three days. An example of this is when you call your broker and buy common stock or other securities. When a farmer sells corn in the spot market, he delivers it to his local grain elevator.

Forward markets were developed because of the uncertainty associated with future spot market prices. For instance, the farmer mentioned above has planted corn, which he will harvest and deliver to the elevator in three months. He sees the price of corn today but isn't sure what it will be when he harvests. The price of corn when it is harvested will depend upon the demand for corn compared to the quantity harvested worldwide. If farmers produce surplus crops, the price of corn may fall due to the abundance of corn.

Regardless, the farmer would like an idea of the price he will receive before he determines how much corn to plant. To lock in a selling price for his corn, the farmer can enter into a forward contract to deliver a set amount of corn at a predetermined price. In this way, the farmer knows in advance the price he will receive. If he waits until delivery to find out the price he will receive, the price per bushel may have dropped significantly.

You might have noticed the uncertainty involved in this transaction. For example, what if the farmer sells 10,000 bushels in a forward contract and has a yield of 20,000 bushels? In this case, he would have locked in a price for only half his yield. However, he might have sold 20,000 bushels in the contract and harvested only 10,000. Since he agreed to deliver 20,000 bushels, he would actually have to buy 10,000 bushels in the spot market and deliver them against the contract. If his yield was reduced, there is a distinct possibility that the overall corn crop was low. Under these conditions, the price in the spot market would be very high. Losses would accrue on the corn that he had to purchase to deliver on the contract.

A problem with forward contracts is the lack of a **liquid market** in which holders can buy and sell contracts quickly. If possible, the farmer could buy and sell forward contracts as the harvest date neared to **hedge** most of his risk. Since such a forward market doesn't exist, **futures markets** were developed. **Futures** are standardized contracts traded on organized exchanges. In this case, they specify the grade of corn, the bushels in one contract, the delivery price per bushel, and the delivery location.

Delivery is included in every contract as a matter of convention and for the infrequent necessity to actually deliver or take receipt of the commodity or financial instrument specified in the contract. Most futures positions are actually established by speculators. Speculators enter the market when they believe that a futures position is currently mispriced. Our farmer would actually deal in two separate markets. His profits (losses) in the spot market would be offset by losses (profits) in

In a **forward market** both parties agree to transact at a future date.

Futures contracts on commodities, currencies, and other financial instruments are liquid, standardized contracts traded on futures markets facilitated by a clearing corporation.

Hedging is the reduction of risk.

The futures price is an estimate of the future spot price. As the maturity date nears, the futures price must **converge** to the spot price until they are equal on the maturity date.

the futures market. Because of **convergence**, the final net price received is the price specified in the contract.

Assume the farmer sells one futures contract for 5,000 bushels of corn at $3.00 per bushel, with a maturity date the same as his expected harvest date. He has locked in a price of $3.00 per bushel, or $15,000 for the contract. Because of convergence, the futures price must converge toward the spot price as delivery time (harvest) nears. If the spot price is $4.00 at the harvest date, our farmer would receive less for his corn than if he had waited and sold in the spot market. If the spot price is $2.00, however, he is much better off having sold the futures. Let's see how it works.

The futures price will be the same as the spot price at the maturity of the contract. In the first scenario, we assumed that the spot price of corn at the maturity of the contract would be $4.00 per bushel, and the farmer can take the opposite position in the futures to close out his contract (i.e., since he sold corn futures three months ago, he simply buys the same futures contract today and his net position in the contract is zero). At the date he sold the futures contract, the farmer expected to receive $15,000 for his corn. When he delivers the corn on the spot market he receives $20,000 (i.e., $4.00 × 5,000 bushels). In the futures market, however, he must buy at $4.00 per bushel what he sold at $3.00 per bushel. Since the contract covers 5,000 bushels, he loses $5,000. His net position for *both* transactions is $15,000.

If the spot price is $2.00 at maturity, the farmer will deliver his corn on the spot market at $10,000. Simultaneously, however, he will buy the futures contract at $2.00 per bushel, which he originally sold at $3.00 per bushel, making $1.00 profit per bushel or $5,000 total on the futures contract. Again, his net position for *both* transactions is $15,000.

The futures markets act as *insurance* against uncertain spot prices. The actual cost of the futures transactions can be considered insurance premiums paid for protection against swings in spot prices. Second, the farmer did not actually deliver his corn to fulfill his obligation under the futures contract. Rather, he traded corn in the spot market and simultaneously traded in the futures market. He was actually involved in two separate transactions.

To help ensure highly liquid, smooth flowing futures markets, a **clearing corporation (CC)**, oversees every transaction. The CC does not actually buy or sell contracts, but it matches every buyer to a seller. Since the CC acts as the middleman, buyers and sellers need not even know each other. The CC also ensures each side performs as required under the contract, effectively eliminating any risk of nonperformance.[3]

The price at which a futures contract is closed on a given day is the **settlement price**. Every trading day, all futures contracts are **marked to market** based on the settlement price. If the futures contract has lost value, those who bought the contract have lost the same amount (as with any investment, the owner loses money when the value of the investment falls). Their account will be reduced by the difference, and they may be required to deposit the difference between the price they paid and the settlement price. Those who sold the contract have actually made that amount and may withdraw it. In this fashion, profits and losses on futures contracts are settled every trading day.

> During every trading day, all futures contracts are **marked to market** at the **settlement price**.

SECTION 2: PRIMARY CAPITAL MARKETS

Firms obtain long-term capital by selling their securities in the primary markets. They typically utilize the services of an investment-banking firm to privately place their securities or sell them publicly. In a **public offering**, securities are offered to the general investing public through **investment bankers**.

> All **public offerings** of securities must be registered with the SEC.

All securities sold publicly in the United States must be registered with the Securities and Exchange Commission (SEC). This includes common stock and bonds issued by corporations. To register their securities, firms must publish a prospectus, which discloses information as specified by the SEC.[4] The process can be costly both in terms of time and money, and a good deal of information about the firm is disclosed to the general public. A syndicate of investment banking firms, with a few **lead banks**, will help the firm through the process. The lead banks actually meet with management to decide what security to issue, when to issue the security, how much to issue, and at what price.

> **Investment bankers** help firms raise capital through public or private security offerings.

The investment banks will advertise the sale in a **tombstone** in the *Wall Street Journal* and other financial publications. The tombstone

---

[3] For a complete discussion of forward and futures markets, see Reilly and Brown, *Investment Analysis and Portfolio Management, 6 E* (The Dryden Press, 2000), chapter 6.

[4] A discussion on selling securities publicly can be found in the section on Common Stock in the Corporate Finance chapter.

contains the names of the investment banking firms involved in the sale, the main characteristics of the security, and the date of the sale. The tombstone will direct interested investors to the prospectus, which is available through any of the listed investment banking firms.

The lead banks and others listed on the tombstone are part of the **underwriting syndicate**. When an issue of securities is **underwritten**, the investment banks guarantee the proceeds of the issue to the firm before the securities are offered publicly. The prospectus lists all involved investment banks along with the extent of their underwriting obligation (the number of shares or bonds each investment bank agrees to purchase and sell). Often, investment bankers will visit large institutional investors, such as pension funds, mutual funds, and insurance companies, to determine their interest and to get pricing advice.

By **underwriting** an issue of securities, investment bankers guarantee the sale and the proceeds to the issuing firm.

For their efforts, investment banks charge a fee known as the **underwriter spread**. This spread is the difference between the price investment bankers pay for the securities and the price at which they sell them to investors. In effect, the investment bankers buy the securities at wholesale and sell them at retail. The total costs of selling securities publicly (the spread, legal fees, accounting and financial costs, and printing costs) are known as **flotation costs**. The magnitude of the investment banks' fees will depend upon the work the banks have to do to sell the securities as well as the risk associated with selling them. For example, if a very large, well-known firm sells securities, total flotation costs are minimal (as a percentage of the proceeds). For a smaller, less well-known firm, the spread alone can be as high as 20–30 percent of the proceeds. This is mostly due to the extra efforts the banks must expend to sell these securities as well as the risk that they might not sell their total allocation.

Flotation costs are the total costs of issuing securities. They include the underwriter spread and legal, accounting, and printing fees.

To speed up the process of issuing securities and to maintain a certain degree of privacy, many firms place their securities privately. A **private placement** is restricted to a limited number of very large investors, and the issue does not have to be registered with the SEC. This avoids the necessity of disclosing great amounts of information about the firm and its owners.

In a **private placement**, the investment banker acts as a broker and brings the firm and the investors together. The issue is not underwritten

An investment banking firm, acting only as a broker, facilitates the meeting of representatives of the firm and the investors to discuss the details of the issue. In this fashion, only those investors actually involved in the private placement get the inside information that would be disclosed in a prospectus for a public offering. The investors take large positions (i.e., buy a large amount of the debt) in the offering and typically hold it to maturity. The interest rate (coupon) on the bonds is usually slightly higher than if the bonds were sold publicly, because the investors cannot sell their bonds to the public. However, due to the flotation cost savings and the lack of publicly disclosed information, private placements are the method of choice for selling corporate bonds.[5]

SECTION 3: SECONDARY CAPITAL MARKETS

In secondary markets, investors buy and sell securities that have already been issued by firms through primary market transactions. In a primary market transaction, the firm receives the net proceeds from the sale of new securities. Although firms will occasionally buy their own stock in secondary market transactions, the vast majority of secondary market transactions involve investors trading among themselves.

> In **secondary markets**, investors trade securities which have been previously issued in the primary market.

Equity Markets

Common stock and other equity securities are traded on various exchanges, the best known of which is the **New York Stock Exchange** (**NYSE**). The NYSE traces its origins back more than 200 years to the signing of the Buttonwood Agreement by 24 New York City stockbrokers and merchants in 1792. Only NYSE-listed securities are bought and sold on the NYSE, and only by its more than 1,300 members.[6] About 3,000 stocks—valued at nearly $12.5 trillion—are traded weekdays from 9:30 A.M. to 4:00 P.M. (EST). To have their common stock and other securities listed on the NYSE, firms must meet the following criteria:

<u>NYSE Listing Criteria:</u>[7]

Minimum Quantitative Standards: Distribution and Size Criteria

- Round-lot[8] holders totaling 2,000 or total shareholders totaling 2,200.
- Average monthly trading volume of 100,000 shares or total shareholders of 500.

---

[5] A quick glance at the *Wall Street Journal* confirms this. You will see that a very limited number of bonds are publicly traded.

[6] Memberships on the NYSE are referred to as "seats," which have sold for as much as $1,500,000.

[7] Source: NYSE.com

[8] A round lot is typically 100 shares.

- Average monthly trading volume of 1,000,000 shares.
- Public shares outstanding totaling 1,100,000.
- Market value of public shares of $100,000,000.

Minimum Quantitative Standards: Financial Criteria

Aggregate pretax earnings over the last three years of $6,500,000 achievable in one of the following ways:

- Most recent year of $2,500,000 and each of two preceding years of $2,000,000.
- Most recent year of $4,500,000 with all three years profitable.
- For companies with at least $500,000,000 in global market capitalization and $200,000,000 in reserves in the last twelve months, aggregate operating cash flow for the past three years of $25,000,000. Each individual year must be profitable.

Global Market Capitalization

- Revenues for the last fiscal year of $100,000,000.
- Average Global Market Capitalization of $1,000,000,000.

As illustrated above, firms listed on the NYSE tend to be very large. Some of the best-known companies in the world are listed on the NYSE, including almost all the firms listed in the **Dow Jones Industrial Average** (**DJIA**), by far the best known and most widely followed **stock index**.

A **stock index** is used to estimate movements in the overall market.

The **Dow Jones Industrial Average** is the most famous stock index.

Charles H. Dow developed the DJIA in 1896. Determining the overall movement in the market is difficult due to frequent and varied changes in the prices of stocks.[9] He collected trading data[10] on twelve stocks, which acted as a sample of the stock market. He used movements in the average price of his sample as an indicator of movements of the stock market as a whole. If the average price in his sample increased, the market was up. In the same fashion, if the average price decreased, the market was down. **Exhibit 1** shows the original twelve stocks in the DJIA.

[9] Movements in the market, as with individual stocks, indicate changes in value. If the market is up, the overall value of the stocks being traded has increased. When the market is down, the overall value of the stocks being traded has declined.

[10] **Trading data** include prices, the number of shares traded, and the number of shares per trade.

Exhibit 1: Original Twelve Stocks in the Dow Jones Industrial Average[11]

American Cotton Oil	Laclede Gas
American Sugar	National Lead
American Tobacco	North American
Chicago Gas	Tennessee Coal and Iron
Distilling and Cattle Feeding	U.S. Leather Preferred
General Electric	U.S. Rubber

Exhibit 2 shows the current composition of the DJIA. The list has changed significantly since its inception, primarily because most of the original companies no longer exist. General Electric is the only one of the original firms that is still in the DJIA. Today, the number of firms has increased to thirty, twenty-eight of which are NYSE-listed stocks with the remaining two coming from the **NASDAQ** (**National Association of Securities Dealers Automated Quote System**). In addition to its Industrial Average, the Dow Jones Company publishes its Transportation and Utilities Averages.

Exhibit 2: Current (Thirty) Stocks in the Dow Jones Industrial Average

Alcoa, Inc.	International Business Machines Corp.
American Express Co.	Intel Corp. (NASDAQ)
AT&T Corp.	International Paper Co.
Boeing Co.	J.P. Morgan Chase & Co.
Caterpillar Inc.	Johnson & Johnson
Citigroup Inc.	McDonald's Corp.
Coca-Cola Co.	Merck & Co.
DuPont Co.	Microsoft Corp. (NASDAQ)
Eastman Kodak Co.	Minnesota Mining and Manufacturing Co.
Exxon Mobil Corp.	Phillip Morris Cos.
General Electric Co.	Proctor and Gamble Co.
General Motors Corp.	SBC Communications
Home Depot	United Technologies Corp.
Honeywell International Inc.	Wal-Mart Stores Inc.
Hewlett-Packard Co.	Walt Disney Co.

---

[11] Information on all the Dow Jones Company averages is available on the Internet at http://averages.dowjones.com.

Originally, the DJIA was calculated by adding the stock prices of the original twelve firms and dividing by 12 (the number of original stocks). This calculation took place each day and allowed interested parties to compare stock price performance over time. However, adjustments had to be made periodically for non-economic events (e.g., stock splits that change a firm's stock price without affecting its overall value). Without this adjustment, after a stock split, the price of the affected firm's stock would drop precipitously, causing a drop in the DJIA. The drop in the average would give the impression that the market was dropping, when there was actually no change in value.

To account for stock splits and dividends greater than 10 percent, the DJIA uses an **adjusted divisor approach**.

To be an effective indicator, changes in the DJIA have to represent true economic changes (i.e., changes in value). To ensure this, Mr. Dow devised a method of adjusting the divisor (i.e., denominator) to account for noneconomic events, such as stock splits or stock dividends.[12]

Let's look at a very simplified example of this approach. We will assume there are only four stocks in the DJIA and their price histories are as follows:

Stocks

	A	B	C	D	DJIA
Day 1	20.00	15.00	20.00	30.00	21.25[b]
Day 2	21.00	16.00	18.00	29.00	21.00[c]
Day 3	12.00[a]	17.00	19.00	31.00	22.57[d]

[a] Stock A had a 2:1 stock split during day 3.

$$^{b}DJIA_1 = \frac{20 + 15 + 20 + 30}{4} = 21.25$$

$$^{c}DJIA_2 = \frac{21 + 16 + 18 + 29}{4} = 21.00$$

$$^{d}DJIA_3 = \frac{12 + 17 + 19 + 31}{3.5} = 22.57$$

[12] The divisor is adjusted for stock dividends or splits greater than 10 percent. A 10 percent stock dividend means the company sends you ten new shares for every 100 shares you already own, bringing your total to 110 shares. With a 10 percent stock split, you are sent 110 new shares to replace each 100 shares you hold, and the par value of the stock is adjusted. Par value is not adjusted with a stock dividend.

At the end of day one, the **closing prices** of the four stocks are added together and divided by four, resulting in a DJIA of 21.25. This figure represents the average price of the stocks at the end of day one. At the end of day two we see mixed results. Stock A is up $1.00, B is up $1.00, C is down $2.00 and D is down $1.00. By simply looking at the individual price movements it is very difficult to determine the general movement of the market, if any. Since there have been no non-economic events, the DJIA is calculated as for day one. The DJIA at the end of day two is 21.00, indicating a minor downward movement in the market.

On day three, we observe that stock B has increased $1.00, C has increased $1.00, and D has increased $2.00. Stock A appears to have dropped $9.00, but A has experienced a 2:1 stock split.[13] Theoretically, the stock split should affect only the price and par value of the stock, not the value of the firm (though under normal circumstances, changes in the price of a stock indicate changes in the market value of the company). However, if we calculate the DJIA without adjusting for the split, we get:

$$DJIA = \frac{12 + 17 + 19 + 31}{4} = 19.75$$

When observing a value of 19.75 for the DJIA, a casual observer would think the market is down. However, upon closer scrutiny, he would be somewhat perplexed. All the stocks in the average have increased in price except stock A, and the split caused the drop in A, not a drop in the market value of the firm. In fact, with a 2:1 split, the theoretical post-split price for A should be half of $21.00 or $10.50. Since A closed at $12.00, it actually closed up along with the other stocks!

To account for the split in stock A, we have to adjust the divisor before calculating DJIA. First, we use the day two DJIA value of 21.00 and adjust the price of A to its theoretically correct post-split price. Leaving the other stocks unchanged, we solve for the denominator that would leave the DJIA unchanged. This is done in the following way:

A **closing price** is the last recorded trade for the stock. It could be a buy (bid) or sell (ask).

---

[13] 2:1 (2 for 1) stock split means you receive two new shares to replace every old share you hold. For example, if you hold 100 shares with a market value of $50.00 each, your shares were worth a total of $5,000. After the split you will hold 200 shares but their price will be halved to account for the split. They will each be worth $25.00, so your wealth has not changed. Before, you held 100 shares of stock worth $50 per share, and now you hold 200 shares of stock worth $25 per share. In each case you hold $5,000 in stock.

$$DJIA_2 = 21.00 = \frac{10.50 + 16.00 + 18.00 + 29.00}{d'}$$

where d' is the new denominator (i.e., the denominator that would leave the DJIA average unchanged if A had split and all other prices remained unchanged).

Rearranging and solving for the new denominator, we get:

$$d' = \frac{10.50 + 16.00 + 18.00 + 29.00}{21.00} = 3.50$$

Using the closing prices for the day three and the adjusted divisor, the true value of the DJIA at the end of day three is:

$$DJIA_3 = \frac{12 + 17 + 19 + 31}{3.5} = 22.57$$

After adjusting the denominator to account for the split in stock A, we confirm that the DJIA has actually increased.

The DJIA is currently at 10,629.24 and the divisor is 0.15369402.[14] Obviously, there have been many adjustments made to the divisor over the years to account for stock splits and dividends as well as replacement of companies when they are acquired or removed from the index.[15] The divisor is listed every day in the third section of the *Wall Street Journal* under the charts and figures for the Dow Jones Industrial, Transportation, and Utilities Averages.

Other physical exchanges (those with a physical location and a trading floor) in the United States include the American Stock Exchange, the Arizona Stock Exchange, the Boston Stock Exchange, the Chicago Stock Exchange, the Cincinnati Stock Exchange, the Pacific Exchange, the Philadelphia Stock Exchange, and the San Diego Stock Exchange. International exchanges include the Australian Stock Exchange, the Budapest Stock Exchange, the London Stock Exchange, the Tokyo Stock Exchange, and many others throughout the world.[16]

[14] 11:00 A.M. Wednesday, April 18, 2001.

[15] Adjusting the divisor for replacing a stock is done exactly as it is for splits. In this case, the divisor is calculated for the previous day with the new stock's price in place of the stock being removed. The divisor typically gets smaller with each adjustment, but it will get larger if a stock is replaced with a higher-priced stock.

[16] For a complete listing of the more than 100 exchanges worldwide, see http://dir.yahoo.com/Business_and_Economy/Finance_and_Investment/Exchanges/Stock_Exchanges/.

The National Association of Securities Dealers Automated Quotation System (NASDAQ) was the world's first cyber-trading floor. NASDAQ, once referred to as the over-the-counter market, is actually a network of over 350,000 computers linked worldwide. Where listing on one of the national exchanges (e.g., NYSE or AMEX) was once considered a mark of distinction, many companies are now choosing to list on NASDAQ's National Market System (NMS) instead. The importance of NASDAQ is becoming evident also in the DJIA, where two NASDAQ-listed stocks, Microsoft and Intel, are now among the thirty stocks in the average. For complete information on NASDAQ and the NMS, visit www.NASDAQ.com.

Rather than purchasing memberships to trade on the NASDAQ, membership is achieved by subscription. *Level 1* subscription is information only. The subscriber member receives only representative prices of listed stocks, not bid and ask prices, which are typically delayed by 15 minutes. *Level 2* members act as brokers. They receive information and can trade at live bid-ask quotes, but they are not allowed to enter their own quotes. *Level 3* subscribers are **market makers**.

> **Market makers** stand ready to take the other side of any order.

Making the market means the subscriber/member is required to post bid and ask prices on the network. A **bid**, also called an offer, is the price the market maker (dealer) will pay for the security. The market maker sells at the **ask**. The difference between the two prices, referred to as the **bid-ask spread**, represents the market maker's profit.

By standing ready to take the other side of any buy or sell order, the market maker ensures a smooth running market for their stocks (e.g., if the market maker receives many buy orders and there are few or no corresponding sell orders, he will deliver stocks from his inventory to fill the orders). The market maker is required to post the transaction on the network so the investing public knows of it. Trading on the NASDAQ system can take place almost instantaneously. Often the broker will know the price at which the trade took place while the investor is still on the telephone.

> A stock listed on NASDAQ can have an unlimited number of market makers.

In contrast, the NYSE utilizes a **specialist** system, in which each stock is allocated to one specialist. Members acting as specialists can trade only in their assigned stocks at a specific location on the trading floor called a **trading post**, where **floor brokers** come to present orders for their customers. In addition to the floor brokers who handle public

> On the NYSE, the **specialist** acts as a market maker. Every stock on the NYSE has only one specialist.

> On the NYSE, **floor brokers** present orders for customers at the specialist's **trading post**.

A **market order** is an order to buy or sell at the best available price.

A **limit order** is an order to buy at a price below the current market price or sell at a price higher than the current market price.

A **stop order** is a defensive trading strategy. It is used to buy above the market or sell below the market.

orders, **floor traders** trade their own accounts and help the floor brokers when asked.

The most common type of trade is known as a **market order**, an order from a customer to trade at the best possible price. Brokers present bids to buy and offers to sell by open outcry to any interested party at the trading post. In this fashion, floor brokers and others among the trading crowd have the opportunity to participate, thus facilitating the competitive pricing of stocks. When the highest bid (buy) meets the lowest ask (sell), a trade is executed and the customer's order is filled.

Specialists manage this auction process by electronically quoting and recording current bid and ask prices for the stocks assigned to them. This enables current price information to be transmitted worldwide, keeping all market participants informed of the total supply and demand for any particular NYSE-listed stock.

According to the NYSE, the role of the specialist can be divided into five vital functions: to act as agents, catalysts, and auctioneers; to stabilize prices; and to provide capital.[17]

Act as Agents. One of the specialist's jobs is to execute orders for floor brokers. A floor broker may get an order from a customer who only wants to buy a stock at a price lower than the current market price or sell it at a price higher than the current market price. In such cases, the broker may ask the specialist to hold the order, known as a **limit order**, and execute it if and when the price of the stock reaches the level specified by the customer. Limit orders are considered aggressive because they will be filled only at the specified price, which is always better than the market price when the order is placed. By holding limit orders, the specialist acts as an agent for the floor broker.

Likewise, the specialist acts as an agent by holding more defensive orders called **stop orders**, or **stop-loss orders**. These are orders to sell below or buy above the current market price. Let's assume you hold a stock, which has appreciated greatly while you've held it. To protect your profit, you can submit an order to sell the stock if it drops below a certain price. Once the stock falls to the stop price, the order is executed. The stop order is considered a defensive trade, since it is used for protection rather than for aggressive trading.

[17] Source: http://www.nyse.com.

Act as Catalysts. Specialists serve as the contact point between brokers with buy and sell orders in the NYSE's two-way auction market. In this respect, the specialists act as catalysts, bringing buyers and sellers together.

Act as Auctioneers. At the start of each trading day, specialists establish a fair market price for each of their stocks. They base that price on the supply and demand for the stock as indicated by the number of buy and sell limit orders and the limit prices. A large number of limit orders grouped around a certain price indicate what the market anticipates for that stock. For example, many sell orders at a price below the market would indicate the investors feel the stock is overpriced. Throughout the day, specialists quote the current bids and offers in their stocks to other brokers.

Stabilize Prices. Specialists are also called upon to maintain "orderly markets" in their assigned stocks. That is, they ensure that trading in their stocks moves smoothly throughout the day, with minimal price fluctuations between trades. Large gaps in trading prices creates uncertainty around the stock's true value, so the specialist will trade intermittently at prices in between those on the limit orders.

Provide Capital. Specialists act as a market maker. If buy orders temporarily outnumber sell orders, or if sell orders outnumber buy orders, the specialist is required to use his firm's own capital to minimize the imbalance. This is accomplished by buying or selling against the trend of the market until a price is reached at which public supply and demand are once again in balance. Specialists act as *dealers* in this capacity. However, specialists actually participate in only about 10 percent of all shares traded. The rest of the time, orders clear without the participation of specialists.

Debt Markets

In addition to the markets for equity capital, there is an extensive secondary market for various types of debt securities, which are issued by corporations, states, municipalities, and federal governments. Long-term borrowing by the U.S. Treasury is by Treasury Notes (T-Notes) with original maturities from one to ten years, and Treasury Bonds (T-Bonds) with original maturities from ten to thirty years. They are issued in denominations starting at $1,000, pay interest semiannually, and return the principal at the stated maturity.

With U.S. government **strips**, the interest and principal payments of notes or bonds are stripped apart and sold individually.

A fairly new concept is the **strip**. If you visualize the cash flows associated with T-Notes and T-Bonds, you will see a stream of coupon payments and a relatively large payment (i.e., the principal) at the end. For example, a six percent, 20-year T-Bond would pay $60 per year ($30 every six months) and return the $1,000 principal (face value) in twenty years. With strips, all the payments are "stripped" apart and sold separately. Investors can buy individual coupons, a specified set of coupons, or even the principal payment. Each individual cash flow, whether coupon or principal, becomes a **zero coupon bond**.

A **zero coupon bond** pays no interest. It is purchased at a discount from face value and the face value is paid at maturity.

Zero coupon bonds (also known as **zeros**) are pure discount instruments. You buy the zero at a discount from the face value and receive the face value at maturity, with no interest payments between the purchase and maturity dates. For example, let's assume that we are buying a $1,000 principal payment which has been stripped from a T-Bond and will be received in one year. If the rate on this zero is six percent, you will pay $943.40 and in one year receive $1,000. The $943.40 grows to $1,000 over the year, and your return would be six percent as illustrated below:

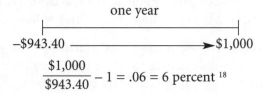

$$\frac{\$1,000}{\$943.40} - 1 = .06 = 6 \text{ percent } [18]$$

An advantage to zeros is that interest rate risk is virtually eliminated. Interest rate risk consists of two types of risk: **price sensitivity** and **reinvestment risk**. When interest rates rise (fall), the prices of fixed income securities fall (rise). However, reinvestment of the interest payments is made at the new rate. If rates rise (fall), the price of the bond falls (rises), but the coupons you receive are invested at a higher (lower) rate.

[18] We have simplified the pricing of this zero-coupon bond by using an annual discounting assumption. In the real world, a semiannual discounting convention would be used and this bond would be priced at $942.60. In the next chapter, we will illustrate the use of a financial calculator to make these types of computations. The keystrokes for this example on a TI BA II Plus would be: 2 → [N], 3 → [I/Y], 1,000 → [FV], [CPT] → [PV] → 942.596.

If held until maturity, pure discount instruments (e.g., strips) should pay the **stated** or **nominal rate** promised. This would make it appear that interest rate risk has been eliminated. However, if inflation changes during the holding period, the actual real return will be different from the promised real return. Let's consider the following equation:

$$R_i \cong RR + IP$$

where R_i is the **expected return** on investment, RR is the real rate of interest (i.e., the true increase in buying power after adjusting for the effects of inflation),[19] and IP is the premium added for *expected* inflation.

The expected return is the return implied by the price paid and the amount to be received at the end of the holding period. For example, the strip above had a price of $943.40, which implied an expected return of six percent. Had the price been different, the expected return would have been different, also. For example, if the price of the $1,000, one-year strip had been $952.38, the expected return would be:

one year

$-$952.38 \longrightarrow $1,000$

$$\frac{\$1,000}{\$952.38} - 1 = .05 = 5 \text{ percent}$$

Returning to our original example, let's assume that at the beginning of the year you expect inflation to be two percent for the year. With a nominal rate of six percent, your expected real return (RR) is four percent (i.e., 6 percent – 2 percent = 4 percent). If at the end of the holding period, inflation turns out to have been five percent over the year instead of the expected two percent, the actual real return (RR) would only be one percent (i.e., 6 percent – 5 percent = 1 percent).

As long as they are held until final maturity, U.S. government strips are essentially riskless. Strips and U.S. Treasury Bills (T-Bills) (also discussed in Section 4, Money Market Securities), protect the investor from every type of risk, *except the risk of changes in inflation.*

The **nominal rate** of interest is the rate promised or stated on the security.

The **expected return** is the return implied by the price paid and the amount to be received at the end of the holding period.

---

[19] The real rate of interest, RR, is the return on risk-free investments when there is no inflation (there is no risk or inflation premium). RR can also be called the "pure time value of money" or "compensation for delayed consumption."

For example, assume you purchased the T-Bond strip above for $943.40. Instead of holding it until maturity in twelve months, you find you must sell it in six months. The return on the strip has changed to eight percent, so the prevailing price would be:

$$\frac{\$1,000}{1 + \frac{.08}{2}} = \$961.54 \text{[20]}$$

And your return for holding the strip for six months is:

$$\frac{\$961.54}{\$943.40} - 1 = 1.92 \text{ percent}$$

When you originally purchased the strip, your *expected* twelve-month return was six percent, which would imply a six-month return of three percent. However, since the return demanded by the market on the strip increased after you bought it, its price was pushed down and your actual six-month return was only 1.92 percent. This demonstrates that the only time the nominal return is guaranteed is when you buy the strip (or any pure discount instrument) and hold it until it matures. If you must sell the security before it matures, your return is subject to interest rate risk.

U.S. T-Notes and T-Bonds are issued[21] regularly with initial maturities of 2, 5, 10, and 30 years. Although not strictly forbidden, U.S. T-Notes and T-Bonds have not been callable since those issued in 1984. They are quoted in the *Wall Street Journal* and other financial publications at a percentage of par or face value. For instance, you might see a 20-year T-Bond quoted at 97.27. The numbers to the left of the decimal (a dash may be used in place of the decimal) represent percent, in this case 97 percent. The numbers to the right of the decimal (or dash) are 32nds of a percent. This bond is therefore quoted at 97 and 27/32 percent of par (97.84375 percent). Thus, a Treasury bond with a $1,000 face value would sell for $978.44 (.9784375 × $1,000 = $978.44).

Other fixed income capital instruments include those issued by U.S. federal agencies to support their lending and/or mortgage buying operations. In 1938, the U.S. government established the **Federal National Mortgage Association**, (FNMA or "Fannie Mae"), to

---

[20] Since there are six months remaining until the strip matures, the price of the strip is the face value discounted at the six-month rate, which is 4 percent.

[21] The Treasury actually auctions its debt securities. See F. J. Fabozzi, *Fixed Income Analysis for the Chartered Financial Analyst® Program* (Frank J. Fabozzi Associates, 2000), 68–69.

increase the availability of mortgage money by creating a secondary market for home mortgage loans. These mortgage associations purchase mortgages from lenders, package them into securities, and sell them to investors. In 1954, Fannie Mae became a "mixed-ownership" corporation owned partly by private stockholders. In 1968, U.S. President Lyndon Johnson signed legislation amending Fannie Mae's Charter, which established Fannie Mae as a private, shareholder-owned company. Fannie Mae stock was listed on the New York and Pacific Exchanges in 1970.

In 1968, Fannie Mae was partitioned into two separate entities: the **Government National Mortgage Association** (GNMA or "Ginnie Mae"), and Fannie Mae. Ginnie Mae remains a wholly owned government association catering to low and moderate-income buyers. **The Federal Home Loan Mortgage Corporation** (FHLMC or "Freddie Mac") is a stockholder-owned corporation, created in 1970 and chartered by the U.S. Congress to increase the supply of funds to homebuyers.

The single largest supplier of home mortgage credit in the U.S. is the partnership of the **Federal Home Loan Banks** (FHL Banks). FHL Banks are privately capitalized, government-sponsored agencies that were created by Congress in 1932. The FHL Bank System consists of twelve regional banks and is regulated by the Federal Housing Finance Board. The mission of the FHL Banks is to support residential mortgage lending by their members/stockholders. Eligible members include commercial banks, savings institutions, credit unions, and insurance companies.

Cities and municipalities borrow publicly by selling municipal bonds. These bonds, referred to as **munis**, are exempt from federal income taxes (and in some cases state and local income taxes). For example, a municipal bond issued by a city in Ohio is typically exempt from Ohio state income taxes as well as federal taxes. Because of differences in tax treatment between municipal bonds and other bonds, comparing such investments should be conducted on an after-tax basis.

> Due to varying tax rates and tax treatments, investments should be compared by their **after-tax yields**.

Let's consider an investor trying to decide between a fully taxable corporate bond and a totally tax-free muni. If the corporate bond pays 10 percent and the muni pays 7.5 percent, the investor might actually be better off with the muni. Assume the investor is in the 33 percent marginal tax bracket. His after-tax yield on the corporate bond is 6.7 percent [i.e., 10 percent − .33(10 percent) = 6.7 percent]. His after-tax yield on the muni is 7.5 percent, since it is tax-free. If the muni is otherwise equivalent to the corporate bond (meaning that from a risk perspective the two investments are equivalent), it is actually a better investment for this particular investor. Of course the after-tax yield is dependent upon both the before-tax yield and the investor's tax rate.

Many corporations have issued long-term debt. Even though most long-term debt is sold privately, there are bond issues listed on the NYSE and the AMEX as well as a small number of NASDAQ-listed bonds.

SECTION 4: MONEY MARKETS

Short-term, low-risk debt securities are traded in the **money markets**. As the name implies, securities traded in the money markets are *nearly* "money" or cash insofar as they are extremely **liquid** (i.e., they can be bought or sold very quickly at their fair market value). Because of their short-term nature, they are not as susceptible to interest-rate risk as longer-lived debt securities. The biggest "players" in the money market are institutional investors, because money market securities are typically traded in very large denominations. Individuals can invest in the money market by buying money market mutual funds.

U.S. T-Bills are by far the most actively traded money market instrument. Individual investors can buy T-Bills from government securities dealers, at auction, from Federal Reserve Banks, brokers, or financial institutions, or through **Treasury Direct** in $1,000 denominations up to $1,000,000. Institutional investors can purchase T-Bills in much greater denominations through government securities dealers or government auctions.

The following is a representative T-Bill quote as it might have appeared in the *Wall Street Journal*. Data in the quote would be closing figures for the previous trading day (data in a Monday quote are for the previous Friday).

Maturity	Days to Maturity	Bid	Asked	Chg.	Ask Yld.
June xx, 'XX	120	3.73	3.71	+0.01	3.81

Sidebar:

Securities with initial maturities less than one year are traded in the **money markets**.

All **money market instruments** have short maturities, low risk, and high liquidity.

Treasury Direct is the Internet site maintained by the U.S. Treasury to facilitate trading in U.S. government securities. See http://www.publicdebt.treas.gov.

The **maturity** of the bill is the day the bill matures or expires (i.e., the date the Treasury sends holders the face value of the bill through Treasury Direct or through a commercial book entry, effectively an electronic transfer to your bank account). Treasury Direct also allows the holder to reinvest or roll over the principal via the internet. If a holder lives near a government securities dealer or Federal Reserve Bank, he or she can simply take it there for redemption.

Due to the **skip day settlement process**, it is assumed transactions will clear two business days later. The T-Bill quoted above matures in 120 days. If you compared the actual date of the quote with the maturity date, it would appear two days longer than the stated maturity in days.

> T-Bills are quoted using the **bank discount yield**. It differs from the true yield because it is a discount from face value and it assumes a 360-day year.

As with other dealer-handled securities, T-Bill prices are quoted in **bid** and **ask** prices. These quotes differ from conventional price-based bid and ask quotes and are stated as a percentage discount, the **bank discount**, from face value. Also, the number of days in one year is assumed to be 360. Of course, the bid represents the price dealers will pay for a bill, and the ask is the price at which they will sell to you. Note that the bid exceeds the ask due to the inverse relationship between price and yield. In the quotes above, the bid price is lower than the ask price.

Chg. is the change from the previous day's bid discount. This bill's previous day closing bid discount was 3.72.

> The **bond-equivalent yield** is the true expected yield on a T-Bill. It is based upon price paid and a 365-day year.

Ask Yld. is the **bond-equivalent yield** or the actual yield on the T-Bill if purchased at the quoted ask discount, based on a 365-day year.

Let's assume you can actually trade at the closing figures in the quote above. Prices are calculated as follows:

Price = Face Value – Dollar Discount

Dollar discount is the discount off the face value based upon the stated bank discount rate. This is represented by:

$$\text{Dollar Discount} = r_b(FV) \frac{n}{360}$$

r_b is the bank discount rate (bid or ask) stated on an annual basis (i.e., the discount from face value if the bill was to be held for a year).

FV is the face value of the bill (we will assume $1,000).

n is the number of days until maturity (360 is the number of days in a year for pricing T-Bills).

$\frac{n}{360}$ is the holding period stated as a fraction of one year. It is the portion of the bank discount received based upon the actual holding period.

If you want to purchase the bill, the price you pay is based upon the (portion received of the) **ask** discount of 3.71 percent off the face value of the bill.[22]

Price = Face Value – Dollar Discount (ask)

$$= \$1,000 - .0371(1,000)\frac{120}{360}$$

$$= \$1,000 - 37.10(.3333)$$

$$= \$1,000 - \$12.37 = \$987.63$$

You would receive a dollar discount of $12.37 and pay $987.63 for the bill. When the bill matures in 120 days, you would redeem it or receive electronically the $1,000 face value, and your annualized return will be:

$$\frac{\$12.37}{\$987.63} \times \frac{365}{120} = .038096 = 3.81\%$$

You have probably noticed this is the **Ask Yld.** (i.e., bond-equivalent yield) from the quote. It is different from the **ask discount** for two primary reasons. First, the ask discount is a percentage of face value, while the ask yield is a percentage of price paid. Next, the actual yield is based upon a calendar of 365 days (or 366 days for a leap year). Let's take a closer look at how we calculated the Ask Yld.

The return on any investment can be calculated as:

$$\text{Holding Period Return} = \frac{V_1 + \overset{\text{Cash}}{\underset{\text{Received}}{\text{Flows}}} - V_0}{V_0}$$

---

[22] Since the bill has 120 days remaining, you receive 1/3 of the annual bank discount.

V_0 and V_1 are the values of the investment at the beginning and end of the holding period, respectively. The **holding period yield** is the change in value as a percentage of the original value (i.e., the price you paid for the investment) over the period of time the investment was held.

The change in the T-Bill's value over the holding period is the face value minus the price you paid or the **dollar discount**. By dividing the dollar discount by the original price, we obtain the return for the holding period, which in this case is 120 days. By convention, we state the returns in annual terms. In this example, we multiply the 120-day return by the number of 120-day periods in one year, $\frac{365}{120}$.

Let's now assume you already hold the T-Bill and want to sell it to a dealer. The price the dealer will pay you for the T-Bill is based upon the bid discount, but otherwise the price calculation is identical.

> Price = Face Value – Dollar Discount (bid)
>
> $$= \$1,000 - .0373(1,000)\,\frac{120}{360}$$
>
> $$= \$1,000 - 37.30(.3333)$$
>
> $$= \$1,000 - 12.43 = \$987.57$$

Liquidity, low risk, and short maturity are characteristics of all money market instruments. Some other popular money market instruments include certificates of deposit (CDs), commercial paper, banker's acceptances, Eurodollars, Repos, and Federal Funds. Most of these are listed daily in the *Wall Street Journal* in a column called "Money Rates."

CDs are short-term time deposits with commercial banks. They are available in almost any denomination and usually have maturities from 90 days to one year (although CDs can be purchased in multi-year maturities, these longer-lived CDs are not technically money market instruments). There is typically a penalty for early withdrawal of the funds in a CD.

The **holding period yield** is the total change in value over the period divided by the price paid.

Certificates of Deposits (CDs) are short-term time deposits with commercial banks.

Commercial paper is a short-term IOU issued by strong, creditworthy corporations.

Commercial paper is a short-term security issued by a strong, credit-worthy corporation. They are used with maturities up to 270 days (to avoid SEC registration requirements) and are noncollateralized. Since they are short-term, very liquid, and very low risk, there is an extensive market for commercial paper. For example, if a firm finds itself with a temporary excess amount of cash, the firm can buy commercial paper issued by another firm, hold it for the desired time period, and resell it in the commercial paper market. The holding period can be anywhere from a few days to several months. In the same fashion, a firm with a short-term need for cash can sell commercial paper.

Bankers' acceptances are short-term agreements with an importer's bank that guarantee payments of the exporter's invoice.

Bankers' acceptances are utilized in international trade. They are short-term agreements with an importer's bank that guarantee payment of the exporter's invoice. For example, if a U.S. company wants to do business with a company in a less-developed nation, the U.S. firm (the exporter) would have the other firm (the importer) procure a guarantee in the form of a banker's acceptance. This eliminates the credit risk associated with the transaction. Of course, the exporter and importer also have to agree on exchange terms (such as whether the importer must pay in U.S. dollars or local currency).[23]

Eurodollars are U.S. dollars on deposit in foreign banks.

Eurodollars are actually U.S. dollars in foreign countries. Due to its universal acceptance, the U.S. dollar is widely used in international trade, so much so that a tremendous amount of U.S. currency is actually held by foreign banks and companies and used as a medium of exchange. In the 1940s, the Soviet Union had a poor international trade credit reputation. To overcome this problem, they bought U.S. dollars with gold and placed them in European banks, where they earned interest and could be used to pay foreign debts. Other nations did likewise, and the Eurodollar market was created. Even though they are denominated in U.S. dollars, Eurodollars are held in foreign banks and are not subject to the regulations of the U.S. banking system. This enables the foreign banks to pay higher rates of interest on Eurodollars than rates available in the United States.

---

[23] In either case, the U.S. firm would probably have to have U.S. dollars. In some cases, when a U.S. firm does a great deal of trade in another country, it might actually keep an inventory of the foreign currency. This is obviously the case with a foreign subsidiary of a U.S. firm. For a thorough discussion of exchange rates and foreign exchange, see Gwartney, Stroup, and Sobel, *Economics: Private and Public Choice, 9E* (The Dryden Press, 2000).

There are extensive **spot** and **forward** markets for Eurodollars, and time deposits (like CDs) can be as short as overnight to several months. Interest rates on Eurodollars are typically tied to the **London Interbank Offered Rate** (**LIBOR**). LIBOR is the rate offered by the largest London banks to their best customers.

Repo (**RP**) is short for **repurchase agreement**, which is a short-term loan collateralized by marketable securities, such as common or preferred stock, money market instruments, or Treasury securities. Institutional investors, states, and local governments use the RP market as a means to invest short-term excess cash at very low risk. Rather than liquidate inventories of short-term marketable securities and repurchase them later, firms with a short-term need for cash use the securities as collateral to borrow in the RP market. As with commercial paper, there is an extensive secondary RP market.

> A **Repo**, or repurchase agreement, is a short-term loan collateralized by marketable securities, such as common or preferred stock, money market instruments, or Treasury securities.

Federal funds is the name given to the amount of cash a financial institution must keep on deposit at its regional Federal Reserve Bank in the United States. Larger banks also maintain federal funds deposits at correspondent banks throughout the world to facilitate the immediate transfer of funds among banks for very large transactions. Banks with short-term excess federal funds can also loan (i.e., transfer by journal entry) federal funds to banks with a short-term deficit. Due to its nature of being *immediate money*, there is an extensive federal funds market and trillions of dollars may be exchanged in a given day.

> **Federal funds** are the cash a financial institution must keep on deposit at the Federal Reserve Bank in its region of the United States.

CHAPTER SUMMARY

Learning Objective 1: *To understand the differences between direct, broker, and dealer markets and between spot, forward, and futures markets.*

A. In a **direct market**, the buyer and seller contact one another directly.
   1. Benefits include the buyer's ability to inspect the product before purchasing it.
   2. The primary disadvantage to direct markets is the requirement for the buyer and seller to find one another. An example of a direct market includes selling a house or automobile "by owner."
B. In a **broker market**, the broker facilitates the meeting of the buyer and seller.
   1. For a fee, the broker will advertise and otherwise facilitate the purchase or sale.
   2. The buyer and seller need not actually meet.
   3. The broker does not take an ownership interest in the product being sold. Examples of a broker market include the following:
      a. Real estate transactions.
      b. Securities brokers.
C. In a **dealer market**, a dealer facilitates the transaction by purchasing ownership in the product and reselling.
   1. Dealers can sell their goods and services at a central location or through any other means, such as the Internet.
   2. Examples of a dealer market include the following:
      a. Government and corporate securities dealers.
      b. Clothing, food, and other retail stores.
      c. Financial intermediaries.
D. In **spot markets**, securities, commodities, and other goods are traded for immediate delivery.
   1. Spot prices are determined by the existing supply of and demand for the product.
   2. In financial spot markets, investors buy currencies, securities, and commodities for two- to three-day delivery.
E. In **forward markets**, traders agree to transact at a future date at a specified price.
   1. Contracts are customized to fit the needs of the buyer and seller.

Schweser
Study Program™

2. Although extensive, forward markets are not as complete or as liquid as futures markets.

F. In **futures markets**, participants trade standardized contracts.

1. Contracts specify the commodity, currency, or financial instrument and the following information:
   a. Maturity/delivery date.
   b. Delivery location.
   c. Grade or other specifications for the product.
2. Futures contracts are maintained by a **clearing corporation**.
   a. The clearing corporation makes sure each side of the contract fulfills the terms of the agreement.
   b. Futures contracts are **marked to market** (i.e., price changes are reflected in account value) every day at the **settlement price**.
3. Futures contracts are extremely liquid and are often used for hedging risk.

Learning Objective 2: *To understand primary markets and the role of the investment banker.*

A. Corporations, governments, and municipalities raise capital in **primary markets**.
   1. Primary markets are where new securities are issued.
   2. The issuing firm or organization receives the net proceeds from the sale.
B. In a **public offering**, organizations sell securities to the general public.
   1. The securities must be registered with the Securities and Exchange Commission (SEC).
   2. In an **underwritten public offering**, an **investment banking firm** buys the securities and resells them.
      a. The **underwriter spread** is the difference between the price the investment banker pays for the securities and the price at which they are sold.
      b. **Flotation costs** are the total costs of selling the securities, including underwriter spread and legal, accounting, and printing fees, which can total from 5 to 30 percent of the proceeds from the sale.

C. In a **private placement**, the investment banking firm acts as a broker. The issue (usually bonds) is sold to a small number of large investors.
   1. The firm receives the proceeds faster than with a public offering.
   2. It is not as expensive as a public offering.
   3. It is not registered with the SEC.
   4. It is not as liquid as a public offering.

Learning Objective 3: *To understand secondary markets and the securities traded there.*

A. In **secondary markets**, investors trade securities among themselves.
   1. As a rule, the firm is not involved in secondary markets.
   2. Firms sometimes buy their own stock or the securities of other firms in the secondary markets.
B. The best-known secondary markets deal in **equity** securities. They are traded **over the counter** and on over 100 **floor exchanges** worldwide.
C. The **New York Stock Exchange** (**NYSE**) is the most famous floor exchange.
   1. Firms must meet rigid criteria to be listed on the NYSE and other exchanges.
   2. Only members can trade on the NYSE. Memberships, known as "seats," are purchased.
   3. The NYSE utilizes a **specialist** system.
      a. Every listed stock has one specialist.
      b. Specialists are members of the NYSE.
      c. Acting as brokers, they provide a means for the buyer and seller to meet and present **market orders** (i.e., orders to trade at the best possible price).
      d. Acting as dealers, they hold inventories of their assigned stocks.
      e. They trade only in their assigned stocks.
   4. The specialist holds the **limit book** for all their assigned stocks.
      a. **Limit orders** are orders to buy below the current market price or sell above the current market price.

    b. **Stop orders** (defensive limit orders) are orders to buy above the current market price or sell below the current market price.

D. **NASDAQ**, the **over the counter market**, is the most famous "cyber trading floor."

  1. Over 350,000 computers linked worldwide.

  2. Listing criteria are less strict than with NYSE.

  3. Membership is by level of subscription.

    a. A Level 1 subscription is for information only.

    b. A Level 2 subscription allows trading at bid and ask prices.

    c. A Level 3 subscription allows **market makers**, similar to specialists on the NYSE, to enter their own bid and ask price quotes.

    d. Individual stocks can have an unlimited number of market-makers.

E. There is an extensive secondary market for **debt securities** issued by corporations, states, municipalities, and federal governments.

  1. The U.S. Treasury borrows in maturities from 91 days to 30 years.

    a. T-Bills have initial maturities from 91 days to one year.

    b. T-Notes have initial maturities of one to ten years.

    c. T-Bonds have initial maturities of ten to 30 years.

  2. T-Bills are **pure discount instruments**.

    a. They are purchased at a discount from face value and pay face value at maturity.

    b. T-Bills are priced using the bank discount method.

    c. Individuals can purchase T-Bills at the ask discount.

    d. Individuals can sell T-Bills at the bid discount.

    e. T-Bills always pay the nominal or stated rate as long as they are held until maturity.

    f. T-Bills are the most heavily traded money market instruments.

    g. The only risk associated with T-bills is inflation risk (if held to final maturity).

  3. **Strips** are T-Note and T-Bond interest and principal payments, which have been stripped apart and sold separately.

    a. This creates individual pure discount bonds or **zeros**.

    b. They are purchased at a discount from face value and pay face value at maturity.

F. Debt and other fixed income securities are subject to **interest rate risk**.

   1. When interest rates rise, the prices of fixed income securities fall, but interest payments are reinvested at higher rates.

   2. When interest rates fall, the prices of fixed income securities rise but interest payments are reinvested at lower rates.

   3. In either case, the actual return earned from holding the fixed income instrument will be different from the expected return when the instrument was initially purchased.

G. There is also an extensive market for U.S. federal agency debt instruments.

   1. The **Federal National Mortgage Association** (FNMA or "Fannie Mae") was created in 1938 to develop a secondary market for mortgages.

      a. This increased the amount of mortgage money available.

      b. Fannie Mae is privately owned.

      c. Fannie Mae stock is listed on the NYSE and Pacific Exchange.

   2. The **Government National Mortgage Association** (GNMA or "Ginnie Mae") was created as an offshoot of Fannie Mae in 1968. Ginnie Mae is wholly owned by the federal government and caters to low and moderate-income homebuyers.

   3. The **Federal Home Loan Mortgage Association** (FHLMA or "Freddie Mac") was chartered by the U.S. Congress in 1970 and is stockholder-owned.

   4. The **Federal Home Loan Banks** (FHL Banks) are the largest supplier of mortgage credit in the United States, composed of twelve regional banks and regulated by the Federal Housing Finance Board.

Learning Objective 4: *To understand the most active markets in the world, the money markets, and some of the instruments traded in them.*

Money Market securities are short-lived, low risk, very liquid instruments.

   1. **U.S. T-Bills** are the most heavily traded money market instruments. T-Bills are sold through auction by competitive or noncompetitive bid in denominations from $1,000 to $1,000,000.

2. **Commercial paper** is uncollateralized, short-term (up to 270 days) borrowing by very large, creditworthy firms.
   a. Firms with short-term excess cash buy commercial paper.
   b. Firms with a short-term need for cash can sell commercial paper.
3. **Bankers' acceptances** are used in international trade. They are short-term agreements with an importer's bank, which guarantee payment of an exporter's invoice.
4. **Eurodollars** are U.S. dollars held in foreign banks.
   a. Eurodollars are not subject to U.S. banking regulations.
   b. Eurodollars are used extensively for international trade.
   c. The rate on Eurodollar CDs and bonds is typically tied to the London Interbank Offered Rate (LIBOR).
5. **Repurchase agreements** (**Repos**) are short-term loans collateralized by marketable securities.
   a. Rather than sell marketable securities when they need cash temporarily, firms can use them as collateral.
   b. The securities are sold with a preset repurchase date and price.
6. **Federal funds** represent the amount of money banks must keep at the Federal Reserve Bank in their region.
   a. Many larger U.S. banks also keep federal funds at international correspondent banks to facilitate immediate transactions.
   b. Banks with short-term excess cash can loan federal funds.
   c. Banks with a short-term deficit can borrow.

PRACTICE QUESTIONS

1. Which of the following is the primary **difference** between a broker market and a dealer market?

    A. In a broker market, the buyer and seller must meet face-to-face.
    B. Dealers are legally prevented from taking possession of the product.
    C. In a broker market, the broker actually takes ownership of the product.
    D. In the dealer market, the dealer actually takes ownership of the product.

2. A farmer with an entire harvest of corn would **most likely** sell it in the:

    A. futures markets.
    B. spot market.
    C. forward markets.
    D. farmer's market.

3. Marking to market means:

    A. settling all contracts at the end of the trading day at a settlement price.
    B. being sure all contracts are constantly at the market price.
    C. that the buyer and seller are forced to buy or sell at the market price.
    D. writing up the prices of all contracts.

4. Which of the following is **true** concerning primary and secondary markets?

    A. Stocks of larger more established firms are traded only in primary markets.
    B. Stocks of newer, smaller firms are traded only in secondary markets.
    C. Bonds are traded only in secondary markets.
    D. Firms issue new securities in primary markets.

5. Which of the following is **not** an example of flotation costs?

    A. The costs of printing stock certificates.
    B. The underwriter spread.
    C. Legal and accounting fees.
    D. Preemptive costs.

6. Which of the following exchanges is **most likely** to have the strictest listing criteria?

    A. NYSE.
    B. AMEX.
    C. NASDAQ.
    D. The Pacific Exchange.

7. Which of the following have initial maturities of **less** than one year?

    A. U.S. Treasury Notes.
    B. U.S. Treasury Bonds.
    C. U.S. Treasury Bills.
    D. All can be issued with an initial life less than one year.

8. Treasury bills:

    A. have an initial life from one year to ten years.
    B. are subject to (coupon) reinvestment risk.
    C. have initial lives of ten to thirty years.
    D. always yield the nominal rate if held to maturity.

9. Which of the following would **not** be a money market security?

    A. U.S. Treasury Bill.
    B. Corporate bond.
    C. Commercial paper.
    D. Banker's acceptance.

10. Convergence is:

    A. the futures price approaching the spot price.
    B. members of the "Road Show" approaching prospective buyers of a large private placement.
    C. the futures and forward prices approaching each other.
    D. the bidding process at the trading post on the NYSE.

11. In a fully underwritten public offering of common stock, the underwriter:

    A. faces the most risk.
    B. only promises best efforts in selling the issue.
    C. spread is the difference between the price the investors pay for the stock and the flotation costs.
    D. guarantees all the shares will be sold but not the price the issuing firm will receive.

12. The duties of the specialist include:

    A. acting as an agent for the issuing firm.
    B. stabilizing stock prices.
    C. making loans to floor brokers.
    D. representing only the sellers in stock transactions.

13. Which of the following types of stock orders would be considered the **most aggressive**?

    A. Market order.
    B. Stop order.
    C. Limit order.
    D. Stop-loss order.

14. By convention, all holding period returns are:

    A. stated in terms of one year.
    B. rounded to the nearest tenth of one percent.
    C. stated for whatever period they are calculated.
    D. stated in whole numbers.

Use the following information to answer questions 15–17.

Maturity	Days to Maturity	Bid	Asked	Ask Chg.	Yld.
June xx, 'XX	140	3.73	3.71	+0.01	??

15. Assuming an investor could trade at the discounts in the quote, what would he have to pay for the T-Bill?

    A. $962.70.
    B. $962.90.
    C. $985.49.
    D. $985.57.

16. Assuming an investor could trade at the discounts in the quote, what would he receive from selling the T-Bill?

    A. $985.49.
    B. $985.57.
    C. $962.70.
    D. $962.90.

17. What is the ask yield (bond-equivalent yield) for the T-Bill in the quote?

    A. 3.71 percent.
    B. 3.73 percent.
    C. 3.82 percent.
    D. 3.91 percent.

18. Which of the following represents the taxable yield that would be equivalent to a 6 percent, tax-free yield, if an investor's tax rate is 35 percent?

    A. 4.88 percent.
    B. 6.00 percent.
    C. 8.44 percent.
    D. 9.23 percent.

19. Six months ago an investor bought a bond for $865. During the last six months she received a $40 interest (coupon) payment. If she sells the bond today for $875, what is the holding period yield?

    A. 5.78 percent.
    B. 10.44 percent.
    C. 11.56 percent.
    D. 11.89 percent.

ANSWERS AND SOLUTIONS

1. D. In a dealer market, the dealer actually takes ownership of the product at one point. In a broker market, the broker brings the buyer and seller together but does not take ownership of the product.

2. B. Since the farmer actually has the harvest of corn, he will sell in the spot market. He may have used futures to hedge part of his risk while the corn was growing.

3. A. At the end of the day, all futures contracts are marked to market. It is the process of settling all futures contracts each day at the settlement price. The seller and buyer of the contract recognize profits and losses every day.

4. D. Firms sell new securities in primary markets and actually receive the net proceeds from the sale. Seasoned securities (previously issued) are traded in secondary markets by investors.

5. D. Flotation costs are all the costs associated with selling securities. This includes printing costs, legal and accounting fees, underwriter's spread, and any other cost the firm might experience.

6. A. NYSE is likely to have the strictest listing criteria.

7. C. T-Bills have maturities of 90 to 360 days.

8. D. Since it pays no coupons, a U.S. Treasury Bill will always yield its nominal or stated rate, as long as it is held to maturity. However, this does not protect the investor from inflation risk.

9. B. Money Market securities are very liquid, very low risk securities with original lives of up to one year.

10. A. At maturity, the futures price *must* equal the spot price.

11. A. When a new issue of securities is fully underwritten, the underwriter guarantees both the price and number of shares to be sold. The underwriter accepts all the risk: price and selling risk.

12. B. The specialist performs five duties: (1) Act as an agent for floor brokers by holding limit orders; (2) act as a catalyst by bringing buyers and sellers together; (3) act as auctioneer by providing a location for trading by the open outcry method; (4) stabilize prices by preventing large jumps in trading prices; (5) provide capital by acting as a market maker to take the other side of orders during temporary imbalances in trading.

13. C. A market order, the most common type of stock order, is simply an order to trade at the best price. A stop order is a defensive order used to protect profits or limit losses. A limit order is aggressive because the trade will take place only at the limit price.

14. A Holding period returns are usually stated in terms of one year.

15. D. Use the **asked** discount to determine the price you would have to pay.

$$P = \$1,000 - .0371\left(\frac{140}{360}\right)1,000 = \$985.57$$

16. A. Use the **bid** discount to determine the price you would receive.

$$P = \$1,000 - .0373\left(\frac{140}{360}\right)1,000 = \$985.49$$

17. C. Use the **ask price** to determine the **ask yield**.

$$\text{Ask Yield (BEY)} = \frac{\$Discount}{Price}\left(\frac{365}{n}\right) = \frac{\$14.43}{\$985.57}\left(\frac{365}{140}\right) = .0382 = 3.82\%$$

18. D. Set the after-tax yields equal to each other:

Taxable Yield – Tax = Non-taxed Yield

$$k_{taxed} - .35(k_{taxed}) = .06$$

$$k_{taxed}(1 - .35) = .06$$

$$k = \frac{.06}{.65} = .0923 = 9.23\%$$

19. C. Holding Period Yield = (Price Received + Cash Flows Received – Price Paid)/Price Paid

$$\text{Holding Period Yield} = \frac{\$875 + \$40 - \$865}{\$865} = 5.78\%$$

This is the yield for six months, so we must convert it to the Bond Equivalent Yield. There are two six-month periods in one year, so:

HPY = 5.78% × 2 = 11.56%

Security Valuation

As long as an asset is expected to generate cash flows, whether in a series or a lump sum or even just an implied value at which it can be sold in the future, we can estimate its current value. The asset could be a stock or bond, an individual piece of equipment, or even an entire firm. The **capitalization of income** approach is the centerpiece for the valuation of any income-producing asset.

Steps in the **capitalization of income** method include:

1. Estimating the amount and timing of all future cash flows.
2. Estimating the risk associated with cash flows.
3. Assigning a required return based upon risk.
4. Finding the total present value (today) of each cash flow.

While future cash flows can be difficult to estimate, assessing the associated risk of cash flows and assigning a required return based upon risk can be even more challenging.

Section 1 opens this chapter with a review of the concepts of time value of money.[1] Section 2 presents the basics of valuing debt and equity securities.

---

[1] For complete coverage see Brigham and Houston, *Fundamentals of Financial Management, the Concise Edition* (The Dryden Press, 1999).

SECTION 1: TIME VALUE OF MONEY

In this section, your learning objectives are:

1. To calculate and interpret the present and future values of a lump sum.
2. To calculate and interpret the present and future values of an annuity.

Present value is the value *today* of a cash flow to be received or paid in the *future*.

A lump sum is a single cash flow.

An **annuity** is a countable number of equal cash flows occurring at equal intervals over a defined period of time.

Future value is the value in the *future* of a cash flow received or paid *today*.

A **perpetuity** is a series of equal cash flows occurring at the same interval forever.

The **discount rate** and **compounding rate** are the rates of interest used to find present and future values, respectively.

One of the most important tools the financial services professional has is the ability to calculate present and future values. In addition, the competent financial services professional is very comfortable calculating the amortization of a loan, the payout from an insurance annuity, or the annual investments necessary to achieve the desired funds available at retirement.

In this section, we will utilize **timelines** to calculate the present and future values of lump sums and annuities. A **lump sum** is a single cash flow. An **annuity** is a countable number of equal cash flows occurring at equal intervals over a defined period of time (e.g., monthly payments of $100 for three years).

Although certainly not a requirement for producing time value of money calculations, timelines are invaluable in visually identifying the timing of cash flows. Let's look at some of the terms we will utilize throughout the discussion:

- **Present value** is the value *today* of a cash flow to be received or paid in the *future*. On a timeline, present values occur before their relevant cash flows.

- **Future value** is the value in the *future* of a cash flow received or paid *today*. On a timeline, future values occur after their relevant cash flows.

- A **perpetuity** is a series of equal cash flows occurring at the same interval forever.

- The **discount rate** and **compounding rate** are the rates of interest used to find the present and future values, respectively.

Future Value

We'll start our discussion with the future value of a **lump sum**. Assume you put \$100 in an account paying 10 percent and leave it there for one year. How much will be in the account at the end of that year? The timeline below represents the one-year time period.

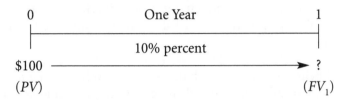

In one year, you'll have \$110. That \$110 will consist of the original \$100 plus \$10 in interest. To set that up in an equation, we say the future value in one year, FV_1, consists of the original \$100 plus the interest it earns.

$$FV_1 = \$100 + (i \times \$100)$$

where i represents the annual interest rate expressed in decimal form.

Since \$100 is the *present value*, the original deposit, we can substitute PV_0 for the \$100 in the equation.

$$FV_1 = PV_0 + (i \times PV_0)$$

Factoring PV_0 out of both terms on the right side of the equation, we are left with:

$$FV_1 = PV_0 (1 + i) \qquad\qquad (1)$$

The result of these mathematical manipulations is the general equation for finding the future value of a lump sum invested for one year at a rate of interest i. Had it not been so easy to do the calculation in our heads, we would have substituted for the variables in the equation and gotten:

$$FV_1 = \$100(1.10) = \$110$$

What if you leave the money in the account for two years? After one year, you'll have $110, the original $100 plus $10 interest. At the end of the second year, you will have the $110 plus interest on the $110 during the second year. The interest earned in the second year consists of interest on the original $100 plus interest earned in the second year on the interest earned during the first year but left in the account. When interest is earned or paid on interest, the process is referred to as **compounding**. This explains why future values are sometimes referred to as **compound values**.

Now our timeline expands to include two years. Although the numbering is totally arbitrary and we could have used any number to indicate today, we are assuming we deposit $100 at time 0 on the timeline. We already know the value after one year, FV_1, so let's start there.

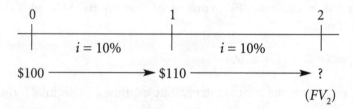

We know from Equation 1 that the future value of a lump sum invested for one year at interest rate i is the lump sum multiplied by $(1 + i)$. We simply find the future value of $110 invested for one year at 10 percent by using Equation 1 (adjusted for the different points in time), which gives us $121.00.

$$FV_1 = PV_0(1 + i)$$
$$FV_2 = FV_1(1 + i)$$
$$FV_2 = \$110(1.10) = \$121$$

To take this example a step further, we make some additional adjustments. We know from Equation 1 that FV_1 is equal to $PV_0(1 + i)$. Let's further develop relationships between future and present value.

We start with:　　　　　　　$FV_2 = FV_1(1 + i)$

Substituting, we get:　　　　$FV_2 = PV_0(1 + i)(1 + i)$

And we end with:　　　　　　$FV_2 = PV_0(1 + i)^2$　　　　　(2)

Equation 2 is the general equation for finding the future value of a lump sum invested for two years at interest rate i. In fact, we have actually discovered the general relationship between the present value of a lump sum and its future value at the end of any number of periods, as long as the interest rate remains the same. We can state the general relationship as:

$$FV_n = PV(1 + i)^n \qquad\qquad (3)$$

Equation 3 says the future value of a lump sum invested for n years at interest rate i is the lump sum multiplied by $(1 + i)^n$. Let's look at some examples. We'll assume an initial investment today of $100 and an interest rate of 5 percent.

Future value in 1 year: $100(1.05) = \$105$

Future value in 5 years: $100(1.05)^5 = \$100(1.2763) = \$127.63$

Future value in 15 years: $100(1.05)^{15} = \$100(2.0789) = \$207.89$

Future value in 51 years: $100(1.05)^{51} = \$100(12.0408) = \$1,204.08$

Regardless of the number of years, as long as the interest rate remains the same, the relationship in Equation 3 holds. Up to this point, we have assumed interest was paid annually (i.e., annual compounding). However, most financial institutions pay and most loans charge interest over much shorter periods. For instance, if an account pays interest every six months, we say interest is "compounded" semiannually. Every three months represents quarterly compounding, and every month is monthly compounding. Let's look at an example with semiannual compounding.

Again, let's assume that we deposit $100 at time zero, and it remains in the account for one year. This time, however, we'll assume the financial institution pays interest semiannually. We will also assume a **stated** or **nominal rate** of 10 percent, meaning it will pay 5 percent every six months.

The **nominal rate** is the annual interest rate stated in the contract.

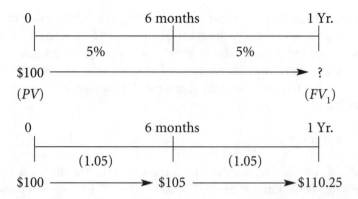

In order to find the future value in one year, we must first find the future value in six months. This value, which includes the original deposit plus interest, will earn interest over the next six-month period. The value after the first six months is the original deposit plus 5 percent interest, or $105. The value after another six months (one year from deposit) is the $105 plus interest of $5.25 for a total of $110.25.

The similarity to finding the *FV* in two years as we did in Equation 2 is not coincidental. Equation 2 is actually the format for finding the *FV* of a lump sum after any two periods at any interest rate, as long as there is no compounding within the periods. The periods could be days, weeks, months, quarters, or years. To find the value after one year when interest is paid every six months, we multiplied by (1.05) twice. Mathematically this is represented by:

$$FV = \$100(1.05)(1.05) = \$100(1.05)^2$$

$$FV = \$100(1.1025) = \$110.25$$

The process for **semiannual compounding** is mathematically identical to finding the future value in two years under **annual compounding**. In fact, we can modify Equation 3 to describe the relationship of present and future value for any number of years and compounding periods per year.

$$FV_n = PV_0\left(1 + \frac{i}{m}\right)^{m*n} \tag{4}$$

With **annual compounding,** interest is calculated and paid once per year.

where:

FV_n is the future value after n years.

PV_0 is the present value.

i is the stated annual rate of interest.

m is the number of compounding periods per year.

$m{*}n$ is the total number of compounding periods (the number of years times the compounding periods per year).

For semiannual compounding $m = 2$, for quarterly compounding $m = 4$, and for monthly compounding $m = 12$. If you leave money in an account paying semiannual interest for four years, the total compounding periods would be $4 \times 2 = 8$. Interest would be calculated and paid 8 times during the four years. Let's assume you left your \$100 on deposit for four years, and the bank pays 10 percent interest compounded semiannually. We'll use Equation 4 to find the amount in the account after four years.

$$FV = \$100\left(1 + \frac{.10}{2}\right)^{4 \times 2}$$

$$FV = \$100(1.05)^8$$

$$FV = \$100(1.4775) = \$147.75$$

where:

$n = 4$ because you will leave the money in the account for four years.

$m = 2$ because the bank pays interest semiannually.

$i = 10$ percent, the *annual* stated or nominal rate of interest.

If the account only paid interest annually, the future value would be:

$$FV = \$100\left(1 + \frac{.10}{1}\right)^{4 \times 1}$$

$$FV = \$100(1.10)^4$$

$$FV = \$100(1.4641) = \$146.41$$

The additional $1.34 (i.e., $147.75 − $146.41 = $1.34) is extra interest earned from the compounding effect of interest on interest. Although the differences do not seem profound, the effects of compounding are magnified with larger values, greater number of compounding periods per year, or higher nominal interest rates. In our example, the extra $1.34 was earned on an initial deposit of $100. Had this been a $1 billion deposit, the extra interest differential from compounding semiannually rather than annually would have amounted to $13,400,000!

To demonstrate the effect of increasing the number of compounding periods per year, let's look at several alternative future value calculations when $100 is deposited for one year at a 10 percent nominal rate of interest. In each case, m is the number of compounding periods per year.

As the compounding periods per year increase, future values increase and present values decrease.

$m = 1$ (annually) $FV = \$100(1.10) = \$110$

$m = 2$ (every 6 months) $FV = \$100(1.05)^2 = \$110.25$

$m = 4$ (quarterly) $FV = \$100(1.025)^4 = \$110.38$

$m = 6$ (every 2 months) $FV = \$100(1.10167)^6 = \$110.43$

$m = 12$ (monthly) $FV = \$100(1.008333)^{12} = \$110.47$

$m = 52$ (weekly) $FV = \$100(1.001923)^{52} = \$110.51$

$m = 365$ (daily) $FV = \$100(1.000274)^{365} = \$110.52$

You will notice two very important characteristics of compounding:

- For the same present value and interest rate, the future value increases as the number of compounding periods per year increases.

- Each successive increase in future value is less than the preceding increase (the future value increases at a decreasing rate).

Effective interest rates are the actual rates earned or paid. They are determined by the stated rate and the number of compounding periods per year.

The concept of compounding is associated with the related concept of **effective interest rates**. In our semiannual compounding example, we assumed that $100 was deposited for one year at 10 percent compounded semiannually. We represented it graphically using a timeline as follows:

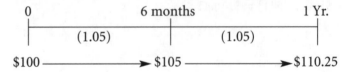

The stated rate of interest (i.e., the announced or advertised rate) is 10 percent. However, determining the actual rate we earned involves comparing your ending value with the beginning value using Equation 5. You can determine your actual or "effective" rate of return by taking into consideration the impact of compounding. Equation 5 measures the change in value as a percentage of the beginning value.

$$\text{Effective return} = \frac{V_1 - V_0}{V_0} \qquad (5)$$

V_0 is the total value of the investment at the *beginning of the year*.

V_1 is the total value of the investment at the *end of the year*.

You will notice Equation 5 stresses using the values at the beginning and the end of the year (actually, any 12-month period). By convention, we always state effective interest rates in terms of one year.[2]

Returning to our previous example, let's substitute our beginning-of-year and end-of-year values into Equation 5. Because the interest was compounded semiannually instead of annually, we actually earned 10.25 percent on the account rather than the 10 percent stated rate.

$$\text{Effective return} = \frac{V_1 - V_0}{V_0} \qquad (5)$$

$$\text{Effective return} = \frac{\$110.25 - \$100}{\$100} = .1025 = 10.25\%$$

Let's employ algebraic principles and rewrite Equation 5 in the following form:

$$\text{Effective return} = \frac{V_1 - V_0}{V_0} \Rightarrow \frac{V_1}{V_0} - \frac{V_0}{V_0}$$

$$\text{Effective return} = \frac{V_1}{V_0} - 1 \qquad (6)$$

Now let's restate Equation 6 in terms of *FV* and *PV*:

$$\frac{V_1}{V_0} \text{ is equivalent to } \frac{FV_1}{PV_0} \text{ and } FV_1 = PV_0\left(1 + \frac{i}{m}\right)^{m*1}$$

$$\text{so } \frac{FV_1}{PV_0} \text{ can be rewritten as } \frac{PV_0\left(1 + \frac{i}{m}\right)^{m*1}}{PV_0} \qquad (7)$$

[2] In fact, to compare any interest rates, including investment returns, we always use this one-year convention.

Remember, we always state effective returns in annual terms. Thus, we can set $n = 1$ in the equation and the PV_0 in the numerator and denominator cancel each other out. Substituting Equation 7 back into Equation 6 we get:

$$\text{Effective return} = \left(1 + \frac{i}{m}\right)^m - 1 \qquad (8)$$

We have arrived at the general equation to determine any effective interest rate in terms of its stated or nominal rate and the number of compounding periods per year. Let's investigate a few examples of calculating effective interest rates for the same stated interest at varying compounding assumptions. You will notice the effective rate increases as the number of compounding periods increases.

> **As the number of compounding periods per years increases, the effective interest rate increases.**

$m = 1$ (annual) $\qquad \left(1 + \frac{.12}{1}\right)^1 - 1 = (1.12)^1 - 1 = .12 = 12\%$

$m = 2$ (semiannual) $\quad \left(1 + \frac{.12}{2}\right)^2 - 1 = (1.06)^2 - 1 = .1236 = 12.36\%$

$m = 4$ (quarterly) $\quad \left(1 + \frac{.12}{4}\right)^4 - 1 = (1.03)^4 - 1 = .1255 = 12.55\%$

$m = 12$ (monthly) $\quad \left(1 + \frac{.12}{12}\right)^{12} - 1 = (1.01)^{12} - 1 = .1268 = 12.68\%$

$m = 365$ (daily) $\quad \left(1 + \frac{.12}{365}\right)^{365} - 1 = (1.0003288)^{365} - 1 = .1275 = 12.75\%$

Next, let's turn our attention to **annuities**. Recall that an annuity is a series of equal payments, equally spaced through time. The series may consist of two or more cash flows. We begin by using Equation 3 for each cash flow in the series. For instance, consider the timeline and associated cash flows shown below in **Figure 1**.

> **When payments come at the beginning of the period, the annuity is called an annuity due.**

Assume the cash flows represent deposits to an account paying 10 percent, and you want to know how much you will have in the account at the end of the fifth year. Point zero on the timeline is when the first deposit is made. Each successive deposit is made at the beginning of each year, so the last deposit is made at the beginning of year five. When cash flows come at the beginning of the period, the annuity is known as an **annuity due**. An annuity due is typically associated with leases or other situations where payments are made in advance of services or products received or rendered. Our goal is to determine the amount we will have in the account at point five (i.e., the end of year five).

> **When loan payments include both principal and interest, we say the loan is amortized.**

The process of finding the future value of an annuity in this manner is equivalent to summing the future value of each individual cash flow. The cash flow stream is illustrated below in **Figure 1**. Each cash flow is assumed to earn a 10 percent return for each of the indicated number of years. For example, the $100 at time 0 will remain on deposit for a total of five years, so we multiply $100 by $(1 + i)^5$ and obtain $161.05. When all the cash flows are compounded to find their future values, we add them to find the total future value of the five cash flows, which totals $671.56. In other words, if you deposit $100 per year in an account paying 10 percent, you will have $671.56 in five years.

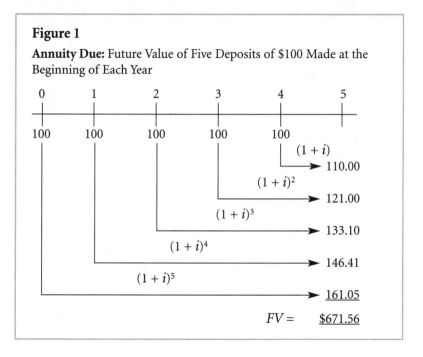

Figure 1

Annuity Due: Future Value of Five Deposits of $100 Made at the Beginning of Each Year

Now we'll consider the same annuity of five $100 deposits, but we'll assume that the deposits occur at the end of each year. When cash flows are at the end of the period, the annuity is known as an **ordinary annuity**. An ordinary annuity, such as the one above, represents the typical cash flow pattern for loans, such as those for automobiles, homes, furniture, fixtures, and even businesses. The timeline and cash flows are illustrated in **Figure 2.**

When payments come at the end of the period, the annuity is called an **ordinary annuity**.

You will notice that the future value of the ordinary annuity is less than the future value of the annuity due, although the number of equal deposits is the same. Upon further inspection, you should notice that the four deposits at points one though four are exactly the same for both annuities. The difference between the two types of annuities is the treatment of the remaining deposit. With the **annuity due** (**Figure 1**), the remaining deposit is made at time zero and earns interest for five years. With the **ordinary annuity** (**Figure 2**), the remaining deposit is made at the end of year five immediately before the account is closed and the money withdrawn. Since the last deposit in the case of the ordinary annuity earns no interest, the difference between the future values of the two annuities must be the interest earned on the deposit made at time 0 in the case of the annuity due. The future value of the ordinary annuity is $610.51. The future value of the annuity due is $671.56, exactly $61.05 greater.

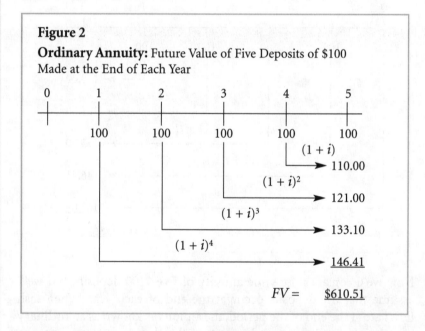

Figure 2
Ordinary Annuity: Future Value of Five Deposits of $100 Made at the End of Each Year

The solutions presented for both annuities were more for demonstration purposes than for actually calculating the future values. If you find yourself needing to calculate the future value of an annuity, you will use one of two other approaches: a financial calculator or a formula.

Let's illustrate the use of a financial calculator to find the future value of an annuity. Our example will rely on the keystrokes using a Texas Instruments (TI) Business Analyst II Plus® calculator.

Ordinary Annuity. Your calculator should be set to end of period payments and one payment per year. To set to end of period payments, press [2nd] → [BGN] and press [2nd] → [SET] until END is displayed, then [2nd] → [QUIT] (since END is default, the display will not indicate end of period payments). To set to one payment per year, press [2nd] → [P/Y] → 1 → [ENTER], [2nd] → [QUIT]. The keystrokes[3] to find the future value are:

−100	[PMT]	The calculator assumes one of the payments is an outflow and one is an inflow. The negative sign indicates an outflow (the deposit).
5	[N]	
10	[I/Y]	
[CPT]	[FV] = $610.51	

Annuity Due. For an annuity due, set the financial calculator for beginning of period payments and one payment per year. To set to one payment per year press [2nd] → [P/Y] → 1 → [ENTER], [2nd] → [QUIT]. To set to beginning-of-period payments, press [2nd] → [BGN] and press [2nd] → [SET] until BGN is displayed, then [2nd] → [QUIT] (BGN will show in the calculator display). The keystrokes to find the future value are:

−100	[PMT]	The calculator assumes one of the payments is an outflow and one is an inflow. The negative sign indicates an outflow (the deposit).
5	[N]	
10	[I/Y]	
[CPT]	[FV] = $671.56	

[3] Calculator Tip: Note that, PV, FV, PMT, I/Y, and N are just memory registers. If there is some data in these values from previous computations, you will need to clear these amounts. There are two ways to do this. The brute force method is to simply put a zero into the register that you're not using. The second and more elegant method is to press [2nd] → [CLR WORK] before you enter the next set of data points.

You can also use a formula for calculating the future value of an annuity. To find the future value of an **ordinary annuity**, multiply the cash flow (payment) by the formula and the result is the future value. Assume the same $100 deposits made each year for five years earning a 10 percent return, compounded annually.

$$FV_5 = PMT \frac{(1 + i)^n - 1}{i}$$

$$FV_5 = \$100 \frac{(1.10)^5 - 1}{.10}$$

$$FV_5 = \$100 \frac{1.6105 - 1}{.10} = \$100(6.1051) = \$610.51$$

The same process would be used to calculate the future value of an **annuity due**, but we must multiply the future value of the ordinary annuity by $(1 + i)$ in order to adjust for the fact that each cash flow is shifted back by one period with the annuity due.

$$FV_5 = \$100 \frac{1.6105 - 1}{.10} = \$100(6.1051) = \$610.51(1 + .10) = \$671.56$$

Present Value. Equation 3 showed us the relationship between the present and future values for a lump sum.

$$FV_n = PV(1 + i)^n \qquad (3)$$

In Equation 3, we find the future value by multiplying the present value by $(1 + i)^n$. To solve for the present value, we can divide both sides of the equation by $(1 + i)^n$.

$$PV = \frac{FV_n}{(1 + i)^n} \qquad (3a)$$

Finding a present value is actually deducting interest from the future value, which we refer to as **discounting**. Returning to the future value examples used earlier, we can demonstrate how to calculate present values. We will assume the same discount rate of 5 percent.

(FV) The value in 1 year of $100 deposited today: $100(1.05) = \$105$

(PV) The value today of $105 to be received in 1 year: $100 = \frac{\$105}{(1.05)}$

(FV) The value in 5 years of $100 deposited today: $100(1.05)^5 = \$127.63$

(PV) The value today of $127.63 to be received in 5 years: $100 = \dfrac{\$127.63}{(1.05)^5}$

(FV) The value in 15 years of $100 deposited today: $\$100(1.05)^{15} = \$207.89$

(PV) The value today of $207.89 to be received in 15 years: $100 = \dfrac{\$207.89}{(1.05)^{15}}$

(FV) The value in 51 years of $100 deposited today: $\$100(1.05)^{51} = \$1{,}204.08$

(PV) The value today of $1,204.08 to be received in 51 years: $100 = \dfrac{\$1{,}204.08}{(1.05)^{51}}$

When we found the future value of an annuity, we compounded each cash flow individually and summed them at a future date. To find the **present value of an annuity**, we **discount** all the future values and sum them up. We'll start with the *annuity due* we used before. The cash flows are assumed paid/received at the beginning of each year, and we want to find the aggregate present value of the five cash flows at point zero on the timeline. Again we assume an interest rate of 10 percent. **Figure 3** illustrates the calculation of the present value of an annuity due.

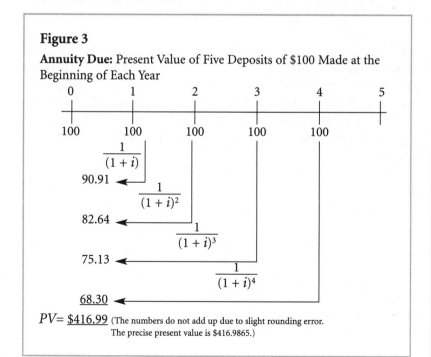

Figure 3

Annuity Due: Present Value of Five Deposits of $100 Made at the Beginning of Each Year

$PV = \underline{\$416.99}$ (The numbers do not add up due to slight rounding error. The precise present value is $416.9865.)

To find the present value of this **annuity due** using a TI Business Analyst II Plus calculator, you would make the following key entries (be sure to turn on BGN):

−100	PMT
5	N
10	I/Y
CPT	PV = $416.99

There are several ways of interpreting the above figure of $416.99. The $416.99 is the present value of the five $100 payments/receipts, but what does *present value* really mean? A simple interpretation is that if you put $416.99 in an account paying 10 percent interest, you will be able to withdraw $100 per year for five years. Another, somewhat more sophisticated, interpretation is that $416.99 is the maximum you would pay for an investment paying $100 per year with a required return of 10 percent. A third interpretation is that if you borrow $416.99 to be paid in five equal annual payments, you will pay $100.00 per payment. Regardless, $416.99 today is equivalent to five annual $100 cash flows, the first cash flow occurring today.

Likewise, the present value of an ordinary annuity may be calculated by summing the present value of each individual payment. **Figure 4** illustrates the cash flow stream for the ordinary annuity. In this case the first cash flow occurs one year from today with the other four coming yearly after that. The present value of each cash flow is found using the appropriate factor and is then added to the others to get a total of $379.08.

Figure 4

Ordinary Annuity: Present Value of Five Deposits of $100 Made at the End of Each Year

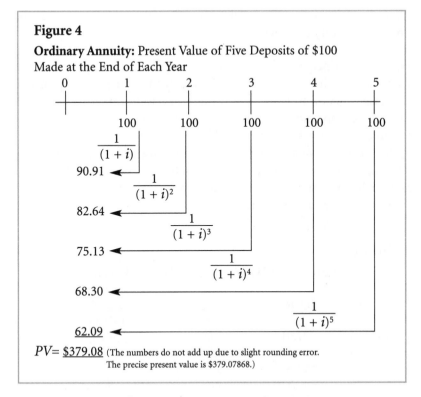

$PV = \underline{\$379.08}$ (The numbers do not add up due to slight rounding error. The precise present value is $379.07868.)

The keystrokes to find the present value of an ordinary annuity are (be sure to turn BGN off):

−100	**PMT**
5	**N**
10	**I/Y**
CPT	**PV** = $379.08

In addition, we may calculate the present value of an ordinary annuity using the following formula:

$$PV_A = PMT\left[\frac{1}{i} - \frac{1}{i(1+i)^n}\right]$$

$$PV_A = \$100\left[\frac{1}{.10} - \frac{1}{.10(1.10)^5}\right]$$

$$PV_A = \$100[10 - 6.2092]$$

$$PV_A = \$100[3.7908] = \$379.08$$

As illustrated above, we are able to confirm the present value of the ordinary annuity is $379.08.[4]

When both principal and interest are included in a loan payment (rather than a series of interest payments followed by the repayment of principal at the maturity of the loan), we say the loan is **fully amortized**. Let's use the ordinary annuity above as an example. Let's assume you have borrowed $379.08 for the purchase of a household item and have agreed to pay for it in five equal payments at 10 percent. We know from the previous example that the payments will be $100 each. **Figure 5** shows how each payment would be broken down into interest and principal if the loan were fully amortized.

Figure 5:

Amortization of $379.08 for Five Years at 10 Percent

Payment	Interest	Principal	Balance
			$379.08
1 $100	$37.91	$62.09	316.99
2 100	31.70	68.30	248.69
3 100	24.87	75.13	173.56
4 100	17.37	82.64	90.92
5 100	9.09	90.91	0 * slight rounding error

Each of the five payments repays a portion of the principal borrowed and pays interest on the balance remaining after the previous payment. The first payment includes 10 percent interest on the entire loan amount of $379.08, or $37.91. The remainder of the payment ($100 − $37.91 = $62.09) is applied to the principal, leaving a balance of $316.99. The second payment includes 10 percent interest on the new balance of $316.99, or $31.70. Again, the remainder of the payment, $68.30, is applied to the principal. This process continues until the loan is fully paid. You can see in **Figure 5** that the interest in each payment decreases while the principal increases.

---

[4] Similar to calculations related to future value, the present value of an annuity due can be calculated from the present value of the ordinary annuity by multiplying the present value of the ordinary annuity by $(1+i)$.

SUMMARY OF SECTION ONE

Learning Objectives: *To calculate and interpret the present and future values of a lump sum. To calculate and interpret the present and future values of an annuity.*

A. **Timelines** help us keep cash flows straight.
   1. The beginning number on the timeline is purely arbitrary.
   2. They indicate the end of the respective period (e.g., days, weeks, months, years, or any other defined period).
   3. Present values always are before their respective future value on a timeline.
   4. Future values always fall to the right of their respective present values on a timeline.

B. A **lump sum** is a single cash flow.
   1. The **present value** of a lump sum is the equivalent value today of a lump sum to be received or paid sometime in the future.
      a. The value depends upon the number of periods and the interest rate.
      b. As interest rates increase (decrease), present values decrease (increase).
   2. The **future value** of a lump sum is the equivalent value in the future of a lump sum to be received or paid today.
      a. The value depends upon the number of periods and the interest rate.
      b. As interest rates decrease (increase), future values decrease (increase).

C. An **annuity** is a countable number of equal cash flows occurring at equal intervals over a defined period of time.
   1. The **present value** of an annuity is the equivalent lump sum value today of a series of cash flows to be received or paid.
      a. The present value depends upon the number of cash flows and the (constant) interest rate between them.
      b. As interest rates increase (decrease), the present value of an annuity decreases (increases).
   2. The **future value** of an annuity is the equivalent lump sum value in the future of a series of cash flows to be received or paid.
      a. The value depends upon the number of periods and the interest rate.

  b. As interest rates decrease (increase), the future value of an annuity decreases (increases).
 D. The **effective interest rate** (i.e., return) depends upon the **nominal rate** and the number of **compounding periods** per year.
  1. The **nominal rate** is the interest rate stated in the contract.
  2. When interest is calculated over periods shorter than one year, we say interest is **compounded**. We refer to the number of times per year interest is calculated as the number of compounding periods per year.
  3. **Effective interest rates** are determined by the number of compounding periods per year. As the number of compounding periods increases (decreases), the effective rate increases (decreases).
  4. Present and future values of both lump sums and annuities depend upon the effective interest rate. As effective interest rates increase, present and future values increase.
  5. Effective interest rates MUST be equal to or greater than their respective stated rates.
 E. When loan payments include both principal and interest, we say the loan is **amortized**.
  1. Each payment includes a portion applied to interest due and a portion applied to the **principal** (i.e., the amount borrowed).
   a. The proportion of each payment applied to interest decreases with each successive payment.
   b. The proportion of each payment applied to the principal increases with each successive payment.

SECTION 2: SECURITY VALUATION

In this section, your learning objectives are:

1. To calculate and interpret the price of debt securities.
2. To calculate and interpret the price of equity securities.

Corporate Bonds

When a corporation issues (sells) bonds, it promises to pay the holder (buyer) a series of coupon payments (i.e., interest) and repay the face value (i.e., principal) at maturity. For U.S. corporations, coupon payments are paid semiannually and resemble the ordinary annuities we discussed in Section 1. The principal repayment is a lump sum payment. Using the **capitalization of income method**, the market value of the bond can be determined by calculating the present value of its cash flows.

Most debt instruments are **fixed income securities**. Their payments are set contractually.

Let's determine the value of a 10-year, 8 percent semiannual bond, yielding 8 percent. Consider each of the bond's characteristics:

- *10-year* indicates that the bond **matures** in 10 years. This should not be confused with the bond's original length of issue, which could be 30 years or longer.
- *8 percent* refers to the **coupon rate** on the bond. The bond pays 8 percent of its face value (typically $1,000) each year, in two equal semiannual payments of $40.
- *Yielding 8 percent* indicates that the bond is priced to yield 8 percent. This means that based upon the risk of the firm and the bond, its **required return** or **discount rate** is 8 percent.

Since the bond pays coupons semiannually, there are twenty (10×2) coupons paid in ten years. Also, since the annual required return is 8 percent, the semiannual required return is 4 percent.

The coupon payments are nothing more than an annuity. Each payment is $40, and they come exactly six months apart. In order to determine the value of the bond, we must find the present value of each coupon and sum them to find the total present value of all the coupons we will receive. This results in an annuity of twenty $40 payments discounted at four percent.

Let's explore two ways of finding this value. First, we could actually find all the individual present values and sum them, which is a very tedious job to say the least. Second, we could use the ordinary annuity formula:

$$PV_A = PMT \left[\frac{1}{\frac{i}{m}} - \frac{1}{\frac{i}{m}(1 + \frac{i}{m})^{m*n}} \right]$$

$$PV_A = \$40 \left[\frac{1}{.04} - \frac{1}{.04(1.04)^{20}} \right]$$

$$PV_A = \$40 [25 - 11.4097]$$

$$PV_A = \$40 [13.5903] = \$543.61$$

where:

> PV_A is the present value of an annuity. The annuity in this case is the series of coupons we will receive.
>
> PMT is the amount of each payment. The payments are the $40 coupons.
>
> i is the annual interest rate.
>
> n is the number of years.
>
> m is the number of coupons per year.

The figure $543.61 represents the present value of the stream of coupon payments expected if we buy the bond. Of course, we would also expect the repayment of the principal in ten years. We know from Equation 4 that the relationship between present and future values of a lump sum can be expressed in the following manner:

$$FV_n = PV \left(1 + \frac{i}{m} \right)^{m*n} \tag{4}$$

Rearranging Equation 4 to solve for PV yields:

$$PV = \frac{FV_n}{\left(1 + \frac{i}{m} \right)^{m*n}}$$

where:

> FV is the future value, in this case the lump sum return of principal (the face value of the bond).

i is the annual interest rate.

m is the compounding periods per year. In this case coupons are paid semiannually.

n is the number of years.

In this example,

$$PV = \frac{\$1,000}{\left(1 + \frac{.08}{2}\right)^{(2)(10)}} = \frac{\$1,000}{(1.04)^{20}} = \frac{\$1,000}{2.191123} = \$456.39$$

Thus, the present value of $1,000 to be received in 20 semiannual periods at four percent is $456.39. Now that we have the present value of both the series of coupons and the lump sum face value, we find the total price of our bond is $543.61 + $456.39 = $1,000.

Two very important points are worth mentioning here. First of all, when the coupon rate and required return on a bond are the same, the bond will always be quoted at par. Secondly, the model assumes you purchase the bond **on a coupon date**. This means both methods assume the next coupon will be received in exactly six months (180 days). This is obviously not the typical case.

Accrued Interest. When you purchase a bond between interest payment dates, you will have to pay **accrued interest**. Even though coupons are paid semiannually, interest accrues daily. The bond in the above example pays $80 in interest every 360 days[5] (in two payments of $40) or 22.22 cents per day. The holder of the bond (the seller) not only wants, but is entitled to the interest accrued since the last coupon payment.

Let's assume the bond last paid interest 115 days ago (65 days before the next interest payment). Since you must pay the seller the interest accrued since the last coupon, you must pay him $0.2222/day × 115 days = $25.55 in addition to the bond's quoted price. While you should be aware of the effect of accrued interest in the bond pricing relationships, further treatment of this topic is beyond the scope of this text.

> Most bonds pay interest **semiannually** on the **coupon dates** established in the indenture.

---

[5]A 360-day year is assumed by convention.

Price vs. Yield. In following examples, we will illustrate the inverse relationship between bond yield and price.

Characteristics of the bond:

- The coupon rate is 8 percent (it pays 8 percent of its face value in two equal, semiannual $40 payments).
- The bond has ten years remaining until maturity.
- The bond has a face value of $1,000.

When the required return is 8 percent, its price is $1,000. This is because its required return equals its coupon rate. Using the TI Business Analyst II Plus® calculator, we'll find the value of our bond at various required returns. The TI BAII Plus keystrokes are as follows:

$40	PMT
4 percent	I/Y
20	N
$1,000	FV
CPT	PV = –$1,000

Let the required return fall to 7 percent and 6 percent respectively:

$40	PMT	$40	PMT
3.5 percent	I/Y	3 percent	I/Y
20	N	20	N
$1,000	FV	$1,000	FV
CPT	PV = –$1,071.06	CPT	PV = –$1,148.77

Let the required return increase to 9 percent and 10 percent respectively:

$40	PMT	$40	PMT
4.5 percent	I/Y	5 percent	I/Y
20	N	20	N
$1,000	FV	$1,000	FV
CPT	PV = –$934.96	CPT	PV = –$875.38

As shown in the illustration, the price of the bond moves in the opposite direction from the change in required return, giving us three important relationships:

- If the required return equals the coupon rate, the bond sells at par (i.e., face value).
- If the required return is less than the coupon rate, the bond sells at a premium (i.e., greater than face value).
- If the required return is greater than the coupon rate, the bond sells at a discount (i.e., less than face value).

Rather than memorize these relationships, just remember that present value always moves opposite the change in discount rate. When a bond's required return is greater than its coupon rate, the discount rate has increased, and the bond's price will fall. When the bond's required return is less than the coupon rate, the discount rate has fallen, and the price will rise.

Another very important bond characteristic is the relationship between maturity and the change in price given a change in required return. We already know that there is an inverse relationship between the bond's price and its required return. Now we'll show that *the greater the time until maturity of the bond, the greater the change in value associated with an interest rate change.* Using the same bond illustrated above, let's assume that the maturity of the bond is 20 years instead of 10 (i.e., there will be 40 semiannual periods).

$40	PMT
4 percent	I/Y
40	N
$1,000	FV
CPT	PV = -$1,000

Again, as long as the required return and coupon rate are equal, the bond sells at par.

> If the required return equals the coupon rate, the bond sells at par (face value).

> When interest rates change, the price of the bond will change in the opposite direction.

Let the required return fall to 7 percent and 6 percent respectively:

$40	PMT	$40	PMT
3.5 percent	I/Y	3 percent	I/Y
40	N	40	N
$1,000	FV	$1,000	FV
CPT PV = –$1,106.77		CPT PV = –$1,231.15	

Let the required return increase to 9 percent and 10 percent respectively:

$40	PMT	$40	PMT
4.5 percent	I/Y	5 percent	I/Y
40	N	40	N
$1,000	FV	$1,000	FV
CPT PV = –$907.99		CPT PV = –$828.41	

In addition to the time until maturity, the change in a bond's price is also affected by its coupon rate. In general, *the higher the coupon rate (i.e., the higher the interest payments), the smaller the change in price for a given change in required return*. Let's revisit our 20-year bond again, but let's now assume it has a 12 percent coupon rate instead of 8 percent (i.e., there will be $60 semiannual payments instead of $40) and that the yield on the bond is 12% (i.e., the bond trades at par value). Using your TI Business Analyst II Plus® calculator:

$60	PMT
6 percent	I/Y
40	N
$1,000	FV
CPT PV = –$1,000	

Let the required return fall to 11 percent and 10 percent respectively:

$60	PMT	$60	PMT
5.5 percent	I/Y	5 percent	I/Y
40	N	40	N
$1,000	FV	$1,000	FV
CPT PV = –$1,080.23		CPT PV = –$1,171.59	

Let the required return increase to 13 percent and 14 percent respectively:

$60	PMT	$60	PMT
6.5 percent	I/Y	7 percent	I/Y
40	N	40	N
$1,000	FV	$1,000	FV
CPT PV = –$929.27		CPT PV = –$866.68	

Let's sum up the results of our findings in **Figure 6**. The first column shows the change in required return from the original coupon rate. Remember, the bond will sell at par value as long as the coupon rate and required return are equal. The second and third columns show us the changes in price are less severe (for both increases and decreases) for the bond with the shorter maturity. The third and fourth columns show us the changes in price are less severe for bonds with larger coupons.

This demonstrates two general rules for all fixed income securities:

Rule 1: The longer the maturity of any fixed income instrument, the more sensitive its price is to changes in interest rates.

Rule 2: The greater the interim cash flows[6] associated with a fixed income security, the less sensitive its price is to changes in interest rates.

Rule 1: The longer the maturity of any fixed income instrument, the more sensitive its price is to changes in interest rates.

Rule 2: The greater the interim cash flows associated with a fixed income security, the less sensitive its price is to changes in interest rates.

---

[6]**Interim cash flows** are received between the purchase date and maturity date, as with the coupon payments for a bond.

Figure 6

Bond Price Reactions to Changes in Required Return (Par = $1,000)

Chg. In Req. Return	Price Change from Par		
	10-year, 8%	20-year, 8%	20-year, 12%
$ −2%	$ +148.77	$ +231.15	$ +171.59
−1%	+71.06	+106.77	+80.23
no chg.	0.00	0.00	0.00
+1%	−65.04	−92.01	−70.73
+2%	−124.62	−171.59	−133.32

These rules give us guidance in establishing investing strategies related to bonds. If you expect interest rates to rise[7] in the near future, you want to hold short-term bonds to minimize the subsequent drop in prices. However, if you expect interest rates to fall in the near future, you want to hold long-term bonds to take advantage of the price increases.

Common Stock

Since dividends are declared, they are not contractual. **Common stock is not a fixed income security.**

As with any other cash flow producing asset, stocks can be valued using the capitalization of income method. When you hold common stock, the only income you can expect are dividends.[8] The problem is that dividends are not fixed. Instead, the board of directors declares them. So, as a stockholder you can predict the timing of the next dividend, but you cannot be certain of its value until it's declared. However, corporate boards usually favor a fairly consistent dividend pattern, so the chore of forecasting dividends might not be as laden with uncertainty as it seems.

The cash flows associated with common stock are **dividends**, which are declared by the firm's board of directors.

Before we begin valuing common stock, we need to introduce some terminology:

- D_t is the dividend expected at time t (on our timeline), which corresponds to the end of year t.

---

[7] A change in the required return on a bond can be caused by a change in inflation or a change in the bond's risk.

[8] There can be special (cash) dividends or even stock dividends. Also, the number of firms that don't pay dividends at all is growing.

- P_t is the price of the stock at the end of year t. For example, we will use P_0, P_1, and P_2 to denote the price today and at the end of years one and two, respectively.

- g is the expected rate of growth in the stock's dividends.

- k_e is the required return on equity (i.e., common stock) for the firm. k_e can be estimated in several different ways, but we will use the dividend discount model and the capital asset pricing model, CAPM.[9]

The formula for valuing a share of common stock calculates the present value of all expected future dividends. Since a firm is assumed to never suspend the payment of dividends, and the firm is assumed to have an infinite life, dividends are expected to continue indefinitely. The general formula appears below as Equation 5. You should notice the summation of present values assumes the dividends stream from the end of year 1, $t = 1$, to infinity, $t = \infty$. All the future dividends are discounted at the investors' required return on the firm's equity, k_e.

$$P_0 = \sum_{t=1}^{\infty} \frac{D_t}{(1+k_e)^t} \qquad (5)$$

Estimating all future dividends and their present values could be a very time consuming process. To overcome the necessity of estimating dividends throughout eternity, we try to estimate them for a few years, then assume at some point in time that they begin growing at a constant rate.

Equation 5 is the general form of the **dividend discount model** for pricing common stock. The equation below shows the expansion of the series showing individual dividend payments:

$$P_0 = \frac{D_1}{(1 + k_e)} + \frac{D_2}{(1 + k_e)^2} + \frac{D_3}{(1 + k_e)^3} + \frac{D_4}{(1 + k_e)^4} \cdots \frac{D_\infty}{(1 + k_e)^\infty}$$

where D_1 is the amount of the first expected dividend. [10]

---

[9] The CAPM shows the relationship between the risk of a common stock, measured by β, and its required return, k_e, as $k_e = k_{rf} + \beta(k_m - k_{rf})$, where k_m is the market return and k_{rf} is the risk-free return. When rearranged, the dividend discount model expresses required return as $k_e = \frac{D_1}{P_0} + g$, where g is the growth in earnings, assets, dividends, and the stockprice.

[10] Even though dividends are typically paid quarterly, the valuation methods used assume annual dividend payments.

We assume that the following dividend, D_2, is a certain percentage larger than D_1. In the same manner, each dividend is estimated as a percentage larger than the previous dividend (the percentage growth would be zero if dividends are expected to remain at the same level and negative if they are expected to decrease). The change in the amounts of the dividends from year to year is called the **growth** in dividends. Assuming that the growth rate in dividends is the same each year, the relationship between the values of the successive dividends may be expressed in the following way:

$$D_1 = D_0(1 + g)$$
$$D_2 = D_1(1 + g)$$
$$D_3 = D_2(1 + g)$$
$$D_n = D_{n-1}(1 + g)$$

In other words, each dividend is the previous dividend multiplied by 1 plus the expected rate of growth. If D_0 is $2.00 and g = 5 percent, $\hat{D}_1$ = $2.00(1.05)$ = $2.10. In this manner we estimate all future dividends. Note: Since $\hat{D}_1$ is not known with certainty we use the carat , ^ , which is the symbol for "expected."

$\hat{} = $ expected

Growth in dividends is typically tied directly to the growth of the firm.[11] Although most firms are assumed to maintain consistency in growth, some firms might be in industries where new innovations result in exceptional growth over varying periods of time. Some might be able to maintain higher than normal growth rates for several years, while others might enjoy higher than normal growth for only months or a few years.

Let's consider Amazing Glass, a glass manufacturing firm that develops a new heat reflective glass for automobiles. This innovation could give Amazing Glass a decided edge over competitors until the competition develops their own glass. During this period, Amazing may enjoy a higher than normal growth rate as sales increase dramatically. When

---

[11] Growth in a firm is usually defined as the percentage growth in earnings per share (EPS), the change in the value of the firm's assets, or the change in its stock price. As long as management pays out a constant percentage of earnings as dividends, the dividend growth rate will be the same as the firm's overall growth rate.

the competition starts producing equivalent (or even better) glass, Amazing will resume a more sustainable growth rate.[12]

The period when firms are expected to perform well above (or below) average is known as the **explicit growth period**,[13] because the growth in earnings and dividends must be explicitly estimated. The period when the firm performs at a more sustainable, long-term rate of growth is called the **implicit growth period**. During this period we assume the firm will perform as most other firms in the industry, and its dividends will grow at the industry average. Of course, not all firms will experience explicit growth periods.

If the firm is expected to grow at a constant rate forever, we can use the **constant growth** dividend valuation model. Without actually showing the derivation, if the growth rate between all dividends into the foreseeable future is expected to be constant, Equation 5 simplifies into Equation 6, which appears below.

$$P_0 = \frac{D_1}{k_e - \overline{g}} \qquad\qquad (6)$$

This means we can estimate the price of the firm's common stock using the next expected dividend, D_1, its required return on equity, k_e, and its **constant growth rate**, $\overline{g}$.

Let's assume the last dividend paid, D_0, was $2.00, the firm's required return on equity is 15 percent, and assets, earnings, and dividends are expected to grow 5 percent per year *forever*. We would estimate the price of the firm's common stock in the following manner:

$$P_0 = \frac{D_1}{k_e - \overline{g}} = \frac{D_0(1 + g)}{k_e - \overline{g}}$$

$$P_0 = \frac{\$2.00(1.05)}{.15 - .05}$$

$$P_0 = \frac{\$2.10}{.10} = \$21.00$$

The **explicit growth period** is the period when the firm enjoys above normal growth in earnings and dividends.

During the **implicit growth period**, the firm performs at a more sustainable, long-term rate of growth.

---

[12] It could be said there are normal rates of growth for firms based upon their industries. All firms in mature industries might have reached a point of zero or very low "normal" growth. Some industries, such as computer software and communications, are prone to rapid innovation.

[13] Some texts will refer to this period as supernormal growth.

If the firm is expected to pay the same dividend over the foreseeable future (i.e., growth is expected to be zero), Equation 6 reduces to the formula for a **perpetuity**. Since the growth rate is zero, each dividend is the same as the preceding dividend, so D_1 is the same as D_0.

$$P_0 = \frac{D_1}{k_e - \overline{g}} = \frac{D_0(1 + g)}{k_e - \overline{g}}$$

$$P_0 = \frac{\$2.00(1 + 0)}{.15 - .0}$$

$$P_0 = \frac{\$2.00}{.15} = \$13.33$$

The difference between the price assuming five percent growth and the price assuming no growth is what we refer to as the **present value of growth opportunities**. This is fitting, since the difference in the prices is caused solely by the increase in our expectations of the future growth of the firm.[14]

> The difference between the firm's stock price assuming no growth and its current stock price is the **present value of growth opportunities**.

Under certain circumstances, the firm might be expected to enjoy "supernormal" growth for a number of years and then revert to its more predictable, normal growth. Perhaps Amazing Glass has developed a new type of glass that would give it a competitive advantage for four years, the time it will take competitors to develop their own glass. In this case, we'll assume that Amazing's assets, earnings, and dividends will grow at an accelerated rate of 10 percent for four years then revert to the normal growth of five percent for all periods after year four.

To assist in the valuation of the stock under this scenario, we will illustrate our expected cash flows on a timeline as we did for bond valuation. The difference is that we are required to estimate each cash flow (i.e., dividend) for the stock instead of plotting the bond coupon payments in the form of an annuity. D_0 is the last dividend declared and paid by the board of directors. Each successive dividend must be estimated as the previous dividend multiplied by $(1 + g)$. Let's see how it looks on the timeline.

---

[14] To estimate the market's assessment of the firm's growth opportunities, compare its current price to its price assuming no growth.

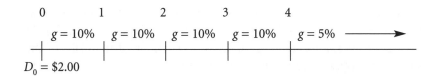

The growth rate for the first four years is 10 percent, meaning dividends one through four are expected to be 10 percent greater than each preceding dividend. We estimate them as:

$$D_1 = D_0(1 + g) = \$2.00(1.10) = \$2.20$$
$$D_2 = D_1(1 + g) = \$2.20(1.10) = \$2.42$$
$$D_3 = D_2(1 + g) = \$2.42(1.10) = \$2.66$$
$$D_4 = D_3(1 + g) = \$2.66(1.10) = \$2.93$$

```
0          1          2          3          4
   g = 10%    g = 10%    g = 10%    g = 10%    g = 5%  ──────────▶
   |          |          |          |          |
(2.00)      2.20       2.42       2.66       2.93
```

In order to complete the common stock valuation, we need to estimate all future dividends, not just dividends one through four. We can simplify the process to estimate dividends five through infinity. Recall that as long as the dividend growth is constant, we can utilize Equation 6 to find their present value. Our example fits this requirement, because starting with dividend five, dividends are expected to grow at a rate of five percent indefinitely.

Equation 6 shows the relationship between the price at time zero (today) and the first dividend, D_1. We can rewrite Equation 6 in its general form that shows the relationship between the price of a common stock at any time and its next dividend:

$$P_0 = \frac{D_1}{k_e - \overline{g}} \tag{6}$$

$$P_n = \frac{D_{n+1}}{k_e - \overline{g}} \tag{6a}$$

A firm is considered an ongoing concern with no maturity. The value of its common stock is the present value of an endless stream of dividends.

Using the general form, Equation 6a, we can estimate the "price" at time four by using the dividend at time five. The word "price" is in quotes because, although it actually is an estimate of the price of the stock in four years, we are using it here to indicate the present value of dividends 5 through infinity at time four.

$$P_n = \frac{D_{n+1}}{k_e - \overline{g}}$$

$$P_4 = \frac{D_5}{k_e - \overline{g}} = \frac{\$2.93(1.05)}{.15 - .05}$$

$$P_4 = \frac{\$2.93}{.10} = \$30.77$$

Our estimate of the present value of dividends five through infinity at time four is $30.77. Instead of actually estimating all dividends occurring beyond dividend four and finding their present values, we can use the $30.77 in their place. Let's place the cash flows on our timeline again.

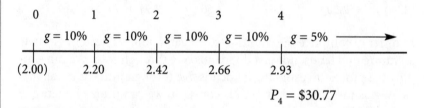

We are now in a position to calculate the present value of all future dividends to find our estimate of the current stock price. The first three amounts on the timeline are the next four dividends, $2.20, $2.42, $2.66, and $2.93, respectively. The fourth figure, $30.77, is the present value (i.e., price) of dividends occurring after constant growth resumes. Together, these two pieces represent the present value of all future dividend estimates. We are now prepared to calculate the estimated stock value of Amazing Glass:

$$P_0 = \sum_{t=1}^{\infty} \frac{D_t}{(1+k_e)^t} \qquad\qquad (5)$$

$$P_0 = \frac{D_1}{(1+k_e)^1} + \frac{D_2}{(1+k_e)^2} + \frac{D_3}{(1+k_e)^3} + \frac{D_4}{(1+k_e)^4} + \frac{P_4}{(1+k_e)^4}$$

$$P_0 = \frac{2.20}{(1.15)} + \frac{2.42}{(1.15)^2} + \frac{2.66}{(1.15)^3} + \frac{2.93}{(1.15)^4} + \frac{30.77}{(1.15)^4}$$

$$P_0 = \frac{2.20}{(1.15)} + \frac{2.42}{1.3225} + \frac{2.66}{1.5209} + \frac{2.93}{1.7490} + \frac{30.77}{1.7490}$$

$$P_0 = 1.91 + 1.83 + 1.75 + 1.68 + 17.59 = \$24.76$$

Given our estimates of the stock's future dividends, we estimate the price of Amazing Glass to be $24.76. This adds further evidence of the value of a firm's growth potential. Let's sum up our findings under various growth assumptions:

- If $g = 0$ percent, then $P = \$13.33$.
- If $g = 5$ percent, then $P = \$21.00$.
- If $g = 10$ percent for four years and 5 percent afterwards, then $P = \$24.76$.

The value of the stock increased with assumptions of greater growth. At a five percent growth, the stock value increased by $7.67 compared to the zero growth estimate. This $7.67 is the present value *per share* of the expected growth in the firm's assets, earnings, and dividends. When we assumed the firm developed a new product that gave it a temporary advantage over its competitors, its stock price increased another $3.76 *per share*. The magnitude of these increases in value is more impressive when you consider that the typical large, publicly traded firm can have several hundred million shares of common stock outstanding.

Other Equity Securities

Preferred stock is another well-known form of equity security.[15] As with common stock, preferred stock prices are calculated by taking the present value of all expected future dividends.

Let's assume you are valuing a preferred stock with a face value of $100 and a 6 percent dividend, D_p. The required return on the preferred stock, k_p, is 6 percent, and it will never be retired. That is, the preferred stock is **perpetual**, which means that the $6.00 in annual dividends is never expected to stop or change.

Perpetual preferred stock has no maturity. It is expected to pay dividends forever.

Equation 5 is the general equation used to value any dividend-paying (equity) security. If dividends are never expected to change, the growth in dividends is zero, and Equation 5 reduces to the **constant growth dividend discount model**, Equation 6.

$$P_0 = \sum_{t=1}^{\infty} \frac{D_t}{(1+k_e)^t} \tag{5}$$

$$P_0 = \frac{D_1}{k_e - \overline{g}} \tag{6}$$

Substituting the appropriate data into Equation 6, we find our preferred stock is selling at par, $100.

$$P_p = \frac{D_p}{k_p - \overline{g}} = \frac{D_p}{k_p - 0} = \frac{D_p}{k_p} = \frac{\$6.00}{.06} = \$100.00$$

Because of the fixed dividend payment, preferred stock prices fluctuate in the same manner as fixed income securities. Recall that a fixed income security's price is inversely related to changes in interest rates. **Figure 7** shows the price of our preferred stock assuming various required returns. In each case the price is found as above using

$P_p = \dfrac{D_p}{k_p}$, the formula for the price of perpetual preferred stock.

You will notice from **Figure 7** that the price of a preferred stock varies much like the price of a bond when its required return changes. As the required return increases, the price decreases. As the required return

[15] In the Corporate Finance chapter, we discussed the equity and debt characteristics of preferred stock. For valuation purposes we are considering preferred stock to be an equity security.

decreases, the price of the preferred stock increases. And as long as the required return is equal to the dividend rate, the preferred stock sells at par.

Figure 7

Perpetual Preferred Stock:
Price Reactions to Changes in Required Return
Face value = $100, Dividend = $6.00 (6%)

k_p	P_p
4%	150.00
4.5%	133.33
5%	120.00
5.5%	109.09
6%	**100.00**
6.5%	92.31
7%	85.71
7.5%	80.00
8%	75.00

SUMMARY OF SECTION 2

Learning Objectives: *To calculate and interpret the price of debt securities. To calculate and interpret the price of equity securities.*

A. To value any security we use the **capitalization of income method**.
   1. Estimate all future cash flows from the security.
   2. Estimate the risk of the cash flows.
   3. Based upon the risk, determine a required return (discount rate).
   4. Find the total present value (today) of the cash flows.
B. The most common debt securities are short and long-term **bonds**.
   1. Almost all debt instruments are fixed income securities. Payments and the payment schedule are contractual.
   2. The U.S. Treasury sells Treasury Notes that range in maturity from one to ten years.
   3. Municipalities and corporations sell bonds with original lives of ten to thirty years.

4. Corporate bonds are typically sold with face values of $1,000.
   a. U.S. corporations usually pay semiannual coupon payments.
   b. The coupon rate is stated as a percentage of face value.
   c. Each semiannual coupon is half of the annual interest payment.
   d. The principal (i.e., face value) is repaid at maturity.
5. The total present value of all coupons and the face value is our estimate of the value of the bond.
6. When bonds are purchased between coupon payment dates, the buyer must pay **accrued interest**.
7. Bond prices are sensitive to changes in interest rates (required return).
   a. When the coupon rate equals the required return, the bond will sell at par (face value).
   b. When the required return increases (decreases), the price of the bond will fall (rise).
   c. The longer the maturity of the bond, the greater the price reaction to a given change in required return.
   d. The greater the coupon rate on the bond, the smaller the price reaction to a given change in required return.

C. **Common stock** is the best-known equity security.
   1. Dividends are the only cash flow associated with common stock. One way to determine the value of a common stock is by calculating the present value of dividends.
   2. Each dividend is estimated as the previous dividend multiplied by one plus the growth between them.
   3. When dividends are never expected to change, we say there is zero growth in dividends.
      a. The dividends can be treated as a **perpetuity**.
      b. The present value of the perpetuity of dividends, D, is found by dividing the cash flow (dividend) by the interest rate (required return, k_e).

$$P = \frac{D}{k_e}$$

   4. When dividends are expected to grow at a **constant rate**, $\overline{g}$, indefinitely, we can value the stock using the **constant growth dividend** discount model. The price equals the total present value of all dividends to be received.

$$P_n = \frac{D_{n+1}}{k_e - \overline{g}}$$

5. Some companies experience an **explicit growth period**.
   a. Dividends grow at a rate above the normal industry growth rate.
   b. This supernormal growth is due to a temporary competitive advantage.
   c. Each dividend during this period is estimated using an explicit growth rate.
6. Following the explicit growth period, the firm will return to its normal growth rate implied by its position in the industry. This is known as the **implicit growth period**.
7. The estimated price of the stock is the present value of all future dividends.
   a. We find the present value of all dividends to be received during the **explicit growth** period.
   b. We find the present value of all dividends to be received during the **implicit growth** period.
   c. Price = (Present value of dividends during the explicit growth period) + (Present value of dividends during the implicit or constant growth period).

$$P = \sum_{t=1}^{n} \frac{D_t}{(1 + k_e)^t} + \frac{\left(\dfrac{D_{n+1}}{k_e - g}\right)}{(1 + k_e)^n}$$

8. The increase in stock price caused by increased growth in dividends is known as the **present value of growth opportunities**.
D. **Preferred stock** pays contractual dividends, stated as percentage of face value.
   1. Preferred stock can be **perpetual**, which means that it has no maturity.
   2. Its price is the present value of all future dividends discounted at its required return.
   3. The present value of a perpetuity is the cash flow (preferred dividend) divided by the required return, k_p.

$$P_p = \frac{D_p}{k_p}$$

PRACTICE QUESTIONS

1. For a given present value and interest rate, the future value:
   A. increases as the number of compounding periods per year increases.
   B. decreases as the number of compounding periods per year increases.
   C. remains the same as the number of compounding periods per year increases.
   D. remains the same as the number of compounding periods per year decreases.

2. For a given future value and interest rate, the present value:
   A. increases as the number of compounding periods per year increases.
   B. decreases as the number of compounding periods per year increases.
   C. remains the same as the number of compounding periods per year increases.
   D. remains the same as the number of compounding periods per year decreases.

3. When a consumer loan is *fully amortized*, the loan payments contain:
   A. principal only.
   B. interest only.
   C. principal and interest in equal proportions.
   D. principal and interest in changing proportions.

4. What is the value of $2,000 after 5 years at an *annually* compounded stated annual rate of 10 percent?
   A. $3,221.
   B $3,258.
   C. $3,277.
   D. $3,297.

5. What is the value of $2,000 after 5 years at a *semiannually* compounded stated annual rate of 10 percent?
   A. $3,221.
   B $3,258.
   C. $3,277.
   D. $3,297.

6. What is the value of $2,000 after 5 years at a *quarterly* compounded stated annual rate of 10 percent?

    A. $3,221.
    B. $3,258.
    C. $3,277.
    D. $3,297.

7. What is the value of $2,000 after 5 years at a *daily* compounded stated annual rate of interest is 10 percent?

    A. $3,221.
    B $3,258.
    C. $3,277.
    D. $3,297.

8. If $5,000 is deposited into an account paying 6 percent, compounded monthly, what is the expected effective rate of return?

    A. 6.00%.
    B. 6.17%.
    C. 6.33%.
    D. 6.50%.

9. For any nominal rate of interest, when the number of compounding periods per year increases, the effective rate of interest:

    A. increases.
    B. decreases.
    C. remains the same.
    D. decreases at an increasing rate.

10. For a nominal rate of 15 percent, compounded quarterly, the effective rate is:

    A. 12.99%.
    B. 14.48%.
    C. 15.25%.
    D. 15.87%.

11. An investor plans to make six deposits of $10,000 into an account paying 10 percent, compounded annually. At the end of six years (at the time of the last deposit) how much will be in the account?

    A. $58,743.
    B. $60,000.
    C. $61,554.
    D. $77,156.

12. An investor plans to make six deposits of $10,000 into an account paying 10 percent, compounded annually. If she makes the deposits at the beginning of each year, how much will she have in the account at the end of six years?

    A. $73,225.
    B. $77,156.
    C. $82,311.
    D. $84,872.

13. If the bank charges 10 percent interest, with annual compounding, what are the six equal, end-of-year, annual payments for a loan of $43,553?

    A. $7,259.
    B. $8,389.
    C. $9,091.
    D. $10,000.

14. The price of a bond can be stated as which of the following?

    A. The present value of the coupons plus the present value of the principal.
    B. The present value of the coupons.
    C. The present value of the coupons less the present value of the face value.
    D. The present value of the face value.

15. Which of the following represents the value of a bond with a $1,000 face value, 10 years to maturity, a 10 percent coupon rate (semiannual coupons), and a required return of 10 percent?

    A. $587.
    B. $924.
    C. $1,000.
    D. $1,065.

16. If an investor purchased only the principal of a bond with a $1,000 face value, a coupon rate of 6 percent (semiannual coupons), 10 years to maturity, and a required return of 8 percent, he would pay:

    A. $407.71.
    B. $456.39.
    C. $864.10.
    D. $1,094.26.

17. Which of the following represents the value of a bond with a $1,000 face value, 10 years to maturity, a 10 percent coupon rate (semiannual coupons), and a required return of 12 percent?

    A. $885.30.
    B. $984.26.
    C. $1,000.00.
    D. $1,125.14.

18. If the required return is greater than the coupon rate, the bond sells at:

    A. a premium.
    B. a discount.
    C. par less any accrued interest.
    D. par.

19. The longer the maturity of any fixed income instrument, the:

    A. more sensitive its price is to changes in interest rates.
    B. less sensitive its price is to changes in interest rates.
    C. sensitivity of its price to changes in interest rates remains same.
    D. lower its coupon rate.

20. The greater the interim cash flows associated with a fixed income security, the:

    A. less sensitive its price is to changes in interest rates.
    B. more sensitive its price is to changes in interest rates.
    C. smaller its coupon rate.
    D. smaller its face value.

21. The only cash flows associated with common stock are:

    A. dividends.
    B. preemptive cash.
    C. par value.
    D. retained earnings.

22. An analyst has gathered the following information about a firm:
    - The last dividend was $5.00.
    - The required return on equity is 15 percent.
    - Its assets, earnings, and dividends are expected to grow 6 percent per year indefinitely.

    The firm's stock should sell at:
    - A. $42.68.
    - B. $58.89.
    - C. $72.46.
    - D. $83.33.

23. A firm's $100 par preferred stock pays an annual 6 percent dividend and has a required return of 9 percent. The estimated market value is **closest to**:
    - A. $66.
    - B. $81.
    - C. $89.
    - D. $101.

24. A firm has experienced some difficulties lately. As a result, dividends are expected to grow at a reduced rate of 2 percent for the next two years and return to its historical rate of 5 percent after that. If the last dividend was $2.00 and the cost of equity capital is 15 percent, you can estimate the stock's market value to be:
    - A. $19.85.
    - B. $20.80.
    - C. $21.84.
    - D. $22.84.

ANSWERS AND SOLUTIONS

1. **A.** As illustrated in the equation $(1 + \frac{i}{m})^m - 1$, the effective interest rate increases as the number of compounding periods per year, m, increases. As the effective rate increases, the future value increases, since you are compounding at a higher rate.

2. **B.** This is the opposite of question 1. As the effective rate increases, the present value must decrease, since you are discounting at a higher rate.

3. **D.** When a consumer loan is fully amortized, the payments are typically equal for the life of the loan. Each payment includes interest on the amount of the loan still outstanding (remaining principal) with the rest of the payment applied to the principal. Since the amount of interest in each successive payment is computed on a declining principal, the amount of interest in each payment must decline. Since the interest portion of the payments declines over the life of the loan, the portion applied to principal must increase.

   Note: For problems 4 through 7 you can use the following formula:

   $$FV_n = PV(1 + \frac{i}{m})^{m*n}$$

   m is the number of compounding periods per year.

   i is the stated or nominal rate of interest.

   n is the number of years.

   PV is the beginning amount or present value, $2,000.

   FV is the ending amount or future value.

   Alternatively, you can plug the values into your TI BA II Plus® as shown. If you prefer to do that, set your P/Y value to 1.0 and enter the values. Remember, unless you enter –$2,000 for PV, you will obtain a negative FV, because the calculator will assume one cash flow is an inflow and the other an outflow.

4. **A.** Formula: $PV = 2,000$, $n = 5$, $m = 1$, $i = .10$, and $FV = \$3,221$

Calculator strokes:	–2000	PV
	10/1	I/Y
	5 × 1	N
	CPT	FV = $3,221

5. B. Formula: $PV = 2,000$, $n = 5$, $m = 2$, $i = .10$, and $FV = \$3,258$

    Calculator strokes: −2000   **PV**

                            10/2 =   **I/Y**

                            5 × 2 =   **N**

                          CPT   **FV** = $3,258

6. C. Formula: $PV = 2,000$, $n = 5$, $m = 4$, $i = .10$, and $FV = \$3,277$

    Calculator strokes: −2000   **PV**

                            10/4 =   **I/Y**

                            5 × 4 =   **N**

                          CPT   **FV** = $3,277

7. D. Formula: $PV = 2,000$, $n = 5$, $m = 365$, $i = .10$, and $FV = \$3,297$

    Calculator strokes: −2000   **PV**

                            10/365 =   **I/Y**

                            5 × 365 =   **N**

                          CPT   **FV** = $3,297

8. B. The effective return for an account is the same regardless of the amount of money deposited. Using the effective interest rate formula:

$$(1 + \frac{i}{m})^m - 1.0$$

$m = 12$, $i = .06$, effective rate = $1.0617 - 1 = 6.17$ percent

9. A. See the formula in the answer to question 8.

10. D. Using the effective rate formula again:

$$(1 + \frac{i}{m})^m - 1.0$$

$i = .15$, $m = 4$, effective rate = 15.87 percent

11. D. These are end-of-year payments. Your calculator should be set to END.

Note: Since it is default, END does not display on your calculator. If BGN is displayed, perform the following keystrokes:

[2nd] → [BGN]

[2nd] → [SET]

[2nd] → [QUIT]

Calculator strokes:

−10,000	[PMT]
10	[I/Y]
6	[N]
[CPT]	[FV] = $77,156

12. D. These are beginning-of-year payments. Your calculator should be set to BGN.

Note: BGN must be displayed on your calculator to use beginning-of-year cash flows. If BGN is not displayed, perform the following keystrokes:

[2nd] → [BGN]

[2nd] → [SET]

[2nd] → [QUIT]

Calculator strokes:

−10,000	[PMT]
6	[N]
10	[I/Y]
[CPT]	[FV] = $84,872

13. D. The present value of the payments must equal the amount borrowed. Be sure your calculator is set to END.

Calculator strokes:

−43,553	[PV]
10	[I/Y]
6	[N]
[CPT]	[PMT] = $10,000

14. A. The price of a bond is the present value of the coupons plus the present value of the principal.

15. C. When the coupon rate and the required return are the same, the bond will sell at par.

16. B. This is equivalent to a zero-coupon bond and is calculated just like a lump sum present value calculation.

Calculator strokes:

−1000	FV	
10 × 2 =	N	
8/2 =	I/Y	
CPT	PV	= $456.39

Please note that it is market convention to compute the value of zero-coupon bonds using a semiannual periods assumption.

17. A. Bond price without accrued interest.

Calculator strokes:

−1000	FV	
−100/2 =	PMT	
12/2 =	I/Y	
10 × 2 =	N	
CPT	PV	= $885.30

18. B. When required return increases, the bond price falls.

19. A. The longer the maturity of any fixed income instrument, the more sensitive its price is to changes in interest rates.

20. A. The greater the interim cash flows associated with a fixed income security, the less sensitive its price is to changes in interest rates.

21. A. Dividends are the only cash flows associated with common stock.

22. B. The firm's dividends are expected to grow at a rate of 6 percent forever, so we can use the constant growth dividend valuation model.

$$P_0 = \frac{D_1}{k_e - \overline{g}} = \frac{\$5.00(1.06)}{.15 - .06} = \$58.89$$

23. A. The dividend is $100*.06 = $6. Hence, the valuation is $6/.09 = $66.67.

24. A. Using a timeline:

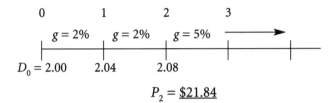

$$P_2 = \$21.84$$

Since dividend 2 is at the beginning of the infinite period of constant growth, we can use it to find the price at time 2 by growing D_2 at the assumed constant rate to find D_3.

$$P_2 = \frac{2.08(1.05)}{.15 - .05} = \$21.84$$

$$P_0 = \frac{2.04}{1.15} + \frac{2.08}{(1.15)^2} + \frac{21.84}{(1.15)^2} = \$19.85$$

$$P_0 = 1.77 + 1.57 + 16.51 = \$19.85$$

Portfolio Theory

When choosing investments, the old saying, "Don't put all your eggs in one basket," should come to mind. The investing equivalent of this expression is that you should not use all your money to buy the common stock of only one firm, since the success or failure of this investment strategy depends solely upon the fortunes of that one firm. However, if you purchase the common stock of several firms, the fate of one company has far less impact on the value of your portfolio.

In his Nobel Prize–winning work of 1959, Harry Markowitz[1] proved mathematically what investors had wisely assumed for decades. Using variance to measure risk, Markowitz demonstrated that the covariance between securities is a more important component of portfolio risk versus an individual security's variance. By combining securities that exhibit low covariance with each other, you can significantly reduce the risk of your portfolio. This process is known as **diversification**. The key to diversification is that **unsystematic risk** may be lowered or even eliminated. **Systematic risk**, or **nondiversifiable risk**, is embedded in all risky securities and is the risk that remains in a well-diversified portfolio.

Total risk, which consists of both systematic and unsystematic risk, is a measure of the variability of the returns in a portfolio. When the stock market is up, individual securities may tend to follow the market

Unsystematic risk can be reduced or even eliminated through diversification.

Systematic risk is immune from the effects of diversification.

[1] Harry Markowitz, *Portfolio Selection: Efficient Diversification of Investments* (John Wiley and Sons, 1959).

to varying degrees. However, some stocks may drop in price due to labor, production, or other problems associated with just those firms.

The inability to predict the impact of systematic and unsystematic risk on a stock's price is the cause of our inability to accurately forecast stock prices and investment returns. As you might guess, the more variable the returns on a common stock, the more inherent uncertainty there is in forecasting its performance. This increases the importance of risk management. If we can minimize risk (i.e., the variability in future stock price movements), we can more accurately predict the future for individual stocks and portfolios.

Section 1 begins with a discussion of risk aversion, a critical assumption in portfolio theory. Section 2 covers expected returns and probability distributions for individual stocks. Section 3 extends this discussion to include expected returns and standard deviation for portfolios (although portfolios can contain any type of investment, we will focus on common stock portfolios). Section 4 discusses the relationships between risk, return, and market prices.

In this chapter, your learning objectives are the following:

1. To understand the concept of risk aversion.
2. To calculate and interpret the expected return and standard deviation for a portfolio.
3. To calculate and interpret the covariance and correlation between two stocks.
4. To calculate the expected return and standard deviation for a portfolio.
5. To interpret and apply the CAPM to find the expected return for an individual stock and for a portfolio.

SECTION 1: RISK AVERSION

The assumption of **risk aversion** is crucial to our understanding of portfolio theory. In Section 3 of the Corporate Finance chapter, we discussed the relationship between risk and return. We argued that the rational investor will always minimize risk for a given level of return or maximize return for a given level of risk. This assumption implies investors are *risk averse*.

Aversion to risk does not mean investors will totally avoid risk, only that they will avoid *unnecessary* risk. If a method exists to reduce risk with minimal impact on expected return, the rational investor will use it. An example will make it clear that, to varying degrees, all investors are risk averse.

Assume you are offered a choice between equal amounts of money in two different rooms, which are clearly marked:

Room one: There is absolutely no risk. You open the door, enter the room, take the money, and enjoy it to your heart's delight.

Room two: There is a very large, ferocious dog in the room. You can have the money, but only if you can get in the room and leave with it.

Which room would you choose? Obviously, you would select room one, demonstrating that you are risk averse. In fact, anyone would make the same decision, because the expected return is the same for either decision, but the money in room two (the return from selecting room two) is risky.

If we leave the same amount of money in room one and gradually increase the amount of money in room two, we will reach a point where you will find it more difficult to make a choice. At some point, we will reach your **indifference point**, which is the exact amount of money (i.e., increased return) necessary to offset the risk associated with entering room two. Of course, the amount of additional return to make different individuals indifferent to the choices will vary based upon a number of characteristics (e.g., age, current wealth, and income). The increased amount of money necessary to compensate for risk is referred to as a **risk premium**. A rational investor will always demand an increased return (i.e., a risk premium) for increased risk.

We'll continue our discussion with an example that demonstrates another characteristic of risk aversion, **decreasing marginal utility**. You're with friends at a party and someone comes up with a new party game. He'll flip a coin one time. If it lands on one side, he'll pay you $0.10. If it lands on the other side, you must pay him $0.10. Would you play? Sure, losing $0.10 isn't considered a major loss and you might even win $0.10.

All investors are **risk averse**. They will always avoid unnecessary risk.

An **indifference point** is reached when the risk and return of two investments makes an investor indifferent between them.

All rational investors demand a **risk premium** to compensate for the risk of an investment.

Decreasing marginal utility means each new dollar gives the individual less utility (satisfaction) than the preceding dollar.

After playing the game once with almost everyone at the party, the originator of the game changes the rules. If the coin lands on one side, he will pay you $1,000; if it lands on the other side, you must pay him $1,000. Would you play the game now? Probably not.

Stated simply, the pain from losing $1,000 is far greater than the pleasure from winning $1,000. This is because you have **decreasing marginal utility**.[2] Each dollar you receive increases your utility (i.e., satisfaction), but to a lesser degree than the previous dollar did. Since each new dollar increases your utility (happiness) at a decreasing rate, as you lose dollars, each dollar takes away increasing amounts of utility.

Utility is measured in units called **utils**.

Let's look at the following representation of marginal utility. The utility of each dollar, measured in **utils**, is indicated beneath the line in **Figure 1**. Your current wealth is $W and your utility from that amount of money is 1,000 utils. If you win, you move to the right on the line, indicating an increase in your wealth and utility. If you lose, you move to the left, indicating a decrease in your wealth and utility.

Figure 1: Increases and decreases from current wealth, $W, and the accompanying increases and decreases in utils from the current 1,000.

-$6	-$5	-$4	-$3	-$2	-$1	$W	+$1	+$2	+$3	+$4	+$5	+$6
-13	-12	-11	-10	-9	-8	1,000	+6	+5	+4	+3	+2	+1

For example, if you win $1.00, you collect an additional six utils. If you win another $1.00, you collect five more utils. If you lose $1.00, you give up eight utils; and if you lose another $1.00, you give up nine more utils, and so on. If you lose $6.00, your final utility is $1,000 - 8 - 9 - 10 - 11 - 12 - 13 = 937$ utils. If you win $6.00, your final utility is $1,000 + 6 + 5 + 4 + 3 + 2 + 1 = 1,021$ utils. By losing $6.00, you give up 63 utils; but by winning $6.00, you only gain 21 utils. Losing hurts. Although the increments of utility between successive dollars are exaggerated, this example clearly shows the phenomenon of decreasing marginal utility.

We will continue with our discussion of portfolio theory by first concentrating on expected returns for individual stocks.

[2] For more on utility theory, see Gwartney, Stroup, and Sobel, *Economics: Private and Public Choice, 9E* (The Dryden Press, 2000), 495.

SECTION 2: EXPECTED RETURN

The expected return for any investment depends upon the price you initially paid for it and the promised cash flow(s) in the future.[3] For instance, assume you pay $100 for an investment that promises to pay $110 in one year. Your expected return is 10 percent.

$$\hat{R} = \frac{V_1 - V_0}{V_0} = \frac{\$110 - \$100}{\$100} = .10 = 10\%$$

$\hat{R}$ = is your expected return.

V_0 is your initial investment.

V_1 is the value of your investment in one year.

Ten percent is the *expected* return because the $110 cash flow is due in one year, and many things could happen to interfere with receiving it *exactly as expected*. A change in how the $110 is received, such as receiving it later than promised, receiving it in installments, or receiving a smaller amount, may make your actual return less than the expected return.

Think of the difference between expected and actual return in the following way. The **expected return** is *estimated* at the beginning of the investment period (i.e., looking into the future), and is based upon the price you *pay* and the cash flow(s) you expect. The actual return, often referred to as the *historical return*, is the calculated return on the investment (i.e., looking back from the end of the investment period) based upon the price you paid and the cash flow(s) you *received*.

The expected return on a share of common stock is not based totally upon the price you pay and the expected cash flow(s). Instead, the expected return is based upon the price you pay, dividends you expect to receive, and price appreciation (i.e., capital gains). Although you might be able to predict with some accuracy the amount of dividends you will receive, the amount of price appreciation is subject to the effects of many different factors. Depending upon events between the day you purchase the stock and the day you sell it, the price could increase, decrease, or stay the same.

The **expected return** is estimated at the beginning of the investment period (looking into the future), and is based upon the price you pay and the cash flow(s) you expect to receive.

The **actual return**, often referred to as the historical return, is the calculated return on the investment (looking back from the end of the investment period) based upon the price you paid and the cash flow(s) you received.

---

[3] From our discussion of risk and return, we know the *required* return on any investment is based upon the investment's risk. In the current discussion, we assume the required and expected returns are the same.

Figure 2 shows the **probability distribution** of *possible* one-year returns for Meyer's Manufacturing (MM) common stock. We assume MM will operate without any unexpected firm specific events, but we will allow different states of the economy over the period: boom, normal, and recession.[4] In calculating the expected return for MM stock, we must estimate the probability of each state of the economy as well as the stock's performance if that state occurs.

Figure 2: Probability Distribution of Returns for Meyer's Manufacturing

State of the Economy	Probability of this State Occurring	Expected Return in this State
Boom	.30	20%
Normal	.40	15%
Recession	.30	10%

If a "normal" economy exists over the next year, we expect MM stock to earn 15 percent. If the economy goes into a recession, the expected return for MM drops to 10 percent. A boom economy will result in a 20 percent return for MM. Based upon our predictions for the economy and MM, the expected return for MM stock for the coming year is:

$$\hat{R} = \sum_{i=1}^{n} P_i R_i \qquad (1)$$

$\hat{R}$ is the expected return for MM.

R_i is our estimate of the return on MM if economic state i occurs.

P_i is the probability that economic state i will occur.

n is 3, the number of possible states of the economy.

$$\hat{R} = (.3)(.10) + (.4)(.15) + (.3)(.20) = .03 + .06 + .06 = .15 = 15\%$$

We have estimated the *expected* return for MM based upon our estimates of possible states of the economy and the return on MM if each condition should occur. Now we will estimate the accompanying risk using the standard deviation of *possible* returns for MM.

[4] Of course, there are many degrees of boom and recession creating infinite possible states of the economy. For simplicity, however, we assume only three possible, distinct states of the economy.

$$\sigma_{MM} = \sqrt{\sum_{i=1}^{n} = P_i(R_i - \hat{R})^2} \qquad (2)$$

σ_{MM} is the standard deviation of the possible returns for MM stock.[5]

R_i is our estimate of the return on MM if state i occurs.

$\hat{R} =$ is the average of the three possible returns for MM.

P_i is the probability that economic state i will occur.

$$\sigma_{MM} = \left(.30(.20 - .15)^2 + .40(.15 - .15)^2 + .30(.10 - .15)^2\right)^{1/2}$$

$$\sigma_{MM} = (.0015)^{1/2} = .0387 = 3.87\%$$

We now have MM stock's expected return and standard deviation. What does that give us? If our estimates are reasonably accurate, we can calculate the **range** of all possible actual returns for the stock. From the **empirical rule**, we know that approximately 68 percent of all possible returns will lie within one standard deviation of the mean (i.e., expected return). Ninety-five percent will lie within two standard deviations, and 99 percent of all possible returns will lie within three standard deviations of the mean. Since one standard deviation for MM equals 3.87 percent, we calculate the following ranges:

$\pm$ one standard deviation = 15 percent $\pm$ 3.87 percent = 11.13 percent to 18.87 percent

$\pm$ two standard deviations = 15 percent $\pm$ 2(3.87 percent) = 7.26 percent to 22.74 percent

$\pm$ three standard deviations = 15 percent $\pm$ 3(3.87 percent) = 3.39 percent to 26.61 percent

Given the ranges we calculated using the expected return and standard deviation, we can estimate the following probability distribution of possible returns for MM. At the beginning of the year we *expect* our actual return to be 15 percent for the year, but due to its risk (i.e., variability), we estimate there is:

- A **68 percent probability** that the actual return for MM will be between 11.13 percent and 18.87 percent.

The **empirical rule** uses the expected return and standard deviation to determine the distribution of possible returns.

[5] This is the formula for the *ex ante* (expected) standard deviation. In the Corporate Finance chapter, we found the *ex post* (historical) standard deviation.

- A **95 percent probability** that the actual return for MM will be between 7.26 percent and 22.74 percent.
- A **99 percent probability** that the actual return for MM will be between 3.39 percent and 26.61 percent.

Based upon projections for MM, your expected return for the coming year is 15 percent, and you are 99 percent certain that the actual return will not be below 3.39 percent or above 26.61 percent.

SECTION 3: PORTFOLIO ANALYSIS

Return

Let's now assume MM is just one of six different stocks you hold in a portfolio with a total value of $50,000. We'll assume you have already estimated the expected return for all six of your stocks as shown in **Figure 3**. In a manner very similar to calculating the expected return for an individual stock, the expected return for your portfolio is a weighted average of the expected returns of the individual stocks in the portfolio. The **weight** of each stock is the amount invested in the stock as a percentage of the total value ($50,000) of the portfolio.

The **portfolio expected return** is a weighted average of the expected returns for the individual stocks in the portfolio.

$$\hat{R}_p = \sum_{i=1}^{n} W_i \hat{R}_i \qquad (3)$$

$\hat{R}_p$ is the expected return for the portfolio.

$\hat{R}_i$ is the expected return for stock i.

W_i is the "weight" of stock i in the portfolio.

n is 6, the number of stocks in the portfolio.

Figure 3: Composition of a Portfolio of Six Stocks

Stock	$\hat{R}$	Investment	Weight
AA	12%	$9,000	0.18
BB	11%	6,000	0.12
CC	10%	8,000	0.16
DD	14%	9,000	0.18
EE	13%	8,000	0.16
MM	15%	10,000	0.20
		$50,000	1.00 = 100%

$$\hat{R}_p = .18(.12) + .12(.11) + .16(.10) + .18(.14) + .16(.13) + .20(.15)$$

$$\hat{R}_p = .0216 + .0132 + .016 + .0252 + .0208 + .03 = .1268 = 12.68\%$$

The expected return on your portfolio of six stocks is 12.68 percent. We know that estimating the expected return on any investment does not give us complete information. We must also estimate the associated risk. Unfortunately, from a mathematical standpoint, the risk (i.e., standard deviation) associated with the expected return of a portfolio is not simply a weighted average of the risk of the individual stocks.

Risk

In previous discussions, we measured the risk of MM stock using the standard deviation of its possible returns. We also assumed MM's return would not be affected by unexpected firm-specific events. However, we know from the earlier discussion of risk and return that the factors which cause variability in the returns on any common stock can be divided into two categories: systematic risk, also known as market risk or nondiversifiable risk; and unsystematic risk, also known as firm specific or diversifiable risk, because it can be significantly reduced or even eliminated when we combine the stocks of many different firms in a portfolio.

The **portfolio standard deviation** is based upon the standard deviations of each stock, the weight of each stock in the portfolio, and the **correlations** between each stock.

For simplicity, we will now consider a portfolio containing only two stocks. The expected return and standard deviation for the stocks are shown in **Figure 4**.

Figure 4: Expected Returns, Standard Deviation, and Weights for a Two-Stock Portfolio

Stock	Expected Return	Std. Dev.	Weight
a	.12	.040	.40
b	.14	.055	.60

$$\hat{R}_p = .4(.12) + .6(.14) = .048 + .084 = .1320 = 13.2\%$$

The expected return for the portfolio, 13.2 percent, is a weighted average of the expected returns for the two stocks. In contrast, the standard deviation is based upon the standard deviations of each stock, the weight of each stock in the portfolio, and the **correlation** between the two stocks. Recall that the correlation between two stocks is the degree to which their returns move together. In addition, we previously stated that correlation is the **covariance standardized** by the product of the stocks' standard deviations. That is, we defined the covariance between two stocks' returns as:

$$COV_{a,b} = \sigma_a \sigma_b \rho_{a,b} \qquad (4)$$

and

$$\rho_{a,b} = \frac{COV_{a,b}}{\sigma_a \sigma_b} \qquad (5)$$

$COV_{a,b}$ is the covariance of the returns on stocks a and b.
σ_a and σ_b are the standard deviations of stocks a and b.
$\rho_{a,b}$ is the correlation between the two stocks. Since correlation is the ratio of the covariance of the stocks and the product of their standard deviations, it will never be greater than absolute one (i.e., $-1 \leq \rho \leq +1$).

To demonstrate the effects of correlation on the standard deviation of the portfolio, we will assume values for $\rho_{a,b}$ and calculate the portfolio standard deviation at each value. The variance for a portfolio of two assets is measured by:

$$\sigma_p^2 = w_a^2 \sigma_a^2 + w_b^2 \sigma_b^2 + 2 w_a w_b COV_{a,b} \qquad (6)$$

σ_p^2 is the portfolio variance.
w_a and w_b are the weights of stocks a and b in the portfolio.
σ_a^2 and σ_b^2 are the variances of stocks a and b.
$COV_{a,b}$ is the covariance between the returns on stocks a and b.

If we substitute $\sigma_a \sigma_b \rho_{a,b}$ for $COV_{a,b}$ in Equation 6, we obtain the following:

$$\sigma_p^2 = w_a^2 \sigma_a^2 + w_b^2 \sigma_b^2 + 2 w_a w_b \sigma_a \sigma_b \rho_{a,b} \qquad (7)$$

$$\sigma_p^2 = (.4)^2(.04)^2 + (.6)^2(.055)^2 + 2(.4)(.6)(.04)(.055)\rho_{a,b}$$

$$\sigma_p = [.001345 + .001056\rho_{a,b}]^{1/2}$$

By substituting the values from **Figure 4** into Equation 7, we observe that the standard deviation of the portfolio depends ultimately upon the correlation of the stocks. **Figure 5** shows the variance and standard deviation for the portfolio at different measures of correlation between stocks a and b.

Figure 5: Variance and Standard Deviation of Portfolio a,b, Assuming Different Values of Correlation, $\rho_{a,b}$

$\rho_{a,b}$	σ_p^2	σ_p
−1.0	.000289	.0170
−0.5	.000817	.0286
0.0	.001345	.0367
+0.5	.001873	.0433
+1.0	.002401	.0490

It is apparent from **Figure 5** that the variance and standard deviation (our measure for total risk) decrease as correlation decreases. This is the mathematical phenomenon known as **diversification**. By combining stocks with less than perfect positive (+1.0) correlation, we can reduce the risk (standard deviation) of the portfolio below that of the weighted average of the individual stock's standard deviations.

For example, when we assume the maximum correlation (+1.0), the standard deviation of the portfolio is a simple weighted average of the standard deviations of the two stocks (i.e., .4(.04) + .6(.055) = .049). When we begin reducing the correlation, the portfolio standard deviation falls until it reaches its minimum value when correlation is −1.0. At the weights specified, 40 percent in stock a and 60 percent in stock b, the minimum standard deviation for our portfolio is .0170, which is considerably less than the standard deviation of either stock on an individual basis.

Please note that actual correlations among asset returns are quite unpredictable and subject to dramatic changes from period to period.

Figure 6 shows the relationship of portfolio risk, measured by standard deviation, and the number of different stocks in the portfolio. Although the reduction of risk with the inclusion of each additional stock decreases as the number of stocks in the portfolio increases, it is clear that when a large number of stocks are combined in a portfolio, the risk of the portfolio is dramatically reduced.

Diversification reduces the unsystematic risk in a portfolio.

You will also notice there is a value below which we cannot drive the portfolio standard deviation, no matter how many different stocks we hold. At this point, all the unsystematic risk has been eliminated, and we are left with only systematic risk, σ_m, or market risk. The exact number of different stocks at that point is uncertain, but after about 50 stocks, the gain from adding more stocks is very small.

The **portfolio standard deviation** gets smaller as each additional stock is added to the portfolio.

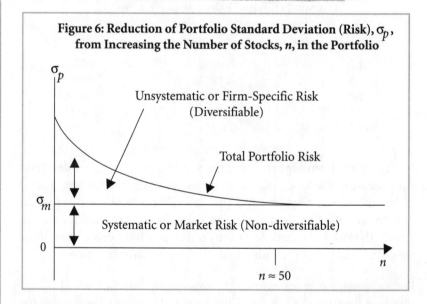

Figure 6: Reduction of Portfolio Standard Deviation (Risk), σ_p, from Increasing the Number of Stocks, n, in the Portfolio

Market Risk

Although combining a large number of different stocks in a portfolio can reduce or even eliminate unsystematic risk, we cannot diversify away systematic or market risk. Systematic risk is caused by economy-wide factors (e.g., inflation), which affect all stocks (and portfolios) to varying degrees. The reasons stocks are affected differently by macro-economic (economy-wide) events are numerous. For example, a firm's reaction to changes in inflation expectations will depend upon, among other things, how quickly the firm can recoup the increased cost of its inputs by increasing the price it charges for its output. Let's take a look at some of the more important market factors that affect all stocks: the macroeconomic factors.

Inflation. All required returns, k_i, include the risk-free rate of interest, r_f, plus a risk premium (RP_i). In turn, the risk free rate includes the real rate of interest (RR) and a premium for expected inflation (IP). Hence, we can express any required return as:

$$k_i = r_f + RP_i \tag{7}$$

and $\quad r_f = RR + IP \tag{8}$

so $\quad k_i = RR + IP + RP_i \tag{9}$

When inflation expectations change, the *indirect* impact on k_i, the impact on the risk premium, is very hard to quantify.[6] Its direct impact, the change in IP, is much more obvious. If inflation expectations increase, all investors will demand an increased inflation premium, IP, which will increase all required returns. If inflation expectations decrease, investors will lower required returns. The reaction in stock prices is almost immediate in either case.

Remember that the **expected return** on an investment is based upon the price we pay and the cash flows we expect to receive. The **required return** is based upon the real rate of interest, the premium for expected inflation, and the risk of the investment. Until now, we have assumed that expected returns and required returns are equal. That is, assets are priced such that their required and expected returns are the same and the market for stocks is in equilibrium.

When inflation increases, the required return will rise immediately, but the expected return remains unchanged. The result is that we have a short-run disequilibrium because the stock price is too high (its

Systematic or **market risk** is immune to the effects of diversification.

Inflation is a macro-economic variable that affects all stocks to varying degrees.

---

[6] With minor adjustments in inflation expectations, most risk premiums are not affected. With large adjustments, however, the change in default, liquidity, and maturity risk premiums can be significant.

return is too low). The price must fall to bring the expected return up to the required return.[7] In addition, the cost of the firm's inputs will rise as suppliers raise their prices, and operating expenses and wages will increase, reducing the firm's short-run cash flows and profits. If the firm is able to increase its output prices, its cash flows will increase, and its stock price will recover.

If you give this scenario some thought, you will understand why changes in inflation affect all firms, but does so to varying degrees. For instance, labor contracts fix wages for a period of time, so wages may take many months to react to changes in inflation. Rent and other real estate contracts usually don't have inflation clauses, so they will not change with inflation in the short term. Input prices might be contractual, meaning they cannot be adjusted for inflation, either. The ability to affect output prices depends on the nature of the product sold. Prices for gasoline seem to react almost immediately to announcements related to changes in supply. Suppliers can increase prices almost at will without much reduction in demand. However, if manufacturers of consumer durables (e.g., washing machines, refrigerators, etc.) increase prices, demand for their products may fall dramatically as consumers postpone purchases. In summary, the impact on some firms can be immediate and strong, while the impact on others is more gradual and less severe.

Risk Aversion. A rational, risk-averse investor will avoid unnecessary risk. He or she will require a higher return to compensate for increased risk. The level of risk aversion will determine the level of return necessary to satisfy a given investor. As a result, different investors may analyze an investment and arrive at different required returns.

> Individual investors have varying degrees of risk aversion.

You could respond to this by saying the degree of risk aversion of one investor has almost nothing to do with the return required by the market, and you would be correct, for the most part. The price of a stock is based upon the equilibrium of its required and expected returns. That equilibrium is reached through a very dynamic relationship between the firm's expected cash flows, the risk of those cash flows, and the price investors, as a *whole*, are willing to pay.

---

[7] We refer to an **equilibrium price** for a product, which is when supply equals demand. If a product is overpriced, its demand will fall and suppliers will be left with large inventories. To sell the product, suppliers will reduce prices until equilibrium is reached again.

The **market price** of a stock is the highest price at which the stock can sell at any particular point in time. Investors who feel a stock is under-priced believe the stock's expected return is higher than its required return and are eager to purchase it, driving its price up. When equilibrium is reached, the stock's expected return equals its required return.

If all investors' aversion to risk increased suddenly, each investor would require a relatively higher return. If this situation occurs, the required return for all stocks would increase above their expected returns, and all stock prices would fall. Conversely, an aggregate decrease in risk aversion would lead to price increases.

> If investors become more risk averse, the risk premium on all stocks will increase.

For instance, let's assume the economy is expanding rapidly, and there is no sign of a slowdown anytime soon. With the general success of the stock market, investors may tend to get overconfident. They know risk is always present, but they may have become less averse to risk, instead focusing their attention on seemingly unlimited returns. The recent experience of Internet stocks is a prime example: Because of the explosive growth in Internet stocks, investors poured billions of dollars into the industry without paying much attention to downside potential (i.e., risk).

In recessions, the opposite occurs. Investors become much more aware of risk and may become more protective of their wealth. For an equivalent amount of risk, investors now require higher risk premiums.

Macroeconomic Shocks. Shocks to the economy can be totally unexpected or they can be longer-term abnormalities. A good example of an economy-wide shock that can last for years is war. Anticipated or not, a war changes the focus of the entire economy. For example, during World War II, most American men of military age were sent off to war, while most women stayed home and ran the factories. Gasoline and many food and textile items were rationed at home, so the military would have adequate supplies.

> **Macroeconomic shocks** are economy-wide events that affect all stocks, to varying degrees.

In other words, the economy moved from peacetime production and growth to a military focus. Instead of making cars, factories made airplanes and military armament. Instead of making material for clothing, textile mills turned out nylon and silk for parachutes. The tremendous growth in manufacturing output made many companies' stock prices climb. As long as the government provided unending demand for output along with the funds to pay for it, some factories made abnormally high profits, and some investors made abnormally high returns.

National disasters (e.g., earthquakes and huge storms) are another example of economy-wide or macroeconomic shocks. When these disasters befall a small country, the resources of the government must be diverted toward humanitarian efforts. Large amounts of money are poured into the affected areas and commercial activities in those areas may be severely restricted. The economic impact on these nations can be enormous, as the interruption in the forces of supply and demand can take years to resolve.

The two economic shocks we have presented are both major, but not all shocks are as extreme. Some shocks may be significant but short-term; while others might be minor but last for years. Some macroeconomic factors will affect only some industries or regions of a nation, and some affect entire continents and eventually spread to all nations. Today, the word *macroeconomic* almost means *global*. With the degree of interdependence among the major economies of the world, macroeconomic events in one nation are often felt in the others. For instance, stock market movements in Japan are quickly interpreted into similar movements in the American markets. The point is that there are factors well beyond the control of the individual firm, and these factors impact all stock prices.

SECTION 4: RISK, RETURN, AND MARKET PRICES

Since only systematic risk is used to estimate required returns, it is the only relevant risk for pricing stocks.

From our previous discussions, we know that as long as stock returns are not perfectly positively correlated, we can diversify away most, if not all, unsystematic risk. This implies that unsystematic risk of a stock is irrelevant in a diversified portfolio. Thus, unsystematic risk is not used to determine the stock's required return.

Since even investors with small portfolios can eliminate unsystematic risk by holding shares of mutual funds, unsystematic risk will not be "priced" in the market. For simplicity, assume a stock has five "units" of systematic risk and five "units" of unsystematic risk. Also, assume investors require one percentage point of return for every unit of risk.

If the stock's total risk were used to set its required return, investors would discount its expected cash flows at 10 percent to determine the price they would pay. Wise investors, who will hold the stock in a diversified portfolio, will use only the stock's systematic risk, resulting in a required return of five percent. The result is that they will be willing to pay a higher price for the stock. In fact, investors who "price" systematic risk only will always be willing to pay more for any common stock. This means all stocks' required returns are set according to systematic risk. In turn, only systematic risk determines stock prices.

The Characteristic Line

We now know that general movements in the stock market affect all stocks, but we also know the effects vary from stock to stock. To estimate the reaction of an individual stock to market movements, we use the **characteristic line**. The characteristic line quantifies the relationship between the returns on a single common stock and the entire stock market through simple linear regression.[8] Equation 8 is the general form of the characteristic line.

The **characteristic line** is the regression model used to estimate betas for individual stocks and portfolios.

$$R_i = \alpha + \beta R_m + e \qquad (10)$$

R_i is the dependent variable, the returns on stock i.

R_m is the independent variable, the returns on the market.

α is the intercept of the regression line.

β is the regression coefficient.

e is the error term.

Simple linear regression finds the straight line that best describes the relationship between the independent and dependent variables. It assumes movements in the independent variable are related to the movements in the dependent variable. Since we assume the return on the stock market is the independent variable, the characteristic line estimates the movement in the individual stock that is related to market movements.

[8] For a complete discussion of regression analysis, see Mason, Lind, and Marchal, *Statistical Techniques in Business and Economics, 10 E* (Irwin, McGraw-Hill, 1999), 424.

To show how this regression works, we will assume we have calculated seven weekly returns for our stock and for the stock market (we use past or historical returns in the regression). We line up the returns—week one for both, week two for both, week three for both, etc.—and run the regression. **Figure 7** shows the observations (the weekly returns) plotted on a graph and the regression line that best fits them.

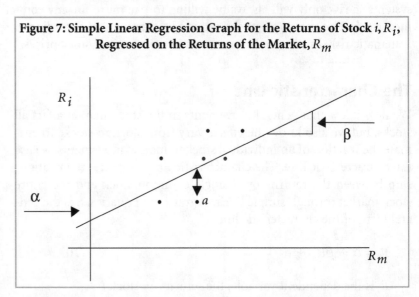

Figure 7: Simple Linear Regression Graph for the Returns of Stock i, R_i, Regressed on the Returns of the Market, R_m

The "best fit" is determined by using the **least squares method**. Point a on the graph is an individual observation, a combination of the returns on the market and on our stock for one of the seven weeks. The distance between it and the regression line is its **error**. A computer-based statistical application squares the error for each observation and adds them together. When it finds the line that creates the least sum of the squared errors, this result becomes the "best fit" line identifying the relationship between the variables.

Let's assume the following equation from our regression analysis:

$$R_i = 0.6 + 1.2R_m$$

The intercept for our estimated line is 0.6 and the slope coefficient is 1.2. The coefficient, referred to simply as **beta**, is by far the most important outcome from our regression. The beta tells us our stock changes 1.2 percentage points for every one-percentage-point change in the market. Another way of saying this is that our stock is 1.2 times

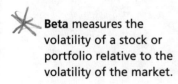

Beta measures the volatility of a stock or portfolio relative to the volatility of the market.

or 20 percent more volatile than the market. <u>Since the beta coefficient measures the influence of the market on our stock's returns, it measures our stock's **systematic risk**.</u>

We now have a way to separate out and designate the systematic risk of an individual stock, so we can now develop a relationship between systematic risk and return. We will assume all investors are risk averse and will demand a higher return for increasing risk. **Figure 8** is our estimate of what this relationship looks like. It shows the required return corresponding to any value of beta. While the line is upward sloping, without its slope and intercept values, the line only shows us that there is a positive relationship of risk and return.

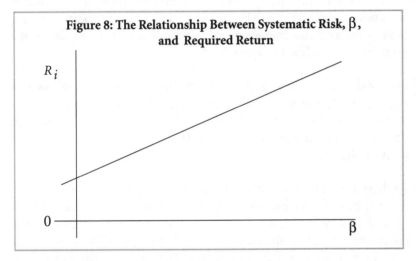

Figure 8: The Relationship Between Systematic Risk, β, and Required Return

Equation 11 shows us the calculation for the regression coefficient β. The equation can be used to find the beta for any asset by substituting its values for asset i in the equation.

$$\beta_i = \frac{COV_{i,m}}{\sigma_m^2} \qquad (11)$$

$$\beta_i = \frac{\sigma_i \sigma_m \rho_{i,m}}{\sigma_m^2} = \frac{\sigma_i \rho_{i,m}}{\sigma_m}$$

β_i is the beta coefficient from regressing the returns from stock i against the market.

σ_i and σ_m are the standard deviations of stock i and the market.

$\rho_{i,m}$ is the correlation of stock i with the market.

Thus, the beta of an asset is the ratio of its standard deviation to the standard deviation of the market, multiplied by their correlation. If we substitute values for a risk-free asset and for the overall stock market, we obtain the following:

$$\beta_{rf} = 0.0$$

$$\beta_m = 1.0$$

Beta for the risk-free asset must be zero, because the standard deviation for the risk-free asset is zero, and its correlation with the market is zero. Beta for the market is defined as being 1.0, because the correlation of the market with itself is +1.0, and the ratio of its standard deviation to itself must also be 1. Now that we know the beta values for the market and risk-free asset, we can move forward and define the properties of the line in **Figure 8**.

Even without risk (i.e., where $\beta = 0$) investors will require the risk-free rate of return, which includes the real rate of return (RR) and a premium for inflation (IP). Since the risk-free asset has a beta of 0.0, we know r_f, the rate of return on the risk-free asset, must be the intercept term in **Figure 9** below.

To determine the slope of the line, we turn to the general algebraic concept of **rise over run**. Starting at the intercept of the line and the vertical axis, and going out to point z on the line; we move out to the point where $\beta_i = 1$ on the horizontal axis, and we move from the point r_f to the point R_m on the vertical axis. The **run**, the distance moved along the horizontal axis, is equal to $1.0 - 0 = 1$. The **rise**, the distance moved along the vertical axis, is ($R_m - r_f$). We can now use the general equation for a straight line to find the equation of the line in **Figure 9**.

$$y = a + bx \tag{12}$$

y is the dependent variable on the vertical axis, R_i.

a is the intercept, r_f.

b is the slope of the line, ($R_m - r_f$).

x is the independent variable on the horizontal axis, β_i.

Beta for the **risk free asset** must be zero.

Beta for the **market** must be 1.0.

Substituting what we have found into Equation 10, we arrive at:

$$R_i = r_f + (R_m - r_f)\beta_i$$

or

$$R_i = r_f + \beta_i(R_m - r_f) \qquad (13)$$

Equation 13 is the equation known as the **security market line** (**SML**).[9] The SML is the graphic representation of the **capital asset pricing model** (**CAPM**). It shows the relationship between systematic risk and required return and is used extensively in investments and portfolio theory.

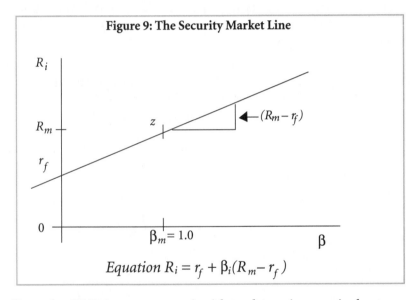

Figure 9: The Security Market Line

Equation $R_i = r_f + \beta_i(R_m - r_f)$

Since the CAPM uses systematic risk to determine required returns, economy-wide shocks can change the CAPM relationship. Both inflation and changing risk aversion impact the CAPM.

Changes in Inflation. Both the independent variable and the intercept term in the CAPM include a premium for expected inflation. If inflation expectations should increase, we see that both r_f and R_m will increase. From earlier discussions we know:

[9] Please note that additional mathematics and theory underlie the concept of the CAPM and the SML which is beyond the scope of this text. See Frank K. Reilly and Keith C. Brown, *Investment Analysis and Portfolio Management*, 6E (The Dryden Press, 2000), 285–312 for a more complete treatment of the derivation of the CAPM.

$$r_f = PR + IP$$

and $R_m = r_f + RP_m$

If **inflation expectations increase**, the intercept of the CAPM will increase (move up), causing an upward shift in the CAPM.

For example, if inflation expectations increase one percentage point, both r_f and R_m would increase the same percentage point. Since $(R_m - r_f)$ is the slope of the SML, and both variables increase the same amount, the slope remains unchanged.

However, the intercept will increase (i.e., move up) by one percentage point, causing an upward shift in the CAPM as illustrated in **Figure 10**. With an increase in inflation expectations, investors will require higher returns on all stocks. Of course, a decrease in inflation expectations would lead to a downward shift in the CAPM, as investors require lower returns on all stocks.

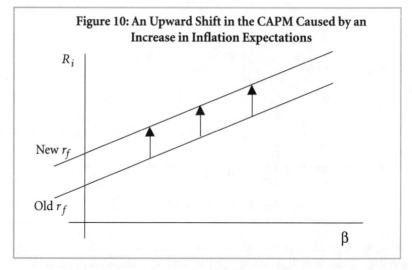

Figure 10: An Upward Shift in the CAPM Caused by an Increase in Inflation Expectations

The **market risk premium** measures the average degree of risk aversion in the market.

An increase in the market **risk aversion** will cause an upward **rotation** of the CAPM.

Changing Risk Aversion. The slope of the CAPM $(R_m - r_f)$ is referred to as the **market risk premium**. It measures the average degree of risk aversion in the market. If investors suddenly required more return per unit of risk, the risk premium would increase. The increased risk premium causes the slope of the CAPM to increase, as illustrated in **Figure 11**.

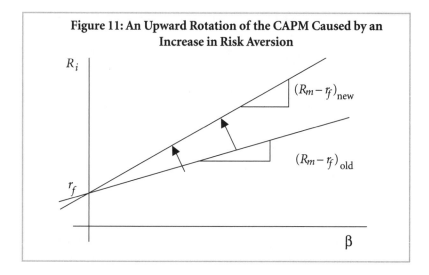

Figure 11: An Upward Rotation of the CAPM Caused by an Increase in Risk Aversion

Portfolio Betas

The beta for a portfolio is calculated much the same way as the beta for an individual stock. To find the beta for an individual stock, we employed the characteristic line in Equation 10. Recall that we regressed the returns of an individual stock against those of the market for the same period of time to obtain the beta value for a particular company. To use the characteristic line to estimate a portfolio beta, we use the same procedure. In this case, we regress the portfolio's returns against market returns (as with the estimation of an individual stock beta, we use historical returns).

Another alternative method of estimating a portfolio beta is to find the weighted average of the betas of the individual stocks using Equation 14.

$$\beta = \sum_{i=1}^{n} w_i \beta_i \qquad (14)$$

β_p is the portfolio beta.
β_i is the beta for stock i.
w_i is the weight of stock i in the portfolio.
n is the number of stocks in the portfolio.

The **portfolio beta** is the weighted average of the betas of the individual stocks in the portfolio.

Assume you hold a portfolio comprised of three stocks as follows:

Stock	Beta	$ Invested
A	1.3	1,000
B	0.8	2,000
C	1.7	2,000

$$\beta_p = w_a \beta_a + w_b \beta_b + w_c \beta_c$$

$$\beta_p = .2(1.3) + .4(0.8) + .4(1.7)$$

$$\beta_p = .26 + .32 + .68 = 1.26$$

If the risk-free rate is six percent and the market risk premium is four percent, we can use the CAPM to find the expected return on your portfolio.

$$\hat{R}_p = r_f + \beta_p(R_{m-} r_f)$$

$$\hat{R}_p = .06 + 1.26(.04) = .1104 = 11.04\%$$

CHAPTER SUMMARY

Learning Objective One: *To understand the concept of risk aversion.*

A. All rational investors are **risk averse**.
  1. They will avoid unnecessary risk.
  2. They will demand a **risk premium** to compensate for risk.
  3. They will always maximize return for a given level of risk and minimize risk for a given level of return.
B. Risk averse investors experience **decreasing marginal utility**.
  1. Each successive dollar earned increases utility less than the preceding dollar did.
  2. Losing an amount of money hurts more than the pleasure from winning the same amount.

Learning Objective Two: *To calculate and interpret the expected return and standard deviation for a portfolio.*

A. The **expected return** is based upon the purchase price and expected cash flows.
  1. The expected return on any investment is uncertain.
  2. Any change in the amount or timing of the expected cash flow(s) will make the actual (historical) return different from the expected return.
B. Whenever there is uncertainty in expected returns, there is a **probability distribution** of different possible returns.
  1. The expected return is the weighted average of the possible returns.
  2. Using the **empirical** rule, we know:
    a. A 68 percent probability exists that the actual return will fall within ± one standard deviation of the expected return.
    b. A 95 percent probability exists that the actual return will fall within ± two standard deviations from the expected return.
    c. A 99 percent probability exists that the actual return will fall within ± three standard deviations from the expected return.

Learning Objective Three: *To calculate and interpret the covariance and correlation between two stocks.*

A. The **covariance** between two stocks measures the tendency for the stocks to move together.
   1. The **correlation** between two stocks is their standardized covariance.
      a. The covariance of two stocks is the product of their standard deviations and their correlation.
      b. Correlation equals the covariance of the stocks divided by the product of their standard deviations.
   2. Correlation will never be greater than absolute one.
      a. Correlation cannot be greater than +1.0.
      b. Correlation cannot be less than –1.0.
B. Correlation between two stocks is a standardized measure of the tendency for two stocks to move together.
   1. Perfect positive correlation, +1.0, means they always move in the same direction.
   2. Perfect negative correlation, –1.0, means they always move in the opposite direction.
   3. A correlation of 0.0 means there is no statistical relationship between the movements of the stocks.

Learning Objective Four: *To calculate and apply the expected return and standard deviation for a portfolio.*

A. The **portfolio expected return** is a weighted average of the expected returns of the individual stocks in the portfolio. The **weight** of a stock in a portfolio is the amount of money invested in that stock as a percentage of the total portfolio value.
B. The standard deviation for a portfolio is not a weighted average of the individual stocks' standard deviations.
   1. **Portfolio standard deviation** depends upon:
      a. The standard deviations of the individual stocks.
      b. The weights of the stocks in the portfolio.
      c. The correlations among the stocks.
   2. The less correlation between stocks, the greater the reduction in portfolio standard deviation. By randomly combining a large number of stocks, investors can reduce or even eliminate the unsystematic risk of the portfolio.

C. As long as unsystematic risk can be eliminated, it is irrelevant for calculating required returns.
   1. Systematic risk is the only risk priced by the market.
   2. Only systematic risk will be considered when determining required returns.
D. Systematic risk is estimated by **beta**, β.
   1. Beta measures an individual stock's or a portfolio's reaction to stock market movements.
   2. Beta is the coefficient obtained by regressing the returns of the stock against the returns for the market over the same period of time.
   3. Beta can be used to estimate required returns for individual stocks and for portfolios by using the **security market line (SML)**. The SML is a graphic representation of the **capital asset pricing model (CAPM)**.

Learning Objective Five: *To interpret and apply the CAPM to find the expected return for an individual stock and for a portfolio.*

A. The CAPM uses beta as the measure of systematic risk in estimating required returns for individual stocks or portfolios.
B. The CAPM assumes all expected returns are the risk-free rate of return plus a risk premium.
   1. The risk premium is the stock's beta multiplied by the market risk premium, $(R_m - r_f)$.
   2. The equation for the CAPM is $R_i = r_f + \beta_i(R_m - r_f)$.
C. The relationship specified in the CAPM is subject to change with macroeconomic changes.
   1. If inflation expectations increase, the CAPM will shift up.
   2. If inflation expectations decrease, the CAPM will shift down.
   3. If the average risk aversion in the market increases, the slope of the CAPM will increase.
   4. If the average risk aversion in the market decreases, the slope of the CAPM will decrease.
D. The beta for a portfolio is a weighted average of the betas of the individual stocks in the portfolio. It can also be estimated through the use of regression analysis.

PRACTICE QUESTIONS

1. When different stocks are combined in a portfolio, which form of risk is reduced?

    A. Systematic risk.
    B. Unsystematic risk.
    C. Systematic and unsystematic risk.
    D. Market risk.

2. A risk-averse investor will:

    A. always avoid risk.
    B. compare investments by looking at their total risk only.
    C. always avoid unnecessary risk.
    D. compare investments by looking at their unsystematic risk only.

3. Which of the following is a characteristic of a risk-averse investor?

    A. Diminishing marginal utility.
    B. Seeking maximum expected return.
    C. Seeking minimum risk.
    D. Seeking maximum return and risk.

4. The mathematical phenomenon that occurs from less than perfect correlation among securities is known as:

    A. investor utility.
    B. diminishing marginal utility.
    C. covariance.
    D. diversification.

Use the following data for Meyer's Manufacturing to answer questions 5 and 6.

State of the Economy	Probability of this State Occurring	Expected Return in this State
Boom	.25	25%
Normal	.50	15%
Recession	.25	−5%

5. What is the expected return for Meyer's Manufacturing?

    A. 11.45%.
    B. 12.50%.
    C. 13.28%.
    D. 15.05%.

6. Assuming that MM'S expected return is 12.5 percent, which of the following is MM's **expected standard deviation?**

    A. 7.2%.
    B. 10.9%.
    C. 11.2%.
    D. 12.3%.

7. The standard deviation for stock a is .066, the standard deviation for stock b is .084, and the covariance between the two is .003. The correlation between stocks a and b is **closest to:**

    A. −0.50.
    B. 0.34.
    C. 0.55.
    D. 0.84.

8. The standard deviation for stock a is .066, the standard deviation for stock b is .084, and the correlation between the two is .75. What is the covariance of stocks a and b?

    A. .004.
    B. .011.
    C. .016.
    D. .025.

9. If the expected return for a stock is 12 percent, and its standard deviation is 8.2 percent, approximately 68 percent of its returns will lie between:

    A. 12% and 20.2%.
    B. 3.8% and 20.2%.
    C. −4.4% and 28.4%.
    D. −12.6% and 36.6%.

10. If the expected return for a stock is 12 percent and its standard deviation is 8.2 percent, approximately 95 percent of its returns will lie between:

    A. 12% and 20.2%.
    B. 3.8% and 20.2%.
    C. −4.4% and 28.4%.
    D. −12.6% and 36.6%.

11. Find the standard deviation for a portfolio comprised of stocks a and b in the specified proportions.
    $\rho_{a,b} = 0.40$

Stock	Expected Return	Std. Dev.	Weight
a	.12	.040	.40
b	.14	.055	.60

    A. .024.
    B. .039.
    C. .042.
    D. .051.

12. The characteristic line can be used to estimate a stock's:

    A. systematic risk.
    B. unsystematic risk.
    C. covariance with the risk-free asset.
    D. total risk.

13. To achieve the most diversification, it would be **best** to combine stocks with which of the following correlations?

    A. −0.5.
    B. 0.0.
    C. 0.5.
    D. 1.0.

14. Which of the following correlations would achieve the **least** diversification?

    A. −0.5.
    B. 0.0.
    C. 0.5.
    D. 1.0.

15. What is the **beta** of the risk-free asset?

    A. −0.5.
    B. 0.0.
    C. 0.5.
    D. 1.0.

16. Which of the following would be **closest** to the beta for the market portfolio?

    A. −0.5.
    B. 0.0.
    C. 0.5.
    D. 1.0.

17. Estimate the beta for the following portfolio.

Stock	Beta	$ Invested
A	1.5	2,000
B	1.8	1,000
C	0.7	2,000

    A. 1.00.
    B. 1.24.
    C. 1.33.
    D. 1.86.

18. An investor's portfolio has a beta of 1.1. Financial analysts predict the market return for the coming year to be 12 percent, and U.S. Treasury Bills (risk-free asset) were just auctioned to yield 5 percent. What is the expected return for the investor's portfolio?

    A. 5%.
    B. 12%.
    C. 12.7%.
    D. 13.2%.

19. An investor's portfolio has a beta of 1.1. Financial analysts predict the market return for the coming year to be 12 percent, and U.S. Treasury Bills were just auctioned to yield 5 percent. What is the market risk premium?

    A. 5%.
    B. 7%.
    C. 12%.
    D. 17%.

20. An investor's portfolio beta is 1.5 and has a required return of 14 percent. If the market risk premium is 6 percent and inflation expectations for the next year are increased from 2 percent to 4 percent, what will happen to the investor's required return? It will:

    A. remain the same because inflation impacts all assets equally.
    B. increase 2 percentage points to 16%.
    C. increase $1.5(2) = 3$ percentage points to 17%.
    D. be indeterminable. Without knowing the risk-free rate, the impact on the portfolio cannot be determined.

ANSWERS AND SOLUTIONS

1. B. Unsystematic risk is reduced through diversification.

2. C. A risk-averse investor will always avoid unnecessary risk.

3. A. Diminishing marginal utility means each new dollar gives the risk-averse investor less utility (satisfaction) than the preceding dollar did.

4. D. Diversification occurs from less than perfect correlation among securities.

5. B. $\hat{R}_{mm} = .25(.25) + .50(.15) + .25(-.05) = .1250 = 12.5\%$.

6. B. $\sigma_p = [(.25 - .125)^2(.25) + (.15 - .125)^2(.50) + (-.05 - .125)^2(.25)]^{1/2} = .10897 = 10.9$ percent.

7. C. $\rho_{a,b} = \dfrac{COV_{a,b}}{\sigma_a \sigma_b} = \dfrac{.003}{(.066)(.084)} = .5411$

8. A. $COV_{a,b} = \sigma_a \sigma_b \rho_{a,b} = (.066)(.084)(.75) = .004158$

9. B. We know approximately 68 percent of all returns will fall within one standard deviation from the expected return.

   $.12 \pm .082 \Rightarrow 68$ percent will fall between 3.8 percent and 20.2 percent.

10. C. We know approximately 95 percent of all returns will fall within two standard deviations from the expected return.

    $.12 \pm 2(.082) \Rightarrow 95$ percent will fall between −4.4 percent and 28.4 percent.

11. C. $\sigma_p^2 = (.4)^2(.04)^2 + (.6)^2(.055)^2 + 2(.4)(.6)(.04)(.055)(.4) = .0017674$

    $\sigma_p = (\sigma_p^2)^{1/2} = (.0017674)^{1/2} = .042$

12. A. The characteristic line is used to estimate a stock's or a portfolio's beta, which is a measure of systematic risk.

13. A. To achieve the most diversification, you want to combine stocks with the least correlation.

14. D. To achieve the least diversification, combine stocks with the highest correlation.

15. B. Since the standard deviation of the risk free asset is 0.0, its beta must be 0.0.

16. D. Beta measures the volatility of an asset's return relative to the market, so the beta for the market must be 1.0.

17. B. $\beta_p \sum_{i=1}^{n} w_i \beta_i = \frac{2}{5}(1.5) + \frac{1}{5}(1.8) + \frac{2}{5}(0.7) = 1.24$

18. C. $\hat{R}_p = r_f + \beta_p(R_m - r_f) = .05 + 1.1(.12 - .05) = .127 = 12.7\%$

19. B. The market risk premium is the slope of the CAPM, $(R_m - r_f)$. Since $r_f = 5$ percent and $R_m = 12$ percent, the market premium is 7 percent.

20. B. When inflation expectations increase, the SML shifts up. The required return on all assets will increase two percentage points, so your portfolio's required return will increase to 16 percent.

Appendixes

Ethics

Whether meeting with clients, answering students' questions, or donating our time to worthy causes, our actions reflect our moral choices. In *Ethics*, M. Thompson defines actions as:

- **Moral**, if they reflect a person's values and those of society.
- **Immoral**, if they go against a person's or society's values.
- **Amoral**, if they are not based upon values or social norms.[1]

Under most circumstances, the average person will not choose to do what she considers immoral. The challenge, of course, is defining what is and is not moral and determining whether the morality of a choice can be interpreted differently depending upon the circumstances. Do we all have the same morals? Obviously not, since we all view our own choices as better than those of just about anyone else. So how do we acquire our morals, and why doesn't everyone share the same set of morals?

We are not born with a set of morals, nor do we study a manual and take a morality test. Morals are learned from different sources as we grow. They are learned through religious and secular education. Probably the most powerful influence on our moral development is the people around us—primarily our family and friends, and to a lesser degree, our co-workers and acquaintances.

"Are you an ethical person?"

"Yes! Of course!"

[1] M. Thompson, *Ethics* (Teach Yourself Books, 1994).

Similar to a structure of federal and state laws, morals can be organized at different levels: individual, group, and societal. Thus, as we go through our day, our morals are subject to change as we interact with different groups of people and play different roles in various situations. For example, a child might begin the day in the comfort and security of his home, under the influence of loving, watchful parents. His moral world may be turned upside down the moment he steps onto the unsupervised school bus, where the morals of the most dominant children may influence the behavior of their peers. When the child arrives at school, he finds himself in a more structured setting dominated by yet another group of children and, of course, his teachers. Whose morals are "correct"? Those of his parents? Those of the other children on the bus? Those of his teachers? This question is not easily answered.

As adults, we find ourselves in similar situations. As businesspeople, for instance, we live in at least two different worlds. How do the morals of our family and professional lives affect one another? Does one dominate or do we strive for a balance? Also, how do these groups develop their morals? Are they the result of a well-defined plan or simply the dominance of those same school children, now grown up?

Any professional (i.e., physician, attorney, financial advisor, engineer, or educator) must work within a set of morals that comprise the code of ethics for his profession. Even within a single organization, employees of different business units can exhibit separate moral codes. Each profession strives, formally or informally, for that balance between the rights of the individual and the collective rights and obligations of the organization. In the paragraphs that follow, we will explore how organizations establish their moral standards, how these standards define the identity of each organization, and how they are vital to the organizations' success.

ETHICS

As discussed in chapter 1, even the most casual decision is a subjective judgment of which economic choice produces the best combination of cost and benefit. Our professional lives are certainly not exempt from this trade-off, especially since the costs and benefits can be real or abstract.

A *real* gain or loss can be described in terms of money or some material object. Right or wrong, *real* is usually the operative word here and is given the most thought prior to making a decision. Often, not enough thought is given to *abstract* costs and benefits, such as increased self-confidence, the respect and trust of others, or bettering the life of someone who depends upon us. While these may receive little or no weight in the decision-making process, they can still be very valuable in our personal, as well as our professional, lives.

Even though the most mundane choices can be described as economic, not every choice we make can or should be thought of in ethical terms. Furthermore, whether a choice is ethical in nature is not always obvious. For instance, while our choice of socks might make a fashion statement, few would consider it a moral question. Under certain circumstances, however, choosing a winter coat might be. Although many consumers might consider a mink coat a legitimate choice for outerwear, there is a segment of society bitterly opposed to the use of any natural fur on moral grounds. By throwing paint or blood on someone wearing a mink coat, this group's moral positions are made quite clear. While not always as obvious, and surely not always as dramatic, our actions speak loudly and clearly.

Whether we intend it that way or not, others tend to judge our moral fiber through our actions. Although some choices come easily with little or no conscious thought, others are far more difficult. Even if you do consider the ethics of a certain action, you might tend to base your decision upon the perceived size or value of any possible transgression. For instance, you might regularly drink coffee at the office without contributing to the coffee fund, but you would never consider taking company funds from petty cash. After all, if you took cash, you would be a thief! Besides, you know of several people who don't pay for their coffee.

So, what are *ethics*? Technically, ethics are a set of moral values or the study of moral choices. However, sometimes it's easier to think of ethics and morals as interchangeable, with either being defined as the "right thing" to do. Think of ethics as the code by which you live. You say you don't have a code? Perhaps you do and just don't know it. Perhaps it controls your life more than you realize.

Ethics: A learned set of moral values; the study of moral choices.

The next section discusses codes of ethics for various organizations. As you read it, stop and think from time to time about the code by which you live. Think about how that code defines you as an individual and how your opinion of others is colored by how you perceive their code of ethics.

A CODE TO LIVE BY

Why have professional codes of ethics become so popular? Why has management come to think of ethical business practices as critically important? The Life Skills Coaches Association of British Columbia states:

Why have a code of Ethics?
- To define accepted/acceptable behaviors.
- To promote high standards of practice.
- To provide a benchmark for members to use for self-evaluation.
- To establish a framework for professional behavior and responsibilities.
- As a vehicle for occupational identity.[2]

Richard T. DeGeorge takes it further:

The very exercise of developing a code is in itself worthwhile; it forces a large number of people to think through in a fresh way their mission and important obligations they as a group and as individuals have with respect to society as a whole.[3]

In referring to codes of ethics, J. Kulten describes them as:

. . . instruments for persuasion both of members of a profession and the public. They enhance the sense of community among members, of belonging to a group with common values and a common mission.[4]

---

[2] Life Skills Association of British Columbia, NDI.

[3] Richard T. DeGeorge, *Military Ethics: A Code of Ethics for Officers* (Washington: National Defense University Press, 1987).

[4] J. Kulten, *Ethics and Professionalism* (The University of Pennsylvania Press, 1988).

What is obvious from the above quotes is that individuals, organizations, and even the societies within which they function cannot wander through time and space without some guidelines, some code by which to live and operate. Most, if not all, firms and professional organizations have a formal, written code of ethics. You will no doubt detect similarities as we look at a few.

Professional Codes of Ethics

The Code of Ethics for the Association for Investment Management and Research, AIMR®, is as follows:

Members shall:

- Act with integrity, competence, dignity, and in an ethical manner when dealing with the public, clients, prospects, employers, employees, and fellow members.
- Practice and encourage others to practice in a professional and ethical manner that will reflect credit on members and their profession.
- Strive to maintain and improve their competence and the competence of others in the profession.
- Use reasonable care and exercise independent professional judgment.[5]

Among other things, the Code of Ethics for the ASC-CA®, the Automotive Service Councils of California, states:

[M]embers of the ASC-CA® are expected to:
- Uphold the high standards of our profession.
- Uphold the integrity of all members.
- Have a sense of personal obligation.
- Employ only the best skilled personnel.[6]

The Code of Ethics for Buckman Laboratories actually lists 12 separate items. Included are:

Most professional organizations have a formal code of ethics. These codes often share many similarities.

[5]© Association for Investment Management and Research, 1999.

[6]© The Automotive Service Councils of California, NDI.

We must:
- Provide high quality products and service.
- Use the highest ethics to guide our business dealings.
- Discharge the responsibilities of corporate and individual citizenship to earn and maintain the respect of the community.
- Endeavor to uphold these standards so that we may be respected as persons and as an organization.[7]

The Code of Ethics for the American Resort Development Association, ARDA*, is quite detailed, specifying exactly how members shall deal with their various constituencies. In a nutshell, their code of ethics states:

> ARDA* and its members are committed to the highest standards and ethics . . . for the benefit of the public.[8]

The ARDA* Code of Ethics, as with most of those surveyed, even spells out sanctions for failure to comply, investigation of complaints by the ARDA* Ethics Administrator (called a compliance officer in some codes), and the appeal of the process by defendants.

From Toledo, Ohio, comes the Code of Ethics for ProMedica Corporation, a large regional medical holding company:

> At ProMedica we are proud of the values that drive our success. These values shape an environment that . . . nurtures the highest standards in business ethics and personal integrity . . . . It is imperative that . . . we . . . adhere to these . . . values in protection of our System's integrity and welfare.[9]

There are similarities among all the codes summarized above, which are worthy of our discussion. Let's look at some of them.

---

[7] © Buckman Laboratories International, Inc., 1997.

[8] © American Resort Development Association, 2000.

[9] © ProMedica Health System, 1996.

Standards

All codes cited above contain language referring to maintaining high standards. In each case, it is made clear that "high standards" means the best possible product, service, or behavior. Why would each code refer to high standards? One only has to think of competition to answer this question.

Whether providing a product or service, businesses want consumers to think of them as upholding the highest standards in their field and in how their representatives portray themselves and the organization. This is particularly important when the product or service is complex enough that the general public is unfamiliar with its true value and there are many sources for the product or service. For example, when shopping for a diamond engagement ring, the typical individual must trust the salesperson and the store from which the ring is purchased. Even with a plethora of information available on the Internet and through other sources, without trust the customer will never be totally confident that the diamond is the quality, size, and value represented by the salesperson (notice how advertisements for jewelry stores tend to emphasize a family-like atmosphere and how long they have been in business).

When considering medical or financial services, much of the same confusion and uncertainty exists. The typical consumer does not have the medical or financial savvy to make a determination of what treatment or product is necessary. And even if they are aware of what they need, they are probably not well acquainted with the details of the products or services. *This is the driving force behind certification.* Certification is an attempt to calm the consumer's apprehension and instill confidence in the surgeon, jeweler, or financial advisor and, through association, in the product or service they provide.

Certification instills consumer confidence in an organization's members and, through association, in the product or service they provide.

By certifying their members and products, organizations declare their members to be of the highest moral fabric and their products or services to be of the highest quality. Since she is assured high standards, the consumer need not consider quality when making a purchase decision; only the price and appropriateness of the product or service are important.

Best People Available

Each organizational code of ethics refers to using only the most competent people. If your product or service is quality certified, the next step is to certify that your people are both honest and highly knowledgeable. By certifying their members' abilities and knowledge, the organization has eliminated another barrier to consumer trust. Consumers can trust that the product or service recommended is exactly what he or she needs. They are now confident of the quality and appropriateness of the product, the quality of the organization, and the quality and ability of the sales representative. If quality and standards are assured, the consumer need only consider price.

Price

Every code of ethics surveyed made reference in one fashion or another to fair pricing. In their code of ethics, The Advertising Federation of Australia states, "We . . . will be straightforward and fair in the tender process."[10] The Automotive Service Councils of California, recognizing their customers are typically skeptical about necessary repairs and the accompanying costs, lists "high quality repair service at a fair and just price" among their standards.[11] The codes have now assured the consumer about standards of the organization, quality and capability of organization representatives, and the price of the product.

Good Neighbor Policy

Without exception, the codes refer to the need to become an accepted member of the community. For instance, the ASC-CA code cites the need "to promote good will between motorists and the industry."[12] The code for ProMedica refers to "corporate citizenship,"[13] while Buckman Laboratories' recognizes "the responsibilities of corporate and personal citizenship to earn and maintain the respect of the community."[14] What should be obvious is that organizations value the concept of being a "good neighbor," or they would not make achieving that status a top priority.

[10] © The Advertising Federation of Australia, 1997.

[11] © ASC-CA

[12] © ASC-CA

[13] © ProMedica, 1996.

[14] © Buckman Laboratories, 1997.

An organization tries to address and alleviate consumers' apprehensions about the quality of the organization, its products or services, and its people. It tries to assure consumers about the fairness of its prices, and strives to become a "good neighbor." There must be sound reasoning behind all the time, energy, and expense that organizations put into developing these codes and assuring that they are disseminated among all of its members or employees. Further, organizations go to great lengths to spell out penalties for noncompliance.

Putting the Pieces Together

From a purely business perspective, the value of an organizational code of ethics becomes evident. The Life Skills Coaches' Association of British Columbia states that a code of ethics is necessary to define accepted and acceptable professional behaviors, promote high standards of practice, and as a vehicle for occupational identity.[15] However, from a more aesthetic perspective, a code of ethics helps develop the organization and the individual in more abstract ways. As DeGeorge points out, the very act of developing a code is worthwhile because it forces people to think through their obligations with respect to society as a whole.[16]

> A code of ethics helps define the identity of the organization and its members.

What is the point of all of this? A code of ethics helps define the identity of the organization and its members. It is a statement of assurance of the quality and value of the products, services, members, and even the organization as a whole. It assures consumers that the organization's members have received sufficient training in the products and services they represent. In short, the code of ethics *is* the organization.

SUMMARY

Technically, there may be a difference in the definition of the words *ethics* and *morals*, but you will probably hear them used more or less interchangeably. You should have a pretty good idea of the meaning, however, when you hear or read either of these words. They are used to refer to acceptable behavior, where "acceptable" means within the laws and norms of society.

[15] LSCABC

[16] DeGeorge, *Military Ethics*.

In the previous sections, you were given examples of the codes of ethics for several organizations. You saw that by developing a code of ethics, organizations are really establishing what they consider acceptable behavior by their members.

We hope the material presented in this appendix has helped you gain insight into why AIMR° has a code of ethics and why you need to be familiar with it. As you study the Schweser Study Program review materials and the AIMR° *Standards of Practice Handbook*, try to think back to what you have read here, and you will approach the material with the interest and respect it deserves. Remember: The CFA° designation tells your clients that you are a well-prepared professional, that your ethics and those of your colleagues with the CFA° designation are exemplary, and that you can be trusted to help them make the best overall financial choices.

Acronyms and Abbreviations

ACRS	Accelerated Cost Recovery System
AIMR®	Association for Investment Management and Research
AMEX	American Stock Exchange
CAPM	Capital Asset Pricing Model
CD	Certificate of Deposit
CFA®	Chartered Financial Analyst
Fannie Mae	Federal National Mortgage Association
FASB	Financial Accounting Standards Board
Fed	Federal Reserve Board
FHLMA	Federal Home Loan Mortgage Association (Freddie Mac)
FNMA	Federal National Mortgage Association (Fannie Mae)
Freddie Mac	Federal Home Loan Bank Corporation

FV	Future Value
GNMA	Government National Mortgage Association (Ginnie Mae)
Ginnie Mae	Government National Mortgage Association
IPO	Initial Public Offering
LIBOR	London Interbank Offered Rate
MACRS	Modified Accelerated Cost Recovery System
MD	Mean Deviation
Muni	Municipal Bond
NASDAQ	National Association of Securities Dealers Automated Quotation
NI	Net Income
NYSE	New York Stock Exchange
PV	Present Value
RP/Repo	Repurchase Agreement
RR	Real Rate of Interest
SCF	Statement of Cash Flows
SEC	Securities Exchange Commission
SML	Security Market Line
T-Bill	U.S. Treasury Bill
T-Bond	U.S. Treasury Bond
T-Note	U.S. Treasury Note

Glossary

Absolute value	The absolute value of a number is its value ignoring its sign.
Accounts payable	A short-term liability (e.g., inventory) that has been received but has not been paid.
Accrual basis accounting	An accounting method that assigns revenues to the accounting period in which they are earned and matches expenses with the revenues generated by those expenses.
Accrued interest	Interest that has been earned but not paid.
Accumulated depreciation	Accumulated depreciation is a contra-asset account, which reduces either an asset or liability on the balance sheet.
Actual return	Often referred to as the *historical return*, it is the calculated return on the investment (looking back from the end of the investment period) based upon the price you *paid* and the cash flow(s) you *received*.
Adjusting entries	Adjusting entries help match expenses to the appropriate revenues.
Affirmative covenants	Actions the borrower of a fixed income security promises to perform.
After-tax yield	The rate of return after taxes have been subtracted from the investment.

Agency costs   Arising from the separation of ownership and management, these are the costs incurred by the company to ensure that management is carrying out objectives related to shareholder wealth maximization.

Amortization   The reduction of debt through periodic payments, such as payments on a home mortgage or car loan. Each payment contains a portion that pays the interest on the loan and a portion that goes toward paying off the principal of the loan. Amortization also refers to the process of systematically writing off costs incurred to acquire an intangible asset such as patents, copyright, or goodwill.

Annual compounding   With annual compounding, interest is calculated and paid once per year.

Annuity   A countable number of equal cash flows occurring at equal intervals over a defined period of time.

Annuity due   When payments come at the beginning of the period, the annuity is called an annuity due.

Arithmetic mean   The sum of all the observations divided by the number of observations.

Ask price   The price at which the market maker is willing to sell. The difference between the bid and ask prices, referred to as the bid-ask spread, represents the market maker's profit.

Bacon, Sir Francis   Sir Francis Bacon was an early philosopher/economist whose writings were based in religious doctrine. He spoke against waste and greed (i.e., wealth for wealth's sake).

Balance sheet   The balance sheet shows the value of assets, liabilities, and owners' equity at a specific point in time. The two sides of the balance sheet must always be equal. Assets = Liabilities + Equity.

Bank discount yield   An annualized interest rate used to price T-Bills and differs from the true yield (i.e., ask yield to maturity) because its calculation is based on the discount from face value and a 360-day year.

Bankers' acceptances Short-term agreements with an importer's bank that guarantee payments of the exporter's invoice.

Barter system	A market system where items are traded rather than bought or sold with currency.
Beta	Beta measures the volatility of a stock or portfolio relative to the volatility of the market.
Bid price	A bid, also called an offer, is the price the market maker (dealer) will pay for the security. The difference between the bid and ask prices, referred to as the bid-ask spread, represents the market maker's profit.
Bond-equivalent yield	The true expected yield on a T-Bill, based upon price paid and a 365-day year.
Broker	A broker helps bring the buyer and seller together.
Broker market	A broker market is where brokers trade shares for the public. It includes the primary, secondary, and third markets.
Business risk	The uncertainty in earnings before interest and taxes (EBIT), or the forces that cause EBIT uncertainty.
C corporation	C corporations can have several thousand investors and their securities can be publicly traded.
Callable security	A callable bond may be retired early to take advantage of falling interest rates. A callable security is a security that is redeemable by the issuer before the scheduled maturity. The issuer must pay the holders a premium price if such a security is retired early.
Capital	Any resource that has value because it helps in the production or supply of goods and services.
Capital assets	Assets having a relatively long life (e.g., land, buildings, and equipment).
Capital markets	Capital markets provide individuals, businesses, and governments with a way to obtain the capital they need for operating and expanding.
Capital structure	Capital structure shows how management paid for the firm's assets and appears on the right-hand side of the balance sheet.
Capitalism	Capitalism is synonymous with and based upon free enterprise.

Capitalized cost	The total cost to purchase and install a piece of equipment or any fixed asset is the asset's capitalized cost.
Cartel	A group who conspires to control the price of a good or service.
Cash basis accounting	An accounting method that recognizes revenues when cash is received and expenses when cash is paid.
Certificates of Deposit (CDs)	Short-term time deposits with commercial banks.
Characteristic line	The regression model used to estimate betas for individual stocks and portfolios.
Classical economics	The belief that the government should not interfere with the economy.
Clearing corporation	Also known as the clearinghouse, the clearing corporation guarantees that traders in the futures market will honor their obligations; ensures there is a buyer for every seller acting as the middleman; eliminates the need for buyers and sellers to know each other; and eliminates the risk of the trade defaulting.
Closing price	The last recorded trade for the stock on a given day. It could be a buy (bid) or sell (ask).
Commercial paper	A short-term IOU issued by strong, creditworthy corporations.
Common stock	Common stock signifies ownership of a corporation. If the common stock of the firm is registered with the SEC, it can be traded publicly.
Communism	Under communism, there is no formal government. Allocation is "from each according to his abilities, to each according to his needs."
Compound values	Future values are sometimes referred to as compound values due to the compounding effect of interest.
Compounding	Compounding occurs when interest is paid on interest.
Compounding rate	The discount rate and compounding rate are the rates of interest used to find present and future values, respectively.

Constant growth rate   Refers to the rate at which dividends will grow in the constant growth dividend discount model; one assumption in this model is that dividends will grow at a constant rate.

Continuous variable   A continuous variable can have an infinite number of outcomes.

Converge   As the maturity date nears, the futures price must converge to the spot price until they are equal on the maturity date.

Convergence   When a futures contract matures, the futures price equals (i.e., converges) the spot price.

Conversion price   The dollar value or price at which convertible bonds, debentures, or preferred stock can be converted into common stock. The conversion price is announced when the convertible is issued.

Conversion ratio   The conversion ratio specifies the number of shares received at the time of conversion.

Convertible   Convertible refers to preferred shares or bonds that are exchangeable for a set number of common shares at a prestated price.

Convertible bond   A convertible bond may be exchanged for common or preferred stock of the issuing firm.

Corporation   A legal entity separate from its owners.

Correlation   Correlation, also called the coefficient of correlation or correlation coefficient, refers to the relative degree to which investment returns move together and must have a value from –1 to +1. A correlation coefficient with a value less than zero indicates the returns move in opposite directions. A value greater than zero indicates the returns move in the same direction.

Cost of goods sold   Cost of goods sold includes the costs of all "raw" inputs, which are combined into the final product.

Coupon payment   The periodic payment of interest received by the bondholder.

Coupon rate   The stated percentage of par or face value of a bond that determines the interest payment.

Covariance	The statistical term for the correlation between two variables multiplied by the standard deviation for each of the variables. The covariance measures the absolute amount of co-movement between the returns of two stocks.
Credit entry	A credit entry increases a liability and decreases an asset.
Cumulative	Most preferred stock is cumulative; all preferred dividends must be paid before the firm can pay common dividends.
Current or short-term assets or liabilities	Assets or liabilities with expected lives of less than one year.
Cyclical unemployment	Cyclical unemployment is due to lack of aggregate demand; it usually involves layoffs.
Data distribution	Data distribution is the way data is described as a whole. The distribution is the way the individual data points or observations are scattered or distributed.
Dealer	A dealer actually takes ownership before reselling a product.
Dealer market	A dealer market is when the buyer and seller submit their orders to dealers, who either buy the stock for their own inventory or sell the stock from their own inventory.
Debentures	Bonds that are not backed by collateral; they are guaranteed only by the firm's promise of payment, and they are subordinated to the mortgage bonds.
Debit entry	A debit entry increases an asset and decreases a liability.
Declaration date	The date that the board of directors of a corporation declare the payment of dividends at their quarterly meeting.
Decreasing marginal utility	The concept that each new dollar gives the individual less utility (i.e., satisfaction) than the preceding dollar.
Demand	The total amount of a good or service society wants. The higher the price, the lower the demand. If demand is greater than supply (i.e., excess demand), prices rise.

Depreciation	The means by which the costs of long-term (or capitalized) assets are expensed. Although depreciation expense is not a cash flow, it reduces taxable income and the company's income tax liability. To recognize this tax break as quickly as possible, managers want to speed up the rate of depreciation as much as possible.
Direct market	In a direct market, the buyer and seller must actually contact one another.
Discount rate	The discount rate carries two meanings: the rate the Fed charges member banks for short-term loans, or the rate of interest used to find present values.
Discrete variable	A discrete variable can only have a countable number of identified values.
Diversification	Diversification reduces the unsystematic or unique risk in a portfolio by placing money in different asset classes (e.g., cash, bonds, and stocks) and varying securities within each category.
Diversifiable risk	Diversifiable risk (i.e., firm-specific, unique, or unsystematic risk) is the risk that can be substantially lowered in a portfolio by adding securities of varying correlations.
Dividends	The portion of net income paid out to the owners, the stockholders. The firm's board of directors decides whether dividends will be paid. Since dividends are declared, they are not contractual.
Dollar discount	The difference between the face value and current price of a security issue.
Double taxation	Dividends are distributed after the firm pays incomes taxes. Double taxation occurs because the stockholder pays income taxes on the dividends he receives.
Dow Jones Industrial Average	The Dow Jones is the most famous stock index in the United States and is a price-weighted index.
Dual entry system	An accounting method in which for every debit there is a corresponding credit.
Economies of scale	The ability to produce more efficiently as the size of the company increases.

Effective interest rates   The actual rates earned or paid. These rates are determined by taking into consideration the stated rate and the number of compounding periods per year.

Empirical rule   The empirical rule uses the expected return and standard deviation to determine the distribution of possible returns for a symmetrical (i.e., bell-shaped) distribution.

Equal sign (=)   Signifies that everything on the left side of the equation is equal to what's on the right.

Equal to or greater than sign (≥)   Signifies that the left side of the equation must be greater than or equal to the right side of the equation. Solving an equation with an equal to or greater than sign (≥) gives a range of possible values along with a minimum value for the unknown.

Equal to or less than sign (≤)   Signifies that the left side of the equation must be less than or equal to the right side of the equation. Solving an equation with an equal to or less than sign (≤) gives a range of possible values along with a maximum value for the unknown.

Equilibrium   Equilibrium is reached when supply equals demand. Supply and demand must be in equilibrium for prices to be stable.

Ethics   A learned set of moral values; the study of moral choices.

Eurodollars   U.S. dollars on deposit in foreign banks.

Ex-dividend date   The ex-dividend date is two days before the date of record. If you buy the share on or after the ex-dividend date, you will not receive the dividend.

Expected return   The expected return is *estimated* at the beginning of the investment period (looking into the future), and is based upon the price you pay and the cash flow(s) you *expect* to receive.

Explicit growth period   The period when a firm is expected to perform well above or below average. Not all firms experience explicit growth periods.

Exponent   An indication of how many times a number or letter or quantity is to be multiplied by itself. An exponent is also referred to as a *power*. When a number or letter has more than one exponent, the exponents should be multiplied together.

Face value	Face value, also called par value, is the amount an investor receives when a bond matures.
Federal funds	The cash a financial institution must keep on deposit at the Federal Reserve Bank in its region of the United States.
FHLB	The Federal Home Loan Bank System supplies credit services for savings and loan associations, cooperative banks, and other mortgage lenders.
FHLMC	The Federal Home Loan Mortgage Corporation (Freddie Mac) buys residential mortgages from lenders, packages them into new securities backed by those pooled mortgages, and resells the securities on the open market.
Financial intermediary	A financial intermediary borrows money from a saver or investor and lends it to others.
Financial leverage	The percentage change in net income given a percentage change in earnings before interest and taxes (EBIT).
Financial risk	The added risk borne by the stockholders due to management's use of debt.
Fiscal policy	Fiscal policy refers to the government's use of spending and taxation to attain macroeconomic goals.
Fiscal year	Any 12-month period, not necessarily beginning January 1.
Fixed costs	Costs that are incurred regardless of the level of output (e.g., rent). In the short run, fixed costs cannot be changed.
Fixed income securities	Fixed income securities require the firm to pay specified cash flows on specified dates. Most debt instruments are fixed income securities; their payments are set contractually.
Floor brokers	On the NYSE, floor brokers present orders for customers at the specialist's trading post.
Flotation costs	The total costs of issuing securities; they include the underwriter spread and legal, accounting, and printing fees.
Forward market	In a forward market, both parties agree to transact at a future date.

Fourth market The direct exchange of securities between investors without using the services of a broker as an intermediary.

Frictional unemployment Frictional unemployment is caused by the inability to connect the workers to the available jobs. It is due to lack of information.

Full employment The natural level of employment resulting from the efficient utilization of the work force.

Future value The value in the *future* of a cash flow received or paid *today*.

Futures Standardized contracts traded on organized exchanges for the delivery of a commodity at some future date.

Futures contracts Futures contracts on commodities, currencies, and other financial instruments are liquid, standardized contracts traded on futures markets facilitated by a clearing corporation.

General ledger The book "of original entry" in which all accounts are kept and maintained. It usually has a separate page for each account.

Geometric mean Geometric mean is used for the calculation of interest rates and growth rates. It is a multiplicative mean that shows the historical return to an investment.

GNMA The Government National Mortgage Association (Ginnie Mae) is a government organization that assists in housing finance.

Government strip With U.S. government strips, the interest and principal payments of notes or bonds are stripped apart and sold individually.

Hedging The reduction of risk.

Holder of record date The date on which the shareholders of record are designated for receipt of a declared dividend.

Holding-period yield The change in value as a percentage of the original value (i.e., the price you paid for the investment) over the period of time the investment was held. The holding period yield is the total change in value over the period divided by the price paid.

Human capital The people employed in the supply of goods or services.

Hybrid security	Technically an equity security, preferred stock is a hybrid security. It is called a hybrid because it has characteristics of both equity and debt (i.e., stocks and bonds).
Implicit growth period	During the implicit growth period, the firm performs at a more sustainable, long-term rate of growth.
Income statement	The income statement, sometimes called the statement of earnings, shows the firm's operating results for a period of time.
Indenture	The written contract between the firm and the bondholders.
Inflation	The general increase in prices when spending increases relative to the supply of goods. Inflation can also be thought of as too many dollars chasing too few goods and is a macroeconomic variable that affects all stocks to varying degrees.
Initial public offering (IPO)	The first offering when a firm sells shares publicly.
Interest expense	Since interest expense reduces taxable income, it also reduces income taxes. This reduces the effective cost of borrowed funds.
Investment bankers	Professionals who help firms to raise capital through public or private security offerings.
Invisible hand	Adam Smith's concept describing market pressure, the unseen force that affects individuals' choices due to market prices to direct their efforts into activities that benefit society as a whole while pursuing their own interests.
Keynes, John Maynard	In *The General Theory of Employment, Interest, and Money*, John Maynard Keynes changed the way we look at macroeconomics. Unlike classical economists, Keynes believed that the government should intervene during a recession by increasing its expenditures. Keynes believed the level of employment in a society is determined by the aggregate spending of consumers, investors, government, and foreigners.
Limit order	An order to buy at a price below the current market price or sell at a price higher than the current market price.

Limited liability Owners of corporations enjoy limited liability because they can lose only what they have invested.

Long-term assets or liabilities Long-term assets and long-term liabilities are generally those with expected lives greater than one year.

Lump sum A single cash flow.

Macroeconomic shocks Economy-wide events that affect all stocks to varying degrees.

Macroeconomics Macroeconomics deals with economy-wide factors, such as inflation.

MACRS In 1986, the U.S. Congress approved the modified accelerated cost recovery system (MACRS), which mandates the rate at which assets are depreciated.

Market order An order to buy or sell at the best available price.

Market pressure The tendency of market prices to direct individuals pursuing their own interests into productive activities that also promote the economic well-being of the society. Market pressure is the same as the invisible hand principle.

Marked to market The process of determining the market price of a security or portfolio.

Market-risk premium The market-risk premium measures the average degree of risk aversion in the market.

Marx, Karl Karl Marx believed in a natural social decay toward communism. He argued that capitalism leads to class struggle, which leads to revolution and socialism; unequal distribution within socialism leads to revolution and communism.

Matching principle According to the matching principle, revenues and expenses are matched to each other and the appropriate accounting period.

Mature market A mature market is the longest phase of an industry's life cycle, when competition is fierce, industry growth rates have slowed down to the growth rate of the aggregate economy, profit margins are tight, and return on equity is at a normal level for the industry.

Mean deviation The average of the absolute values of the distances between each observation and the mean.

Median	The middle value in a distribution, above and below which lie an equal number of values.
Microeconomics	Microeconomics deals with factors within a single firm or household (e.g., wages). Generally, individuals or single firms have at least some degree of control over microeconomic factors.
Mode	The value that appears most often in a set of sample observations.
Monetary policy	Monetary policy refers to the government's use of changes in the money supply to attain macroeconomic goals.
Money markets	Securities with initial maturities less than one year are traded in the money markets. All money market instruments have short maturities, low risk, and high liquidity (e.g., T-bills, CDs, banker's acceptances, and commercial paper).
Monopoly	In a monopoly, one supplier controls the entire supply of a good or service.
Natural rate of unemployment	The long-run average unemployment rate caused by structural and frictional factors. In the United States, the natural rate of unemployment is approximately 5% (i.e., 100% minus the full employment rate).
Negative covenants	The restrictions on the borrower of a fixed income security that prohibit the borrower from doing certain things.
Net income	Total sales less total costs and expenses.
Nominal rate	The annual rate of interest promised or stated on the security or in the contract.
Non-cash expenses	Expenses that have no associated cash outflow. Non-cash expenses on the income statement include prepaid items and depreciation.
Oligopoly	A small group of suppliers who collectively enjoy a monopoly.
Operating expenses	Costs associated with keeping the business open and putting together and selling the final product.
Operating leverage	The percentage change in earnings before interest and taxes (EBIT), given a percentage change in revenues. Operating leverage is caused by the use of fixed assets.

Ordinary annuity	When payments come at the end of the period, the annuity is called an ordinary annuity.
Owners' equity	Owners' equity equals total assets minus total liabilities. It represents the portion of total assets owned "free and clear" after deducting what is owed to others.
Partnership	A business with two or more owners. Legally, a partnership is very similar to a proprietorship.
Payment date	The date that the dividend checks are distributed to shareholders.
Perfect correlation	Perfect correlation refers to a correlation coefficient of −1 or +1. A correlation coefficient of +1 indicates that the returns of two stocks move together in perfect unison. A correlation coefficient of −1 indicates that the returns of two stocks move in perfect unison but in opposite directions.
Perpetual preferred stock	Perpetual preferred stock has no maturity. It is expected to pay dividends forever.
Perpetuity	A series of equal cash flows occurring at the same interval forever.
Physical capital	The equipment, buildings, and other physical items used in the supply of goods and services.
Population	A collection of all possible individuals, objects, or other items.
Population variance	A measure of dispersion based on the deviation from the mean. The variance is defined as the mean of the squared deviations from the mean.
Portfolio beta	The weighted average of the betas of the individual stocks in the portfolio.
Portfolio expected return	The weighted average of the expected returns for the individual stocks in the portfolio.
Portfolio standard deviation	The portfolio standard deviation is based upon the standard deviations of each stock, the weight of each stock in the portfolio, and the correlations between each stock.
Preemptive right	Current stockholders must be given the right to purchase new shares in proportion to their current ownership before they are offered to the general public.

Preferred stock	Although preferred stock is technically an equity security, it has both debt and equity characteristics. Preferred stock usually has a maturity date. It can have a sinking fund and can be callable.
Prepaid items	Expenses that are paid before they are recognized as operating expenses. The balance of the item, which has not been expensed, is considered a current asset.
Present value	The value today of a cash flow to be received or paid in the future.
Primary market	The primary market is where the sale of new issues of bonds, preferred stock, and common stock are sold, often with the aid of an underwriter.
Principal	Principal represents the face value of an obligation (e.g., a bond or loan) that must be repaid at maturity.
Principal financial statements	The four principal financial statements are the balance sheet, income statement, statement of cash flows, and statement of owners' equity.
Private placement	An investment offered for sale to a small group of investors, generally under exemptions to registration allowed by the Securities and Exchange Commission. In a private placement, the investment banker acts like a broker and brings the firm and the investors together. The issue is not underwritten.
Probability distribution	A probability distribution represents all the different possible outcomes of an event and the probability associated with each of these outcomes.
Proprietorship	A business owned by a single individual. Legally, the business and the owner are indistinguishable.
Prospectus	A written document that offers the financial details about an investment. To sell securities publicly, the firm must first get the prospectus approved by the SEC.
Publicly traded	Refers to stock of a company that is available for purchase by the public.
Publicly traded corporations	An ownership (equity) claim in some companies is obtained by purchasing shares of common stock. These companies, with many outside owners who are not usually involved with business operations, are known as publicly traded corporations.
Qualitative	Qualitative variables describe attributes of the sample.
Quantitative	Quantitative variables measure numerical values of the sample.

Randomness   Refers to a sample that was drawn from a population using no detectable plan or pattern. Observations are drawn in a random manner with no preference given to any particular value, size, or location.

Range   The "distance" between the largest and the smallest observations in a sample.

Rational investor   When choosing investments, a rational investor will minimize the risk for a given level of return or maximize the return for a given level of risk.

Real income increase   An increase in real income means the percentage increase in income is greater than the rate of inflation (i.e., buying power has increased).

Repo   A repo, or repurchase agreement, is a short-term loan collateralized by marketable securities (e.g., common or preferred stock, money market instruments, or Treasury securities).

Retained earnings   The portion of net income retained for investment.

Revenue recognition principle   According to the revenue recognition principle, only the portion of revenue that has actually been earned can be recognized on the income statement.

Revenues   The cash inflows generated by operations (i.e., the sale of goods or services).

Risk   The possibility that an unfavorable event will occur (i.e., the possibility the return on the investment will be lower than expected). Risk is caused by microeconomic and macroeconomic factors.

Risk aversion   Investors are risk averse, which means that they will always avoid unnecessary risk. Given the choice between two assets with the same rate of return, an investor will choose the asset with the lowest level of risk.

S corporation   S corporations are legally very similar to partnerships and have a limited number of owners. Their securities cannot be publicly traded.

Sample   A portion of a population that is used to estimate characteristics of (i.e., make inferences about) the population.

Secondary market   In secondary markets, investors trade securities that have been previously issued in the primary market.

Security market line   A graphical representation of the capital asset pricing model (CAPM), showing the relationship between return and systematic (or market) risk, which is referred to as beta.

Seniority   Seniority specifies the order in which bondholders will be paid in case of bankruptcy.

Serial bonds   Serial bonds are retired in portions according to their serial numbers (their registration numbers).

Settlement price   During every trading day, all futures contracts are marked to market at the settlement price.

Sinking fund   The money that is accumulated on a regular basis in a separate custodial account used to redeem debt securities. The sinking fund provides assurance that sufficient funds will be available to retire the bond issue as specified.

Smith, Adam   Adam Smith is considered the father of free enterprise. He was a classical economist who believed in strict laissez-faire (i.e., government should not interfere with the natural working of the economy).

Socialism   With socialism, the government owns all income-producing assets. Allocation of wages and goods is done according to effort.

Specialist   The specialist acts as a market maker. Every stock on the NYSE has only one specialist who buys and sells stocks for their own accounts and the accounts of others. They maintain order and provide liquidity to the market.

Spot market   The spot market is where securities, commodities, and other goods are traded for immediate delivery.

Stand-alone risk   Stand-alone risk (i.e., total risk) is the sum of the security's risk caused by microeconomic forces and the risk caused by macroeconomic forces. If a particular security is the only investment you hold, you are subject to that security's stand-alone risk.

Standard deviation   The mean of the squared deviations from the mean. The standard deviation is also the square root of the variance.

Statement of cash flows   The statement of cash flows shows changes in the cash account caused by cash flows from operations, investments, or financing.

Statement of owners' equity	The statement of owners' equity shows the value of any money (or other capital) the owner has invested in the business.
Stock index	A stock index is used to estimate movements in the overall market.
Stop order	A defensive trading strategy used to buy above the market or sell below the market.
Stop-loss order	A sell order placed below the current market price. Stop-loss orders are usually placed to protect a gain from a future price reversal.
Strict equality	Strict equality means a number or symbol is equal to something else and no other possibility exists. For example, $a = 6$ is a strict equality because no value other than 6 could equal a.
Strips	Coupon payments from bonds that have been stripped off the bond and sold separately. This usually occurs with Treasury bonds, resulting in Treasury strips.
Structural unemployment	Structural unemployment is due to changes in the structure of the economy. It occurs when workers are not qualified for the available jobs.
Supply	The amount of a good or service available for purchase.
Systematic risk	Systematic risk is caused by macroeconomic factors. It is also known as non-diversifiable risk or market risk because it cannot be diversified away.
Third market	A segment of the over-the-counter market (OTC) where investment firms who are not members of an exchange trade registered securities to the public through dealers.
Timeline	A graphical representation of when cash flows occur in relation to time. A timeline is used for time value of money calculations such as the present value and future value of varying cash flows.
Tombstone	The tombstone, found in the *Wall Street Journal*, contains the names of the investment banking firms involved in a sale, the main characteristics of the security, and the date of the sale. The tombstone will direct interested investors to the prospectus, which is available through any of the listed investment banking firms.

Treasury Direct
The Website maintained by the U.S. Treasury to facilitate trading in U.S. government securities.

Trend analysis
Trend analysis is performed to detect general patterns in operating results or other accounting measures from one period to the next.

Trustee
The trustee represents the interests of bondholders in assuring that the issuing corporation honors the provisions of the bond issue.

Underwriter spread
The difference between the price investment bankers pay for the securities and the price at which they sell them to investors.

Underwriting
By underwriting an issue of securities, investment bankers guarantee the sale and the proceeds to the issuing firm.

Underwriting syndicate
The group of firms that provide the underwriting services for a security that is issued.

Unemployed
To be classified as unemployed, an individual must be actively seeking employment or waiting to return to work after being laid off.

Unsystematic risk
Unsystematic risk is also called unique risk (or firm-specific risk) and can be reduced or even eliminated through diversification.

Utils
Units used in measuring utility.

Value intensive
If a finished product is considered value intensive, handling, packaging, and shipping are only a small portion of its final value.

Variable costs
Variable costs (e.g., wages and raw materials) move up and down as production rises and falls. In the long run, all costs are variable.

Working capital
Current assets and current liabilities are called working capital. Increases (decreases) in asset accounts are outflows (inflows), while increases (decreases) in liability accounts are inflows (outflows) of working capital.

Zero coupon bond
A zero coupon bond pays no interest. It is purchased at a discount from face value and the face value is paid at maturity.

Schweser
Study Program